Education Under Siege

Frauds, Fads, Fantasies, and Fictions in Educational Reform

Arthur Shapiro

ROWMAN & LITTLEFIELD EDUCATION
A division of
ROWMAN & LITTLEFIELD
Lanham • Boulder • New York • Toronto • Plymouth, UK

Published by Rowman & Littlefield Education
A division of Rowman & Littlefield
4501 Forbes Boulevard, Suite 200, Lanham, Maryland 20706
www.rowman.com

10 Thornbury Road, Plymouth PL6 7PP, United Kingdom

British Library Cataloguing in Publication Information Available

Library of Congress Cataloging-in-Publication Data

Shapiro, Arthur S., 1928–
Education under siege : frauds, fads, fantasies, and fictions in educational reform / Arthur Shapiro.
pages cm
ISBN 978-1-4758-0307-5 (cloth : alk. paper) — ISBN 978-1-4758-0308-2 (pbk. : alk. paper) —
ISBN 978-1-4758-0309-9 (electronic)
1. Public schools—United States. 2. Education—United States. 3. Education and state—United
States. 4. Educational change—United States. 5. Education—Aims and objectives—United States. 6.
Educational evaluation—United States. I. Title.
LA217.2.S52 2013
371.010973—dc23
2013023494

Printed in the United States of America

I dedicate this book, which explores the follies of so-called educational reform, to our two dear friends and colleagues, Dr. Lynne and Vic Menard, who have steadily supported this rather complex enterprise with astute research and careful editing. Such friends are rare treasures who enrich our lives.

In grateful indebtedness,
Arthur

Stein's Law: Things that can't go on forever, don't.
—Paul Krugman, Nobel Prize–winning economist

Contents

Preface

If it moves, we test it.

—Linda Darling-Hammond

The legislature's stampede to significantly expand online learning for students in public schools has nothing to do with offering more options and meeting unmet needs. It has everything to do with creating opportunities for well-connected, for-profit providers to make money at the expense of public schools.

—Editorial, *Tampa Bay Times*, April 12, 2013

American education seems to be chasing rainbows—that is, fads—almost constantly these days. As a matter of fact, Kevin Phillips, a political commentator, once noted that people in three countries seem prone to chase fads—the Dutch (the Dutch tulip bulb craze), the British, and, yes, the Americans (remember the 2008 housing bubble?).

How about education? Do we Americans chase fads?

You bet we do!

- How about tracking kids? Sure has faded.
- How about self-esteem? When was the last time that anyone mentioned it?
- Madeline Hunter? All the rage in the 1980s and 1990s. Forgotten.
- Open schools? (Can work beautifully, but you have to know how they operate.) Gone.

We can go on, but why bother? The point is clear. How does this apply to American education right now?

Let's turn to Diane Ravitch, who notes that reform in American education seems at times to be driven by a Big Idea. But what if the Big Idea is a fantasy—or worse, a fraud? If so, we have a heck of a problem.

Unfortunately, that's exactly where we are presently. We have a heck of a problem. We are racing down the yellow brick road in Oz, based on a fantasy. And what is that fantasy? Simply this: that education ought to be based on the free market and, therefore, privatized. And that came from what appears to be a pretty good source: Milton Friedman, a Nobel Prize–winning economist who thought that if education were treated as a business, it would flourish.

What does the research tell us?

He was dead wrong. But we're ignoring the research (as we are wont to do).

As a result, we are careening down the yellow brick road chasing reform fantasies, some of which are based on a privatization ideology:

- No Child Left Behind—being abandoned
- Common Core State Standards—no empirical basis
- Failing kids—not only doesn't work but also generates dropouts
- The testing industry—loves our annual testing frenzy, but doesn't improve education
- Evaluating teachers using merit—generates problems and invalid evaluation
- Rating schools by letter grades—simply tells us the socioeconomic level of the school
- Value-added models (VAMs)—lack validity and, particularly, reliability *(two different VAM models can generate two entirely conflicting evaluations of the same lesson)*
- Research on privatization—reveals poor results
- Charters—generally do worse than their matched public schools
- Vouchers—do not produce expected results
- Online virtual charter schools—produce dreadful academic results and huge dropout rates, but wonderful profits for their owners
- The widely publicized educational miracles—mirages for the gullible

What is going on?

We have to speak honestly if we want to improve education and not get suckered in by false ideologically based claims.

Most of these reforms are being driven by ideology—largely of conservative and libertarian beliefs, as privatization guru Henry Levin notes in his article title: "Vouchers and Public Policy: When Ideology Trumps Evidence."

This book deals with the underside of a number of present attempts to reform education in America, many of which are generating the opposite of their supposed intentions—they are undermining public education in order to privatize it.

Each chapter in this book deals with each of the so-called reforms listed above. We'll be honest, looking at the research-based evidence, not what supporters claim. They should stand—or fall—based on what research on each reveals. But we face a major problem: Unlike all other professions, a lot of educational reform literally is being shanghaied by noneducators. Do we tell our dentists how to practice? Of course not. Do we laymen tell physicians how to operate? Certainly not. But we have allowed politicians, statisticians, and economists to tell teachers how to teach and administrators how to operate schools, even though they know little or nothing about schools. Not too wise, we'd say. And boy, does it generate problems!

- Politicians, statisticians, and economists do not understand how kids learn.
- They really do not understand that kids develop—differently.
- Their ideas regarding motivating kids and teachers? Threaten and punish.
- They have no idea of how to run a class.
- They do not understand how to teach and how to reach kids.
- They have no idea how schools operate effectively.

But none of this deters them.

> The mindset of the statistician—test kids.
> The mindset of the economist—test kids.
> The mindset of the politician? Great! Let's test kids a lot!

So we are test crazy and we drive our kids crazy with myriad tests. They give schools letter grades to motivate, to threaten people to work harder. To shame them.

Question: When you are threatened, what do *you* do?

What are the assumptions and beliefs they run on?

- All kids are at the same developmental level.
- Poverty doesn't matter. All you need is hard-working teachers.
- We can force people to work harder and teach better.
- We can threaten them to improve, we can fire 5–10 percent, and things surely will get better.

These are early nineteenth- and twentieth-century psychological behaviorist beliefs—that if you stimulate teachers or kids, then, like dogs, they'll salivate and jump at your command. That's never happened, and it is not happening now.

Teachers are demoralized by these excessive attempts to control and dictate. We see no understanding of the idea that a major function of administration and supervision is to help teachers teach better so that kids will succeed.

I ran these chapters by some colleagues and a couple of graduate classes in educational leadership for editing and commentary. They urged me to include major reforms that *do* work instead of those undermining our public schools. So the last chapter does exactly that.

This book, like this preface, is written pretty much in a conversational tone so as to be easy to read. I hope you'll find it stimulating and appalling—stimulating so that you will read much of it, but appalling because of the concerted effort to undermine our public schools and replace them with for-profit enterprises.

As Deep Throat from former president Richard Nixon's impeachment saga said, "Follow the money."

Enough said.

Acknowledgments

No man is an island, as John Donne once wrote. And I certainly am indebted to my terrific wife, Sue Shapiro, and to a host of good friends, colleagues, grad assistants, and students for their participation in developing this book.

My wife and partner, Sue, listened patiently as we discussed the overall design and each chapter, and then critiqued the conceptual design for each chapter. After that major contribution, she then spent days cheerfully and meticulously editing, time analyzing, and critiquing. Huzzahs to her.

And to our longtime good friends, Dr. Lynne and Vic Menard, who sent sources and articles, critiqued each chapter, and wrote a contribution to the last chapter stimulated by Lynne's dissertation—you guys helped immeasurably. That's why I dedicated this book to you. It's well deserved.

To Heather Holder, who, by contributing an up-to-date section on supervision to the last chapter, enriched our thinking, many thanks. She, along with two grad classes working on masters' degrees in educational leadership, critiqued each chapter and made astute suggestions, ensuring that it would be relevant and timely—you all deserve my thanks and gratitude for taking the time and energy to think through with me how to improve the book. Ms. Holder's realistic comments proved invaluable in making certain that processes and concepts were on target.

Rabecca Hall, my grad assistant, sure spent a chunk of time thinking about the idea, researching various topics way beyond the time she was an assistant, and contributing mightily to the end product. I certainly hope our paths continue to cross so that we both are enriched.

Much gratitude to my colleagues/student in the classes: Sara Acosta, Shefali Bakshi, Sara Bokor, Charlena Boudreau, Mekeisha Brown, David Duquette, Manly Eugene, Brandon Glenn, Aaron Harvey, Heather Holder, Gilene Janvier, Clayton Luzier, Allison Martin, Lisa Miles, Joshua Phillips, Reginald Printemps, Shannon Schultz, Christina Simpson, Fasee Sollars, Shirley Waldy, Emeretta Warren, Charles Watts, Jenna Ball, LaFrance Clarke, Donna Erickson, Carrie Gentner, Kathryn Harrington, Stacy Risinger, Melissa Rivera, Caitlin Ryan, Christina Simpson, Holly Tabak, Robert Bennett, Dave Yogini, Christine Giannetti-Bell, Kristina Kassabaum, Rita Skyers, Kimberly Stache, Megan Trierweiller, and Kali Westphalen.

ONE

No Child Left Behind (NCLB), Race to the Top (NCLB 2.0), and Their Basis— The Accountability Movement

The singular feature of educational reform in the 21st century is a willing suspension of disbelief. Reformers today believe in miracles.
—Diane Ravitch

If you want to improve a prison, just get a better class of prisoners.
—Former Georgia governor Lester Maddox

To put it baldly, NCLB was built on a lie—the mythical "Texas Miracle." Then it was sold to the country by a president and his secretary of education. So, actually, it's a scam.

And has it changed American education! But hardly for the better.

INTRODUCTION AND ORGANIZATION

Now that that's over, let's get organized:

- First, we'll look briefly at the wondrous "Texas Miracle"—comparing and contrasting the myths and the reality.
- Next, we'll take a look at what NCLB and then Race to the Top (RTTT) essentially are—that is, what makes them work (and fail), and their purposes.
- Then we will cite the exact date, November 30, 2006, when NCLB's flaws were exposed—and crashed—at a conference arranged by its most ardent supporters. They agreed that it didn't work. We'll indicate exactly what its unintended consequences are.
- We'll briefly mention the role of poverty in student achievement. We'll do this by comparing our kids' scores with other nations'

1

scores by level of poverty using Program for International Student Assessment (PISA) results.
- We'll also give Race to the Top an analysis, with commentary.
- Last, we'll come up with a summary, some conclusions, and even some challenging and unfortunate implications, wryly wrought.

NCLB AND THE "TEXAS MIRACLE"

The "Texas Miracle" consisted of "the simple strategy of testing and accountability" (Ravitch, 2011). The Houston schools superintendent and Governor George W. Bush reported that those were the twin drivers. That is, they established statewide tests as an accountability measure, and believed that people would respond to their carrot. And they certainly did, but hardly in the way that the two assumed.

Comparing the claims and the reality turns out to be instructive. (Remember, Houston is a big urban school district with a heavy population of impoverished people, including whites as well as minorities.)

The mythical claim: Sharpstown High School (Houston) in 2001–2002 had *zero* dropouts (Leung, 2009).

The reality: The assistant principal went to the newspapers and reported that 463 kids of 1,700 dropped out in 2001–2002, thus attesting to the discrepancy between the report and the reality (Lueng, 2009). Big city schools suffer large dropout rates, so this became a huge red flag.

More reality: In another high school, out of one thousand kids entering, only three hundred graduated (Winerip, 2003).

How does an administration achieve this result? Since reasons given for dropouts are coded by each school, the people doing this simply cited different reasons for leaving, thus avoiding red-flagging students as dropping out. It is well known that dropout rates are very squishy, since students may not reveal their real reasons for leaving and clerks and assistant principals are overworked and may use different coding. However, Houston apparently developed a policy of fudging the accuracy of this figure, as the following reveals.

Myth: The Houston School District reported that it had only a 1.5 percent dropout rate (Leung, 2009).

Reality: Estimates of 40–50 percent are more accurate, as in other metropolitan school districts with large numbers of impoverished kids. The newspaper reported that an assistant superintendent had decreed that the dropout rate for the following year would decline from 1.5 percent to 1.3 percent (Trelease, 2005, p. 2). This turns the usual process of developing dropout rates on its head, which is always from the local school to the central office. So they substituted running the process from the central office, an unusual process, thus ensuring central administrative control of reporting such rates.

Another myth: Scores rose prodigiously on tests. Kids who passed the Texas Assessment of Academic Skills (TAAS) in 1996—61 percent. In 2002—86 percent.

The reality: SAT and ACT scores during that period dropped slightly (and that was during the term of the Houston superintendent, which ran from 1996 to 2001). Such dramatic TAAS increases raise red flags in observers' eyes, causing us to investigate further. One approach they used to increase scores is illustrated by the following process.

The sad reality: Kids were retained in ninth grade until they passed algebra, many for three years, and then they were jumped past tenth grade so they wouldn't take the TAAS (Leung, 2009).

The resultant reality: In 2001, 1,160 kids were in grade 9, but only 281 were in grade 10.

Obviously, the mechanism to achieve this result was to retain kids in freshman algebra classes until they pass. Typically, if students fail a subject, they are still advanced to their sophomore year, but the Houston administrative policy changed that, which served to inflate the percent of students supposedly passing TAAS.

Myth: In 1994, tenth graders' math scores were 26 percent; in 2003, they rose to 99 percent.

Reality: This is so improbable as to boggle the mind. When do all students taking a math test solve all the problems correctly? The superintendent (who was later appointed as the U.S. secretary of education) changed principals' appointments to one year. Thus, they could be released for any reason; he insisted that scores be jacked up, giving big bonuses for such results and dismissals for poor results. The frightened principals then generated three urban high schools, amazingly, with absolutely zero dropouts (Winerip, 2003).

We really could spend more time critiquing the "Texas Miracle," but, unfortunately, this scam was used to generate NCLB, which essentially is fast-tracking the process of nationalizing American education rather than keeping it in its former locally and state-based decentralized form.

WHAT IS NCLB ALL ABOUT?

NCLB is based on several components or tools:

- A choice option—that is, parents or kids could choose another school
- Supplemental educational services (SES), often consisting of tutorial services
- Corrective action—would include developing a plan (see Annual Yearly Progress [AYP] in this section)
- Restructuring—see also AYP

- Annually testing everybody to death (because that's the perceived present American pathway to accountability) in math and reading, expanded recently to science—the "high-stakes" testing obsession/mania currently in vogue
- Each teacher must be highly qualified
- Annual Yearly Progress (AYP)
- 100 percent proficiency academically by *all* students by 2014 (Bush, 2001)

The following paragraphs briefly explain each point.

Choice—This means that parents had a choice regarding what school their kids could attend. But most did not believe that their school was failing and didn't want their kids to be trucked (bused) across town. And they didn't agree that their school was failing. Only 2 percent opted for choice. So most stayed with their local schools (Bracey, 2007).

Supplemental Education Services (SES)—In some districts, few used tutoring or other SES services, 16 percent overall (Bracey, 2007). This, however, turned out to be a huge bonanza to organizations that already were in the business of coaching kids to raise their test scores or to do better in school. A consequence of this provision was that large numbers of organizations were formed to perform this function; however, the limitations placed on getting high-quality teachers were not enacted in the legislation. Consequently, many people employed to tutor students were not uniformly highly qualified.

Corrective action—This involved technical advice (see AYP).

Restructuring—This is turning a school into a charter (to be discussed in chapter 8), turning it over to public or private school organizations, replacing faculty and/or administration.

Annual testing—Starting in 2005–2006, states had to test kids in grades 3–8 annually in math and reading. Starting with 2007–2008, testing was required in science at least once in all three school levels, elementary, middle, and high school. Tests were required to be aligned to state academic standards, and a sample of fourth- and eighth-grade students had to participate in National Assessment of Educational Progress (NAEP) in alternate years in both math and reading in order to compare state and NAEP results.

A reason for this last provision was that, for some reason, test results in some states shot up, but the national NAEP scores did not. Some suspected that state governors and superintendents were rigging the scores to look good and to support their claims that he/she was the "education governor."

Annually testing kids has become an immense source of funding for test preparation companies. Gerald Bracey discussed how at early test conferences leading companies used to serve lemonade and chips. After NCLB made its entrance, such meetings offered ice-carved swans loaded with shrimp, lots of wine, and other indicators of organizations swimming in profits.

However, a significant problem occurred. Test companies had an extremely difficult time grading all the tests, especially written tests, from all the students in an entire state in time for teachers to use the results to do corrective teaching. As a matter of fact, the testing organizations mostly could not pull that off in the United States or in England. Results came back in the summer or even the fall, so teachers could not use them for the classes that were tested.

An unintended consequence was that districts began to start school earlier and earlier in order to get the testing done after the majority of instruction had occurred. Kids thus were starting school in early or mid-August.

More will be provided below in the section "Unintended Consequences Arise."

Teacher qualifications—All teachers, by the end of 2005–2006, teaching in core areas had to be "highly qualified" in each subject he or she taught. That is, the teacher had to be "fully certified by the state or have passed the state licensure exams and have a license to teach in the state . . . [and] must demonstrate their knowledge of the subject they teach through certain credentials or test scores" (Federal Education Budget Project, 2012)—another voyage down the rabbit hole.

*Annual Yearly Progress (AYP)—*This became a serious problem. The kids in *every subgroup* in the school (usually 95 percent)—such as disadvantaged, minority, or English for Speakers of Other Languages (ESOL)—have to pass the comprehensive tests. If even *one* of those groups (usually about thirty of them in a school) does not pass, the entire school is labeled as failing. In most city districts, most schools eventually fell into this category. Thus, there were few schools available for students to be transferred to, even if they wanted to do so.

Even schools with national reputations became ensnared in the stringent criteria in AYP—for example, New Trier Township High in Winnetka, Illinois, a wealthy suburb on the North Shore of the state, and a nationally renowned school. With schools like this being pointed out as failing, many began to question AYP. Even 46.8 percent of the state of Minnesota's well-recognized schools began to fail to meet the requirements of AYP in 2011 (*MPR News*, 2011).

The consequences of failure multiplied with time:

- If a school receiving Title I moneys could not meet AYP two years in a row, it would be provided technical assistance and its students would be offered a choice of other public schools to attend.
- Schools failing to make AYP three years in a row had to offer free tutoring and other supplementary services.

- If a school continued to be unable to meet AYP a fourth year (called continuing failure), it could be subject to outside corrective measures, including possible governance changes, such as restructuring.
- A fifth year of failure would result in restructuring the entire school. This could include kicking out the staff and administration, turning it into a charter, takeover, or other options (Federal Education Budget Project, 2012). This started occurring in the spring of 2013.

(Because of the clever condition that *all* subgroups had to pass, more and more schools began to be labeled as failing. Obviously, people then began to question the way AYP was being implemented.)

Academic Progress—100 percent proficiency by *all* students had to occur by 2014. Obviously, this is an oxymoron. It means that all kids will have to be above average on the tests (like in Garrison Keillor's Lake Wobegon). Why this obviously impossible provision was even considered is mystifying, but its presence led many to question the entire act.

UNINTENDED CONSEQUENCES ARISE: OR WHY IT ISN'T WORKING

First, It's Based on False Assumptions

At the conference reported by Bracey (2007), participants reported that the NCLB choice, SES, corrective action, and restructuring tools were not working too well. The testing provision assumed that the annual tests could be returned to the schools in time for the teachers to be able to use them. But test reports arrived too late, after the school year was over, for teachers to be able to use them with their kids. (One purpose of tests is to see how well the kids have grasped what the teacher thinks they should have understood, so teachers can work on remediation.) But by the fall, the teachers had a new set of kids in their classes, so the test results on last year's classes were useless.

The political scientist in the panel could not find any theory underlying the policy of instituting SES. If you develop a policy, it should have some sort of theoretical base. And it didn't. As for implementing SES, it was quite difficult to pull off, since it had reverse incentives. It cost the districts money to facilitate the use of private or public SES providers, which could seriously reduce their other expenditures, many of which were fixed.

Why the testing mania? Easy—three reasons:

Accountability
Accountability
Accountability

What has become the mechanism for achieving accountability? Testing, of course.

This, despite the fact that highly successful countries like Finland do not test. (More on that in chapter 7.) Yet accountability has become virtually the existential reason driving governors, legislators, school administrators, teachers, and the public in evaluating schools.

But does this emphasis (some might say, mania) for testing work?

The title of an article by Sarah D. Sparks says it all: "Panel Finds Few Gains from Testing Movement" (Sparks, 2011). We've simply gone overboard (some might say over-testing). But what has it gotten us? One of the premier and quintessential values in the American culture is our emphasis on and practice of creativity, exemplified by our passion for music and the arts. Strauss (2010) cites Shemberg, "who has pointed out our obsession with standardized testing has produced one of the best instruments in the nation's history for stifling creativity."

The $64,000 Question—So, Why Isn't Testing Working?

As Ravitch (2010) said, it's naming and shaming. But we know that shaming is a poor motivator. People respond to opportunities for growth and for achievement, they want to take responsibility and to have control over what they do. They want to be involved (Rand, 1975). Shaming simply doesn't operate much as a motivator, although it does create fear.

Let's go back to Ravitch (2010), the *formerly* enthusiastic assistant secretary of education, who summed it up as follows: "None of the prescribed remedies were making a difference. Choice was not working, they all agreed" (p. 99). Only a very tiny percentage of kids were transferring, as noted earlier. She cites Julian Betts (2007), who questions whether choice is even a successful strategy, finding "that choice had little or no effect on student achievement" (p. 99).

Another reason was that in larger cities so many schools were failing AYP that there were no schools available for switching. In small districts with only one or two schools, if one was labeled as AYP, there was no place to go.

As for tutoring? Just place yourself in the shoes of a student who's not doing very well. Do you want to go to school longer than you have to? How do you know it'll be better than what you've experienced and have not been too happy with?

Other Assumptions

Gaining Control over Education

Education, once local (otherwise, why have local school districts run by local school boards?), has certainly become more and more centralized at both the state and federal levels. At state levels, statewide tests, such as Texas's TAAS, are dominating the classroom and curriculum. As for the national levels, NCLB and RTTP obviously are forcing centralization. Common Core State Standards (CCSS) is the newly minted pressure cooker for centralizing American education, just as state tests tend to drive schools to develop similar curricula, a core of common state standards will surely perform the same function nationally. The scale will be national, tending to obliterate the rich local fabric of curriculum developed over the decades.

Privatizing American Education

America has always offered private schools, some religious, some elite, as options. Recently, new vehicles have been created to privatize education, charter schools and vouchers. See chapters 8, 9, and 10 for discussion and analysis.

Other Unintended Consequences

The heavy emphasis on raising test scores, as we saw in the first section on the Texas Miracle in Houston, generated cheating, outright lying, and gaming the system. So principals began focusing on the kids who were just under the passing scores, newly named the "bubble" kids, forgetting about the rest.

Next, governors and superintendents got on the bandwagon by trying to make their state scores look good, so they manipulated the tests and the scores, as we saw in Houston. When researchers compared their scores with the NAEP tests, their kids' scores were way too inflated. That's why the law began to require comparison with the NAEP.

Teachers and students (and principals and superintendents and some board members) felt far too pressured, and are quite bitter about it. Test manuals tell people monitoring the tests how to handle kids who throw up—not the most pleasant chore. Next, the impact on kids can be pretty grim. In Florida, the first year of the tests, about 29,000 third graders failed and faced repeating a grade (Hunt, Benjamin, & Shapiro, 2004, p. 266). The then governor, Jeb Bush (brother of George W. Bush), said, "That breaks my heart. But if we don't deal with it now, going forward there are going to be a whole lot of shattered dreams."

Actually, over 29,000 were retained. The state legislature then threw in another curve, which stated that if a kid failed the third grade test again, they would be held back again. Almost 10,000 third graders were now two years older than their classmates just for that one year. Research on retaining kids indicates that about 65 percent will drop out if retained once; over 90 percent will drop out if retained twice (Smith & Shepard,

1987). It's about how kids *feel* about being failed that is most important. They fear failing a grade just behind losing a parent or going blind.

So, we are generating huge numbers of dropouts, something that was experienced in Houston and across Texas as the procedures were implemented, and it has become a national concern.

THE ROLE OF POVERTY

PISA: It's poverty not stupid.

—Mel Riddle

Poverty has an absolutely enormous impact on kids, teachers, and schools. All one has to do to see it is to look at national and international test scores to see how it plays out in American schools (Riddle, 2010). We'll point to the Program for International Student Assessment (PISA) scores, which are the results of several years of international test comparisons, for our data, and then we'll break out American scores by level of poverty. First, though, we'll develop a picture of PISA scores: "PISA scores are on a scale, with 500 as the average" (Dillon, 2010). Two-thirds of students in participating countries score between 400 and 600. For the purposes of this chapter, poverty is assessed by looking at the percentage of kids who are on free and reduced lunch.

Free and Reduced Meal Rates	PISA Score
Schools with less than 10 percent	551
Schools with 10–24.9 percent	527
Schools with 25–49.9 percent	502
Schools with 49.9–74.9 percent	471
Schools with more than 75 percent	446
U.S. average	500
OECD average	493

(OECD = Organization for Economic and Co-operation and Development)

OK, have we demonstrated the direct relationship of poverty to achievement!

Now, shockingly, the American rate of poverty exceeds that of all other industrialized nations. The lowest rates are as follows:

- Denmark—2.4 percent
- Finland—3.4 percent
- Norway—3.6 percent

The United Kingdom is at 16.2 percent. New Zealand comes in at 16.3 percent. The United States? *21.7 percent poverty.* When we compare our schools that are below 10 percent poverty with nations that have low poverty levels, we do quite well.

- United States—551
- Finland—536
- Netherlands—508
- Norway—503

- U.S. schools with 10–24.9 percent poverty score third behind Korea and Finland.
- U.S. schools with 25–50 percent poverty rank tenth in the world in this category.

Only the United States and Mexico have numbers of schools with more than 75 percent poverty, both ranking in the bottom of the industrialized world's scores.

Riddle notes, "Researchers report that perhaps the only true linear relationship in the social sciences is the relationship between poverty and student performance. While there is no relationship between poverty and ability, the relationship between poverty and achievement is almost fool-proof" (2010, p. 8). We'll pick up on these data in our last section on implications—and there are a number of them.

Another Unintended, But Positive, Consequence

The NCLB act certainly has directed emphasis to kids not doing well in schools, usually the poor, the marginalized, and the special education students who've slipped beneath our high-achievement radar. This is certainly way past due for our thoughtful attention and action.

As a matter of fact, perhaps we should take a look at our institutional structures and expectations for kids, which many perceive as rigged against them. Shall we mention the National Honor Society, honor rolls, the salutatorian, and National Merit Scholarships as examples of meritorious norms that can discriminate against those in poverty, the marginalized, and the special education kids?

Recent NCLB Developments

The Obama administration recently bypassed the original mandates of NCLB, essentially freeing more than half the states from the central provisions of the law (Rich, 2012). The waivers focused states' attention on the bottom 5 percent of low-performing schools and removed the branding accomplished by the AYP provision. This has led to almost half the schools in the country being tarnished as failing. Rich noted that over

80 percent of Massachusetts schools failed to make AYP, with Virginia following behind with 61 percent (Rich, 2012).

RACE TO THE TOP (OR NCLB 2.0)

What is Race to the Top (RTTP) all about?

- Designing and implementing rigorous standards and high-quality assessments, by encouraging states to work jointly toward a system of common academic standards that . . . includes improved assessments
- Attracting and keeping great teachers and leaders in America's classroom, by . . . reforming and improving teacher preparation, revising teacher evaluation, compensation, and retention policies
- Supporting data systems that inform decisions and improve instruction, by fully implementing a statewide longitudinal data system, assessing and using data to drive instruction
- Using innovation and effective approaches to turn around struggling schools by (focusing on) persistently low-performing schools
- Demonstrating and sustaining educational reform . . . to raise student achievement and close achievement gaps, and by expanding support for high-performing public charter schools, reinvigorating math and science education. (White House, 2009)

False Assumptions

As with NCLB, we'd better take a skeptical look at the assumptions supporting RTTP. Obviously, as with any program such as NCLB or RTTP, one of the best ways to analyze it is to uncover the validity of its assumptions. Unfortunately, for RTTP, they're all false, as Marion Brady (2009) notes. We'll cite several:

False Assumption 1: America's teachers deserve most of the blame. Other factors that affect learning—language problems, hunger, stress (poverty), and so on—are minor and can be overcome by well-qualified teachers.

False Assumption 2: Professional educators are responsible for bringing education to crisis, so they can't be trusted. School systems should instead be headed by business CEOs, mayors, ex-military officers, and other accustomed to running a "tight ship." Their managerial expertise more than compensates for how little they know about educating. (*Question*: How would you like to be in a Marine division in combat commanded by a CEO with no military experience? How about your principal?)

False Assumption 3: If the young can't clear arbitrary statistical standards put in place by politicians, it makes good sense to raise those bars.

False Assumption 4: Notwithstanding the failure of vast experiments such as those conducted in Eastern Europe under Communism, history proves that top-down reforms such as No Child Left Behind work well. Centralized control doesn't stifle creativity, imply teacher incompetence, limit strategy options, or discourage innovation.

False Assumption 5: Standardized tests are free of cultural, social class, language, experiential, and other biases.

False Assumption 6: Forcing merit pay schemes on teachers will revitalize America's schools.

My own contribution: U.S. students are not competitive with the rest of the world. (See the previous section on the role of poverty to see how extremely competitive our students are.)

Some Observations, Preliminary Conclusions, and, Even Critiques of RTTP

Obviously, we see lots of similarities to NCLB, such as those listed below:

- Raising achievement
- Emphasis on maniacal testing
- Evaluating teachers and tying student performance to teacher compensation
- Heavy-duty focusing on data
- Focusing on struggling schools, and still closing them, or turning them into public or private-for-profit charters
- Increasing charter schools (despite evidence that they don't deliver on their promise [see chapter 9])

Some differences include the provision that RTTP is based on forcing school systems and states to *compete* for federal grants funded by the stimulus package. Thus, some districts and states will be able and others will not be able to get these grants, a source for criticism. If education is a civil right, the losing districts and states are not going to be able to access the funds to meet the criteria (although, in the end, that may not be so negative).

Another difference includes the notion that RTTP is driving the nation toward Common Core State Standards (CCSS)—see chapter 2 for an analysis and critique of this strange idea for improving America's formerly locally organized schools.

RTTP continues the emphasis on testing kids to death and then proposes to evaluate and compensate teachers by the results of the tests. Ravitch (Strauss, 2010) reasonably insists that teacher evaluation should be resolved by professional associations rather than by politicians.

Additionally, RTTP will generate a number of very interesting but unwelcome consequences. First, it encourages teaching to the test, since so much rides on improving testing results for kids, teachers, and administrators. Some states are setting 40 or 50 percent of any teacher's evaluation to come from their kids' tests, but no research exists to support that rule (Strauss, 2010). RTTP also focuses on encouraging privately managed schools, although no research exists to support their superiority. Chapter 9 on charters will investigate that.

RTTP also will continue to skew the nature of curriculum offerings to state testing decisions. It will continue the process of gaming the system and attempting to enhance scores by cheating, as documented in the Texas Miracle. RTTP neatly undermines both local and state support and control of education. Local school boards' authority is being eroded by the provisions of both NCLB and RTTP, as is state authority. Interestingly, RTTP seemingly drops AYP (hopefully), with all of its toxic impacts.

SUMMARY, CONCLUSIONS, AND IMPLICATIONS

NCLB has been a huge failure (with the excellent exception of forcing us to focus on poverty and minority students). Based on a Texas scam and a series of false assumptions, it has strongly impacted American schools. It is a top-down operation fundamentally forcing a decentralized system to become more centralized.

It has turned schools into testing factories, but, as the literature concludes, we find few gains from the testing movement. We send kids to school for 180 days and then we evaluate them and their teachers and their schools based on one or two days of tests. If they can't pass the tests, they're retained (read: failed). Huge numbers of students have been failed, horrifying our kids (to say nothing of their parents) and increasing our dropouts prodigiously.

Bracey (2008) noted that the great value we place on creativity has been drastically stifled by our increasing stress on standardized testing. Equally, it has demoralized teachers, with the latest focus on reforming education simply by identifying so-called bad teachers and then kicking them out. (Chapter 4 will provide us with the hard data proving that this isn't so easy to do [especially if you operate with normal moral standards and want testing procedures to have some degree of validity].)

NCLB has narrowed the curriculum, relegating science, history, social studies, physical education, arts, music, and other quintessential elements of Western civilization to fifth-rate status. Science, however, is now back in favor, since we are going to start testing it. An implication? Advocate to test any subject field, and, if accepted, it will magically become important.

And Race to the Top?

No research base has been developed, so it's a hope. It is also very much top-down, imposed. Cara Metz (2010) cites a teacher paraphrasing a Columbia graduate who said, "We've gone from no child left behind to every child—except the ones who win—left behind."

We saw the example of test results being doctored in Texas, but the virus has obviously spread to other districts. A crazed focus on test results virtually inevitably generates such foolishness. But it also generates the narrowing of curriculum noted above.

We are now seeing a huge change in public attitudes, from a time when schools and teachers have been respected, even revered, to being scapegoated, criticized, and even considered to be overpaid. We once thought that art, music, history, and civics were necessary to be a well-educated citizen and an active participant in the glories of Western civilization. In less than a mere handful of years, we now find that they're superfluous.

We see teachers and educators being blamed for the difficulty of erasing the huge impact of poverty on achievement. And the United States has the greatest poverty, by far, of nations in the developed world. If we are serious about improving education, we need to focus on reducing our poverty, not blaming educators. However, this implication has not yet gained wide recognition in America. And since it is not happening, we still tinker around the edges of the disease, not coming to grips with the major cause.

Possibly the second most disastrous and dangerous implication of RTTP is that with enough money and clout (Ravitch [2010] refers to the Billionaire Boys Club), anyone can fundamentally change the entire institution of American education from a decentralized structure to a centralized one. All it takes are a few billion dollars and a couple of years. (And we all unquestionably know that we'll drop it shortly, just like we're doing with NCLB and just like Madeline Hunter's 1980s and 1990s model has passed into oblivion.)

What fad is next?

REFERENCES AND RESOURCES

Betts, J. (2007). California: Does the Golden State deserve a gold star? In Hess & Finn (Eds.), *No remedy left behind: Lessons from a half decade of NCLB.* Washington, DC: AEI Press.

Bracey, G. (2007, February). Things fall apart: NCLB destructs. *Phi Delta Kappan, 88*(6), 475–476.

Bracey, G. (2008, December 9). International comparisons: More fizzle than fizz. *Huffington Post.*

Brady, M. (2009, October 23). Educator: "Race to the Top's" 10 false assumptions. *The Answer Sheet.* [Web log post]. Retrieved from http://voices.washingtonpost.com/answer-sheet/guest-bloggers/educator-race-to-the-top-is-be.html

Bush, G. W. (2001, January 31). U.S. Department of Education. Executive summary. http://www2.ed.gov/nclb/overview/intro/execsumm.html

Dillon, S. (2010, December 7). Top test scores from Shanghai stun educators. *New York Times,* A1.

Federal Education Budget Project. (2012, September 12). *No Child Left Behind—Overview*. http://febp.newamerica.net/background-analysis/no-child-left-behind-overview

Hunt, J. J., Benjamin, W. F., & Shapiro, A. (2004). *What Florida teachers say about the FCAT*. Tampa, FL: Ad Hoc.

Leung, R. (2009, February 11). The "Texas miracle." Retrieved from www.cbsnews.com/2100-500164_162-591676.html

Metz, C. (2010, April 1). Panel looks at pros and cons of Race to the Top. *New York Teacher, 51*(13), 9.

MPR News (2011, September 30). More MN public schools missing federal marks: Officials reluctantly release list. *Minnesota Public Radio*. http://minnesota.publicradio.org/display/web/2011/09/29/no-child-left-behind-schools-miss-federal-marks

Rand. T. M. (1975). Diagnosing the valued reward orientations of employees. *Personnel Journal*.

Ravitch, D. (2010). *The death and life of the great American school system*. New York: Basic Books.

Ravitch, D. (2011, April 5). The Texas miracle revisited. *Bridging differences*, [Web log post] *Education Week*. Retrieved from http://blogs.edweek.org/edweek/Bridging-Differences/2011/04/the_texas_miracle_revisited.html

Rich, M. (2012, July 6). "No Child" Law whittled down by White House. *New York Times*.

Riddle, M. (2010, December). PISA: It's poverty not stupid. *The principal difference: Bridging research and policy to practice for school leaders*. [Web log post]. Retrieved from http://nasspblogs.org/principaldifference/2010/12/pisa_its_poverty_not_stupid_1.html

Smith, M. L., & Shepard, L. A. (1987, October). What doesn't work: Explaining the policies of retention in the early grades. *Phi Delta Kappan, 69*(2), 129–134.

Sparks, S. D. (2011, May 26). Panel finds few gains from testing movement. *Education Week*. Retrieved from www.edweek.org/ew/artic.es/2011/05/26/33academcy.h30.html

Strauss, V. (2010, May 26). The Answer Sheet: A school survival guide for parents (and everyone else): Ravitch's 10 reasons to say "no" to Race to the Top. [Web log post]. Retrieved from http://voices.washingtonpost.com/answer-sheet/diane-ravitch/ravitchs-10-reasons-to-no-to-r.html

Trelease, J. (2005). If money talks, is it a miracle? www.trelease-on-reading.com/whatsnu_miracles.html

White House. (2009, November). *Fact Sheet: The Race to the Top*. Washington, DC: Office of the Press Secretary. http://www.whitehouse.gov/the-press-office/fact-sheet-race-top

Winerip, M. (2003, August 13). On education: The "zero dropout" miracle: Alas! Alack! A Texas tall tale. *New York Times*. Retrieved from http://www.nytimes.com/2003/08/13/nyregion/on-education-the-zero-dropout-miracle-alas-alack-a-texas-tall-tale.html

TWO

Common Core State Standards (for 310 Million Americans!)

Have we generated an immense, unstoppable, implacable monolith crashing down through the forests of time?

—Anonymous

The days of a teacher putting her imprint on the curriculum she teaches daily—those days are long gone.

—Reading supervisor in large Florida school district

INTRODUCTION AND ORGANIZATION (WITH SOME PITHY QUESTIONS)

Key Question: Should each school look exactly like every other school in the country?

Second Key Question: Are all kids the same? (Really, are all of *your* kids the same?)

Last Key Question (at least for now): Are all communities the same?

Therefore, how can we have Common Core State Standards (CCSS)?

Some perspective: Until recently, education was pretty much a local affair. Otherwise, why have a local school board, elected locally? Then we began developing programs with national implications, such as the following:

- National Merit Scholarships
- Scholastic Aptitude Tests (SATs) for college entrance purposes
- Preliminary Scholastic Aptitude Tests to prepare for the SATs
- Goals 2000 to establish common goals for all states

17

- No Child Left Behind (NCLB) with state tests to jack up kids' performance in math and reading
- Race to the Top (really NCLB 2.0)

Let's cut right to the chase. What does research say about CCSS?

Answer: Unfortunately, absolutely nothing. There is no research that supports this idea (Tienken, 2011; Ravitch, 2012; Greene, 2011). So why are we even talking about a national program attempting to be implemented in virtually all our states? Americans tend to jump onto faddish bandwagons (as do the Brits and the Dutch [Phillips, 2002]).

We like to follow fashions. We believe in fictions. We love fantasies. *Finally, it's a fraud.* Why would anyone in his or her right mind implement a program nationally, even in a single district, or two or three schools, that has no research basis? Normally, we would establish a pilot program and build a research component to determine if it works. Normally, we build field trials—just as the pharmaceutical industry does. Instead, we've built a runaway train (onto which virtually all states have jumped).

We'll deal with what the standards are, mention the "Overton Window" as a box that boxes us in (if we're not observant), and look at the underlying mythical assumptions underlying CCSS. We next focus on the underlying realities that demolish the validity of CCSS and ask what comprises the mechanism for measuring standards.

Question: Do you want to guess what it is? (I'll bet you have it cold.)

We then look at basic principles of designing curriculum and find that CCSS violates these. We further critique CCSS, using constructivist principles as our prism, and point to the impact of CCSS in nationalizing our presently fairly decentralized curriculum, which we predict will undercut the present dynamism of our system.

SO, WHAT ARE THE COMMON CORE STATE STANDARDS (CCSS)?

First, we have to figure out what educational standards are.

"Standards in public education are specific guidelines for what children should know upon high school graduation. . . . Typically, standards also delineate what students should know at the end of each grade level" (Piccolo, 2012, p. 2). Piccolo notes that "the primary purpose of standards is to establish guideposts that direct all aspects of schooling toward a defined goal" (p. 2).

Next, what are Common Core State Standards?

"The Common Core State Standards Initiative is a state-led effort coordinated by the National Governors Association Center for Best Practices (NGA Center) and the Council of Chief State School Officers. . . . These standards define the knowledge and skills students should have within their K-12 education careers so that they will graduate high school able to succeed in entry-level, credit-bearing academic college courses and in workforce training programs" (Common Core State Standards Initiative, 2012).

While the emphasis appears to be *as a state basis*, this is illusory. CCSS are intended to be *national* standards. Universal. For each and every state.

The title, deliberately or not, fools us.

In other words, this would *centralize American education*. We would develop a *national system of education*. It certainly *is not a bunch of state standards*. This constitutes an immense shift in American education—from a locally and state-run operation to one that is national—just like many centralized countries (France, Japan, Singapore, Iran).

An example?

Years ago I worked with the government of Iran (before the shah was overthrown) to finalize a program for a number of Iranian educators to get their MA at George Peabody College of Vanderbilt University. Of course, I met some of the folks running the centralized educational system. The director of testing for Iran mentioned offhandedly that at that moment (10:21 AM), all the students in their fourth grade (equivalent to the U.S. system) were on a certain page in the math text. When I asked if even those who were slower than the rest were on that page, she replied, "Of course."

A REALITY—THE "OVERTON WINDOW"

"The Overton Window (named after Joseph P. Overton of the Mackinac Center for Public Policy) refers to the boundaries of the limited range of ideas and policies that are acceptable for consideration in politics at any one time. In other words, the Overton Window is the 'box' that we are constantly exhorted to think outside of, only to be ignored or punished if we succeed" (Lind, 2012). OK, let's take a hard, analytic look at a box a number of thinkers want to lock us into.

MYTHICAL ASSUMPTIONS UNDERLYING THIS CCSS MOVEMENT

1. American kids are behind other nations academically. That's because we lack national standards and tests.
2. Our "economic vibrancy and future . . . relies upon American students outranking their global peers on international tests of academic achievement because of the mythical relationship between ranks on those tests and a country's economic competitiveness" (Tienken, 2011).

Let's take a hard look at these. As for the first, middle-class American kids do as well as any nation internationally (Riddle, 2010). Where we have problems is with our disadvantaged kids, largely impoverished white, Latino, and black students (with the last two categories comprising about 35 percent of our school population, who obviously do not do as well).

As for the second part of that first assumption (because we lack national standards and tests), some nations with national standards do very well in international tests, such as France and Japan. But so do other nations with no national standards, such as Finland, Canada, and Australia (Cuban, 1997). Tienken (2011) noted that "McClusky (2010) reported that for the 27 nations with complete data sets that outranked the U.S. on the 2006 PISA (Program for International Student Assessment) science test, 10 of those nations did not have national standards whereas 12 of the 28 nations that ranked lower than the U.S. had national standards. . . . More countries with national standards underperformed the U.S. than did the countries without national standards" (pp. 7–8). To nail this coffin down firmly, Greene (2011) noted, "With respect to nationalized approaches there is no evidence that countries that have nationalized systems get better results."

So, if some nations who've established national standards and tests do not do well (and there are lots of them), it undercuts the whole argument. National standards and tests do not drive academic excellence. So why are we going down this rabbit hole? Are we hemmed in by the Overton Window? Why?

Now, do we have any evidence that assumption #2 (that beating other countries academically will generate global competitiveness) has any validity? Cuban (1997) refutes it, as does Tienken (2011). Cuban points to the excellent test results experienced by Japan for two decades in the 1990s and 2000s, while their economy tanked. Tienken (2011) cites Bracey (2009), Baker (2007), and Tienken (2008) in arguing that a country's rank on international tests hardly "has the power to predict future economic competitiveness."

Hopefully, we're done with that mythical "box."

NOW, UNDERLYING REALITIES UNDERCUTTING THE VALIDITY OF CCSS

Are Standards Behaviorist? If So, We Have Another Hoax in Education Reform

Calling CCSS "another hoax" is quite a statement to make. So first we'll examine what behaviorism is all about—and then the hoax statement can stand on its own (Shapiro & Koren, 2012).

Behaviorism is an early system of psychological thought developed by Pavlov (1927) and Watson (1913). Watson noted, "Psychology was the study of observable, measurable behavior, and nothing more" (Morris,

1982, p. 6). What does this mean? Watson and other stimulus-response psychologists were interested in only observable behavior that could be measured. Nothing else. They did not want to inquire as to how people thought, how they made meanings out of the welter of happenings around them, or how they developed their thoughts and beliefs. (When we get to constructivist thought later in this chapter, we will see another way we have developed our thinking about how we make meaning in our lives.)

Illustrations of behaviorist thinking in education?

- Gold stars, M&M's as rewards (most often used for special education)
- Teachers' belief that lectures are effective modes of instruction
- The accountability movement, based on the testing movement

What else can you point to as an example of behaviorist practices in education?

The mechanism for measuring standards?

Testing, of course.

Ravitch (2010) noted that the testing movement has joined forces with the standards movement. Since no research supports the Common Core State Standards movement, can we consider it to be behaviorist in nature? Relic (2007) cited Vito Perone lecturing at Harvard that the standards movement appears to be "more about standardization than standards, and a great danger is that given all the state mandates, the richness of classroom dynamics, what is studied and talked about, will be narrowed and stunted" (p. 2).

Standards, then, appear to be behaviorist. For such an immense force impacting American education, no research has been developed to support them. They are just flooding across the state legislatures immersing the curriculum of the schools. They have become the only base for developing curriculum and then designing learning experiences.

Cultures, Sub-Cultures, Regional Differences, and Socioeconomic Differences

Let's look at the huge differences in communities and schools in the United States. Does a kid in an inner city have the same experiences as one in posh Beverly Hills? The latter's parents make sure that they are connected with the right financial advisors as kids. How about a kid in a ranching community out west in comparison with one living in a middle-class area of a city? A small town?

How about wealth differences? Well over 20 percent of our kids are now in poverty. This means they might not get enough food on weekends (since school meals are not available). Do they have a place to study? (My daughter was dumbfounded last week when she discovered that I did not have my own room as an adolescent.) How about other cultural differences, age differences, and access to technology?

Regional differences abound. Connecticut usually is number one in educational expenditures per child. How does this impact kids in school settings? What opportunities are provided by an Evanston Township High School, Illinois, which offered six levels of Mandarin Chinese as early as the 1960s? And New Trier Township High School, Illinois, which provided four years of drama and dance programs for students interested in theatrical careers.

What impact do language differences generate on kids and on schools? One elementary school I worked with had fifty-four different languages among its students.

As with every centrifuging force, we should note unifying forces in our country, pointing to the yin-yangs we seem to face in our society. One of the most important unifiers is our common language. Another consists of common customs (although we have enormous differences in some areas).

Tienkin (2011) sums up the thinking in this section: "To think that every student in this country should be made to learn the same thing is illogical—it lacks face validity. The U.S. is just too large and too diverse to engage in such folly" (p. 11).

Another Reality Undercutting CCSS—Basic Principles of Curriculum Construction

This is a dandy when it comes to looking at underlying realities limiting developing national curricula.

Ralph Tyler's (1949) *Basic Principles of Curriculum and Instruction* lays out the fundamental principles for constructing curriculum. Tyler essentially organized the field of curriculum in his book. He pointed to three sources for designing curriculum. The first, and most important, is to figure out the needs and interests of students. The second is to determine the needs and priorities of society. The third—and last—are the contributions of subject matter specialists to the education of the student in developing curriculum. (Note the priority of meeting the needs and interests of students.)

How do Tyler's criteria impact national, centralized curriculum standards?

They trash the idea. Kids vary hugely in their needs, their abilities, and their readiness for learning. Some kids arrive at kindergarten already reading (that is, if the school has a kindergarten).

By kindergarten, some kids already have spent a couple of years in a high-quality nursery school. Some kids come to school without such experiences, having no idea what school is all about (unless they've been to Head Start or some other governmental intervention to facilitate preparing them for school). There they learn to share, to cooperate, to understand that schools have schedules. They learn the fundamental norms of preschool and primary education—for example, that students' and teachers' roles differ.

Christopher Tienkin (2011) cites Wang, Haertel, and Walberg (1993) in arguing "that the closer to the student that the curriculum is designed, deliberated, and created, the greater influence it has on learning" (p. 12). Obviously, we are saying that curriculum has to be a local enterprise.

One doctoral study I supervised indicated that kindergarten teachers pretty well figured out what social class their kindergarteners were by the end of the first or second week of school, and some began to treat their middle-class charges better than those they perceived as being in poverty or working class. (My way of dealing with that was to make sure my own kids entering kindergarten were quite well dressed, and I went in and chatted up these key people. I wanted no one screwing up their educational chances.)

A Critique of CCSS Based on Constructivist Principles and Practices

Actually, an interesting quote says a lot about the power of constructivism: "Constructivism has become the reigning paradigm in teacher education in America today" (S. Hausfather, *Educational Horizons*).

OK, what is constructivism? And why does it pulverize CCSS?

As we grow, we all develop different experiences, different interactions with people, with organizations, with our families. So, we develop attitudes about things; we develop different values, beliefs, perceptions, and ways of looking at things. Where we live in a city, a suburb, a rural area affects us just as our age does (older folks who are retired live differently from twenty-five-year-olds working feverishly to survive).

Brooks and Brooks (1993) note, "Each of us makes sense of our world by synthesizing new experiences into what we have previously come to understand" (p. 4). We face varying experiences with a range of people, which means we become somewhat unique. Even if we're twins, do twins develop the same beliefs, attitudes, values, perceptions, and ways of looking at things? Of course not. We *construct* different perceptions of our families, school, sports, politics, money, and art depending on our experiences and beliefs. We learn to look at things differently.

Simply stated, constructivism means that every one of us *constructs* or builds the way we look at things somewhat or quite differently than others based on our unique experiences. Note that in describing an accident, two people often see things quite differently. Even twins do that, such as my wife and her twin. My wife, the older twin, is interested in the birth order of twins, and nine out of ten times, she can spot an older twin easily. This is not something her younger twin ever thinks about, so she simply ignores it.

For me, the idea of constructivism exploded into reality when I saw the title of Berger and Luckman's 1966 *The Social Construction of Reality*. The implications of that title stopped me in my tracks. We—each of us—*construct our own reality*.

Philosopher D. C. Phillips, asked by the National Society for the Study of Education to solicit various opinions on constructivism in education, wrote, "[T]his . . . type of constructivist view is that learners actively construct their own ('internal,' as some would say) sets of meaning or understandings; knowledge is not a mere *copy* of the external world, nor is knowledge acquired by passive absorption or by simple transference from one person (a teacher) to another (a learner or knower). In sum, knowledge is *made*, not *acquired*" (2000, 7).

Impact of Constructivism on the Validity of CCSS?

Obviously, constructivism absolutely dynamites the underlying assumption of CCSS that a universal set of common core standards will be used effectively to educate all our kids. How can they when we have such enormous variety in any population, let alone 310 million people? How can we develop a set of common standards that apply to everyone in a culture swimming in a sea of diversity? In an ocean of differently constructed individual worlds? We certainly are not an Iran, where all kids in a grade will be forced to work on a certain page of a text in math or English or history at the very same moment. The idea reeks of absurdity.

Besides, Americans are not wimps who are prone to being dictated to by a bunch of bureaucrats trying to ram a program down their throats. Eventually, rebellion breaks out, as has been happening with No Child Left Behind. CCSS is standardized, regulated. This method does not teach to the moment. It sets instruction that does not rest on student needs but rather on needs that people far removed from the classroom think exist. But they don't.

The epitome of CCSS comprises programs in which teachers are to be robots delivering lessons in teacher-proof curricula. Teachers hate it, and kids despise it. But such a structure has appeal to some people who think that it will result in higher test scores, though not necessarily improve learning.

Tienkin (2011) sums up our thinking in this section, "Standardization assumes that children are not active constructors of meaning that bring prior knowledge and experience to the learning situation. It assumes that all students start at the same academic place with the same advantages and set of skills and that they will finish with the same results" (p. 11).

Critiquing the Nationalizing Structure of CCSS

The very structure and size of CCSS makes it extremely difficult to alter (as all systems need to do in their careers). Changing a small school district's curriculum in one area can be quite daunting, usually taking two or three years (that is, if teachers and administrators can look objectively at what they're doing).

In a large system, it becomes quite an enterprise. This is magnified when one is looking at a state. On a national level, resistance to change can become another matter. Greene (2011) notes that "nationalized approaches lack a mechanism for continual improvement" (p. 2). This brings to mind Harold Benjamin's *Saber Tooth Curriculum* (1939), in which the changing Ice Age conditions rendered the former curriculum of scaring saber-toothed tigers and cave bears with fire and catching fish barehanded in clear streams obsolete. The tigers and bears had become pretty moldy, and the streams were slow and murky, so the former curriculum didn't work. But the teachers persisted in their learning activities. Is this the fate of the CCSS?

Next, what about the quality of the CCSS? A number of experts are hardly convinced of their quality. As a matter of fact, the standards are not being vetted by state or local school districts, to the point that this has raised alarm in several quarters (Stotsky & Wurman, 2010). For example, the head of the Massachusetts chapter of the American Federation of Teachers noted that their state standards "are clearly higher than what the federal government is proposing" (Chieppo & Gass, 2012, p. 2).

Greene (2011) states baldly, "The enemy of high standards and improving outcomes is standardization" (p. 2). One can see the difficulty in changing such a massive system in the metaphor of turning an immense ocean liner around as compared to a jet ski. Greene points to the value of different systems trying different approaches as providing the dynamism of the American educational systems. Gigantic systems are much harder to move, to change. Certainly, a teacher's opportunities for differentiated instruction become remote in a system where nationalized and centralized standards have taken over.

SUMMARY, CONCLUSIONS, AND IMPLICATIONS

Well, we've taken the measure of Common Core State Standards and found them severely wanting. First of all, they're *not state* standards, they're *national and centralized* standards. So, it's a fraud. Next, they're being implemented with no field testing. We are leaping aboard an express train with no idea where we're heading. The American culture is prone to jumping aboard fads. This is a glaring and unfortunate example.

They're based on two mythical assumptions. The first is that American kids are behind other nations educationally because we lack national educational standards. We've demolished this notion. Middle-class American kids do quite well in comparison with the top-scoring nations, as chapter 1 reveals. Our kids in poverty do not do well at all.

The second myth is that a nation's economic success rests on its students' academic achievement. We've also demolished this idea.

We've then looked at several underlying realities. First, we've asked if the standards are behaviorist, and concluded warily that they certainly seem to have the properties to appear so. If so, they constitute an even greater hoax perpetrated on American schools. The next underlying reality undercutting the validity of CCSS is the huge variation in cultures and subcultures, wealth, regional differences, urban-suburban-rural lifestyles, school support, and so on in the United States. All of this disparity works against a successful centralized approach. How can we build standards that meet the needs of such a hugely diverse population?

Next, what we know about constructing curriculum is that it must be based on students' interests and needs first—certainly not the wishes of curriculum experts, nor the needs of society. This CCSS approach turns curriculum development on its head, from being based on the needs and interests of the students to being based on the perceptions of politicians and curriculum designers. As we look at the movement of education into constructivist thinking, because we are so unique, constructing a national curriculum not only makes no sense but also violates the integrity of the individual and our values.

Finally, any nationalizing system becomes exceedingly difficult to amend, to alter, so it will inevitably become out of sync with the changing culture and the needs of kids, teachers, and the system itself. Eventually, the quality will suffer.

So, why go down this benighted path?

REFERENCES AND RESOURCES

Baker, K. (2007). Are international tests worth anything? *Phi Delta Kappan, 89*(2), 101–104.
Benjamin, H. (J. Abner Peddiwell). (1939). *Saber tooth curriculum*. New York: McGraw-Hill.
Berger, P. L., & Luckman, T. (1966). *The social construction of reality*. Garden City, NY: Doubleday.
Bracey, G. (2009). U.S. School performance, through a glass darkly (again). *Phi Delta Kappan, 90*(5), 386–387.
Brooks, J. G., & Brooks, M. G. (1993). *The case for constructivist classrooms*. Alexandria, VA: Association for Supervision and Curriculum Development.
Chieppo, C., & Gass, J. (2012, September 3). Intrusive to the core: Feds overreach on ed standards. *Boston Herald*.
Common Core State Standards Initiative (2012). About the standards. http://www.corestandards.org/about-the-standards

Cuban, L. (1997, April 13). Debunking national academic standards. *St. Petersburg Times*.

Greene, J. P. (2011, September 21). My testimony on National Standards before the US House. http://jaypgreene.com/2011/09/21/my-testimony-on-national-standards-before-us-house/

Hausfather, S. (2001, Fall). Where's the content? The role of content in constructivist teacher education. *Educational Horizons*, 15–19.

Lind, M. (2012, September 1). Education reform's central myths. *The Progressive Populist*, p. 12.

McCluskey, N. (2010, February 17). Behind the curtain: Assessing the case for national standards. Policy Analysis no. 661. Cato Institute. Retrieved from http://cato.org/pubs/pas/pa661.pdf

Morris, C. G. (1982). *Psychology: An introduction*. 4th ed. Englewood Cliffs, NJ: Prentice-Hall.

Pavlov, I. P. (1927). *Conditioned reflexes* (V. G. Anrep, Trans.). London: Oxford University Press.

Phillips, D. C. (Ed.). (2000). *Constuctivism in education: Opinions and second opinions on controversial issues*. Ninety-ninth Yearbook of the National Society for the Study of Education, Part I. Chicago: University of Chicago Press.

Phillips, K. (2002). *Wealth and democracy: A political history of the American rich*. New York: Broadway Books.

Piccolo, M. C. (2012). *Common core: Is it best for Utah's children?* Salt Lake City, UT: Sutherland Institute.

Ravitch, D. (2010). *The death and life of the great American school system: How testing and choice are undermining education*. New York: Basic Books.

Ravitch, D. (2012, April 26). Will current school reforms improve education? Paper presented at the National Association of Teachers of Mathematics, Philadelphia, PA.

Relic, P. D. (2007). The trouble with the standards movement. National Association of Independent Schools. http://www.parentsassociation.com/education/standards_movement.html

Riddle, M. (2010, December). PISA: It's poverty not stupid. *The principal difference: Bridging research and policy to practice for school leaders*. [Web log post]. Retrieved from http://nasspblogs.org/principaldifference/2010/12/pisa_its_poverty_not_stupid_1.html

Shapiro, A., & Koren, A. (2012). Are educators lemmings? Now, it's standards—another behaviorist hoax. *EJournal of Education Policy*. http://nau.edu/uploadedFiles/Academic/COE/About/Projects/Are%20Educators%20Lemmings.pdf

Stotsky, S., & Wurman, Z. (2010, May). The emperor's new clothes: National assessments based on weak "college and career readiness standards." (Research Report No. 61). Pacific Research Institute: A Pioneer Institute White Paper. http://pioneerinstitute.org/download/the-emperors-new-clothes/

Tienken, C. H. (2008). Rankings of international achievement test performance and economic strength: Correlation or conjecture. *International Journal of Education Policy and Leadership, 3*(4), 1–15.

Tienkin, C. H. (2011, Winter). Common Core State Standards: An example of data-less decision making. *AASA Journal of Scholarship and Practice, 7,* 4.

Tyler, R. W. (1949). *Basic principles of curriculum and instruction*. Chicago: University of Chicago Press.

Wang, M. C., Haertel, G. D., & Walberg, H. J. (1993). Toward a knowledge base for school learning. *Review of Educational Research, 63*(3), 249–294.

Watson, J. B. (1913). Psychology as the behaviorist views it. *Psychological Review, 20,* 158–177.

THREE

Merit and Teacher Evaluation— Another Fraud

There is nothing more frightful than ignorance in action.

—Anonymous

INTRODUCTION AND ORGANIZATION

Some people interested in reforming education seem to be experiencing a revived love affair with the alluring siren song of merit pay to motivate teachers. This intermittent infatuation has been recurring for over four decades (Lewis, 2010). The first group to try out merit was some suburban school superintendents, who, proud of their widely recognized avant-garde leadership, attempted the idea. Although I was a suburban superintendent (who was skeptical and did not pick up the reform), we rapidly dropped the potential reform because of the havoc it created among faculty. We'll explain this shortly. As this chapter unfolds, this statement will become crystal clear.

First, we will explore the assumptions lurking under the widely held belief about applying the virtues of free market ideology and practice to education. We'll analyze each assumption with empirical studies. Next, we'll examine the immediate impact inherent in setting up merit systems in business, industry, government, and education. And finally, conclusions and implications will be fleshed out (hopefully, to everyone's satisfaction).

Let's fast-forward to the present, where from the 1990s to today, reforming education has been a national and state priority because of the widely agreed-upon—but false—claim that American education is failing. In chapter 1, we analyzed how well we're doing in comparison with

29

other industrial nations and found that our kids who are not in poverty were doing as well as the top nations in international tests when we compare scores on math and language. But we aren't doing so well for our kids in poverty. As a matter of fact, we are doing quite poorly (Riddle, 2010). Chapter 1 dealt with that in presenting data from the Program for International Student Assessment (PISA) scores.

GETTING DOWN TO MEAT AND POTATOES: ASSUMPTIONS SUPPORTING MERIT

Proponents of merit talk of "incentivizing" (read: motivating) teachers, assuming that teachers require stronger motivation (read: money) to become more effective (read: to work harder). The paradigm largely being pushed onto the profession of education obviously is being imported from market-based ideas in business and industry. Thus, Beth Lewis (2010) probably states it relatively boldly:

> Americans value hard work and results, and our capitalist system hinges upon rewarding such results. Most professions offer bonuses and salary increases to exemplary employees. Why should teaching be the exception? The fact that a sloppy teacher and a dedicated teacher earn the same salary just doesn't sit right with most people.
>
> Incentivized teachers will work harder and produce better results. What motivation do teachers currently have to go above and beyond the job's basic requirements? The simple possibility of extra cash would most likely translate into smarter teaching and better results for our children.

Two assumptions underlie this thinking:

1. Money increases the motivation of teachers, presumably to work harder.
2. Teachers want to compete.

Analysis of Assumption 1: Money Is a Motivator for Teachers

We immediately get into intrinsic versus extrinsic motivation, thus asking if money is an intrinsic or extrinsic motivator in education. Or is it a motivator at all? We can turn to Thomas Rand (1977) for some insight into this matter. We'll summarize his empirical findings. Rand examined the reward preferences of three groups: upper management, foremen, and hourly wage earners. He also asked upper management and foremen to *predict* the value rewards of their hourly workers.

Question: What would *you* predict are the motivators for these folks? For everyone? And are they the same?

Rand found that all three groups placed opportunity for growth as their first priority. The second priority was achievement or sense of accomplishment. Obviously, these are major intrinsic motivators. Pay, or monetary reward, was fifth for upper management, and sixth for foremen and hourly wage workers. Such additional extrinsic motivators as recognition by friends, interpersonal relationships, and company status came out last.

Conclusion: Money is not a major, or even an intrinsic, reward for any of these three groups.

But upper management and foremen predicted (obviously wrongly) that achievement would be fourth or fifth and opportunity for growth was predicted as fifth by upper management and ninth by foremen.

What are we to make of this?

Here is the kicker: Patently, because management and foremen have established virtually no relationship with the hourly folks, they simply have no understanding of them. So, they're merely guessing about their motivation. This is a real illustration regarding how the social structure of the workplace, or any organization, works. It isolates social groups from each other. Since managers and foremen have few, if any, meaningful relationships with the hourly people, they consistently believe the extrinsic motivators of pay and job security to be more important, rating them as first (1) and second (2) in priority. But they're way off.

Based on Rand's interesting research, we can dismiss the notion that teachers perceive money as a prime motivator—they do not. Has this study demolished the fundamental assumption by those who have swallowed the (by now apparent) fiction that teachers are universally motivated by money?

It would be useful for people who write or talk about teacher motivation, "incentivizing" teachers, to spend some time in the schools, talking and working with teachers. We might see some more realistic insights emerge that demolish this assumption.

Fortunately, another recent study by Vanderbilt University finishes hammering the nail into this notion that we can "incentivize" teachers by dangling a financial carrot in front of their drooling mouths. Anderson (2010) summarizes "the first scientifically rigorous review of merit pay in the United States [which] measured the effects of financial incentives on teachers in Nashville public schools" (p. 1).

Details are informative. The experiment lasted three years. Half of the math teachers in grades 5 through 8 were randomly assigned half to a control group and half to the experimental group. Those in the latter group were offered bonuses of $5,000, $10,000, and $15,000 if their students reached annual test score targets. "On the whole, researchers found no significant differences between the test results from classes led by teachers eligible for bonuses and those led by teachers who were ineligible" (p. 2).

Rothstein (2011) notes, "There is now substantial evidence that pay for performance [P4P] does not even work on its own terms—reading and math scores don't increase when teachers or entire schools are offered bonuses for higher sscores," going on to add, "But even if pay for performance did work on its own terms, it would harm public education" (p. 5). That's a serious charge. We'll pick up on this shortly.

Analysis of Assumption 2: Teachers Want to Compete with Their Peers

Because this assumption, like the first, is borrowed from business and industry, it is useful to test it by asking if teachers, by and large, like to compete with one another. Figlio (2011) notes, "There's evidence that people who choose to be teachers tend to be more cooperative and tend to wish to avoid competition." This is certainly true of elementary teachers. Secondary teachers tend to want to teach their subjects and, again, do not seem to want to compete.

Since teachers as professionals seem to be intrinsically motivated, it is time to inquire why this patently false perception has persisted in having such a long shelf life, arising like Lazarus from the dead to surface in different tattered attire.

Question: Do you think that perhaps those advocating pay for performance need to talk to teachers and develop an understanding of what drives them?

Research indicates that it does not seem to be salary (Rand, 1977; Marsh, 2011). Teachers work hard because they want their kids to do well. See chapter 1 for the enormous impact of poverty on the educational attainment of our kids (as measured by math and language tests).

This is supported by the findings of New York City's botched attempt to implement merit pay. Marsh (2011) noted that "more than three quarters of teachers surveyed felt that bonus criteria relied too heavily on student test scores . . . [and therefore] the motivational power of the incentive could be greatly compromised" (p. 2). In fact, Marsh states that

> teachers in schools not associated with the bonus program (control) were just as likely as those from assigned schools (treatment) to report undertaking a host of efforts to help their school achieve a high Progress Report grade. . . .
>
> Also, intrinsic motivators—such as seeing themselves improve and seeing their students learn new skills and knowledge—ranked much higher than financial bonuses on the list of potential motivators cited by teachers on surveys. (p. 2)

Often, however, some kids like to compete with themselves, which seems a pretty good piece of information both to be aware of and to utilize in our instructional planning. To this point, the motivational assumptions underlying P4P seem to be hopelessly simplistic—and dead wrong.

*The Impact of Systems Establishing Merit: They Establish Categories
to Cram People Into and Produce . . . a Tragedy*

To hammer the nail in the coffin even more firmly, let's look at *systems*
to implement merit. *Every such system has to establish categories*, otherwise
how do you have merit? Many systems seem to construct three, four, or
five categories into which people must fit (or be jammed into).

One such system in a Florida county uses the Danielson Evaluation
Instrument, revised edition (Danielson, 2007), model with four levels,
which seems to have been borrowed from Microsoft, which seems logical
inasmuch as the district was awarded a Gates grant (remember, Bill
Gates ran Microsoft). Microsoft's approach has been to develop teams of
ten people that are evaluated as follows: one or two people are evaluated
as superior, six or seven are rated as average, and one or two are rated as
bottom feeders, no matter how productive — or not — the team has been
(Eichenwald, 2012).

This has generated competition for survival, which has led Microsoft,
once the world electronics leader, to lose its primacy, since team members now compete on developing products, not on what people/custom-
ers would use and want. Apple now far exceeds Microsoft in products
and income. The system just described has essentially slowed Microsoft,
as can be seen in the number of Apple products and the demand for them
in comparison with those of Microsoft.

The system embraced by Danielson has been that the top level is entered only by a small percent. This top level is treated "as a house you can
only visit, but not reside in." The second level certainly is above average.
The third level was labeled "developing" and was eventually changed
because people placed in that category were so outraged that the administration changed it, but, of course, the label and the symbol stuck. The
lowest category is perceived as "untouchable" (a reference to the lowest
caste in India) and, if not remediated fast, leads to being fired.

This leads to two issues: What are the repercussions of implementing
the system? And how valid are the evaluations? First, the repercussions.

Repercussions

Let's examine Meyer's (1975) basic study regarding professional and
managerial employees' perceptions of how they compare with others in
their field. That is, people were asked in the strictest confidence how they
believed they compared with others.

- They results are fascinating — and disastrous — for the rating scales
  fundamental to merit models. Forty-seven percent believed they
  were in the top 5 percent.
- Thirty-six percent believed they were in the top 10 percent.
- That's 83 percent!

- And the rest of the people? No one, but no one, felt they were under the top 25 percent.

Thus, *everyone* else believed they were in the top 25 percent. Simply put, we are extremely optimistic about ourselves.

So, we have 83 percent of people firmly believing they were in the top 5–10 percent of their peers. And the remaining 17 percent placed themselves in the top 25 percent. Now, in the Danielson model, 100 percent are told they do not place in the top category (where only 2 percent or more may visit occasionally).

The very nature of this model, therefore, *informs everyone that he/she is substandard*. As evaluations were made, teachers actually wrote into the two local newspapers expressing their outrage. One very able woman in my class asked her principal with considerable anger why he didn't place her in the top 2 percent category. He blithely informed her that only 2 percent of teachers fell into that category, enhancing her already considerable anger—and alienation.

Actually, the damage was done merely by setting up the categories. To add to the destruction of morale, Meyer noted that people usually develop one or both of two reactions. First, they reject the evaluator/supervisor to the point of dismissing them as totally incompetent or biased. This completely destroys their relationship. The next reaction was equally disastrous, since people also felt that the work or the profession wasn't worth it. Both results destroyed morale and relationships. People believed that the system was a disaster.

More on the Validity of the System

In the district using the Danielson model, teachers of the year found themselves in the category "needing development" (some teachers thought that that reward was political anyway). When one teacher of the year asked the evaluator "sweetly" to demonstrate how she could improve, the evaluator demurred, saying that such was not her role. Of course, the widely formed conclusion was that the evaluator couldn't.

Another example comes to mind. A newish kindergarten teacher (with three years of experience) was given very strong evaluations by an evaluator. The dean of the kindergarten staff, well recognized for her skill and talent, however, received a far lower evaluation, much to the consternation of her colleagues, destroying their trust of the process.

How is one placed in one of these categories? By teacher evaluators' and the principal's evaluations.

One problem that emerged early was that high school teachers were evaluating primary teachers. If you know anything about education, this produced disastrous results, since the high school folks had no understanding of elementary teaching and generated evaluations that were considered invalid and further outraged people, who felt betrayed.

Measures were taken to avoid such mistakes and to standardize observer perceptions, which, hopefully, may increase perceptions of the validity of the process. We are now into inter-rater reliability as essential to improve the validity and reliability of using such instruments. But the entire process focuses on evaluation, not the more effective process of supervision, which the next chapter lays out.

However, one nagging question remains: In view of the generalization that most principals are selected for their ability to organize and run a bureaucracy, not for their instructional prowess and skills, can all principals become effective evaluators? In the past, a major function of principals was to take care of problems and not let them escalate into crises, which became issues with which the central office would have to become involved. Such skills are not necessarily instructional in nature.

To this point, we have analyzed and then critiqued the American proclivity to apply the business, free market paradigm to education — and, we found it completely inapplicable for use in the schools. Indeed, Rothstein (2011) cites Donald T. Campbell's "law" of performance measurement: "The more any quantitative social indicator is used for social decision-making, the more subject it will be to corruption pressures and the more apt it will be to distort and corrupt the social processes it is intended to monitor."

I promised to provide illustrations of Rothstein's comment that if P4P was used, it would harm education. If the disastrous results of evaluating teachers portrayed above aren't enough, we can add the following.

More Repercussions in Health Care, Government, and Business

We may ask, since the literature, the newspapers, and many political leaders extol competition and try to use it wisely, what are the results of using merit in health care, government, and business? Rothstein notes:

> When health care systems (such as Medicare) attempted to reward cardiac surgeons or their hospitals or practice groups, for survival rates of their patients, medical professionals responded by declining to operate on the sickest patients. When the Department of Labor attempted to reward local agencies for placing the unemployed in jobs, the agencies increased placement rates by getting more workers into more easily-found short-term poorly-paid jobs, and fewer into harder-to-find but more skilled long-term jobs. When prosecutors have been rewarded for the number of cases cleared, more plea bargains based on false confessions resulted. When *U.S. News and World Report* ranks colleges partly by the share of applicants for whom they have no space, colleges respond by soliciting unqualified high school students to apply. (p. 4)

Campbell's Law Lives!

Let's return to education and the impact on education. In chapter 1, we pointed out that No Child Left Behind (NCLB) was a scam founded on a bunch of fictions used by a Texas governor in his quest for the presidency. The system established by NCLB causes cheating (documented in Washington, D.C., and Atlanta) and focusing on the "bubble kids" to jack up their scores so that the principal and teachers can improve their performance ratings. The corrupting impact of the NCLB is exemplified in the excessive focus on math and English, narrowing the curriculum and reducing such areas as history, social studies, the arts, physical education, and recess in elementary school.

The first grade in which kids are tested for academic skills is now the kindergarten. Even reading has narrowed, with oral presentations reduced because standardized tests do not present oral components.

SUMMARY, CONCLUSIONS, AND IMPLICATIONS

Pay for Performance (read: merit) simply does not work: "Reading and math scores don't increase when teachers or entire schools are offered bonuses for higher scores" (Rothstein, p. 5). The free market–based assumptions supporting merit (teachers are "incentivized" by extrinsic goals of money and they are itching to compete with each other) collapse under scrutiny. As the Vanderbilt study reveals, they do not apply to teachers.

In fact, Rand's table reveals that we are all motivated by the same intrinsic goals—a strong wish for opportunity to grow and an equally robust desire to achieve, although upper management and foremen did not understand this was also true for hourly workers. We discovered that systems established to implement merit have proven disastrous, resulting in the opposite—lack of motivation and alienation, because virtually everyone believes he/she is in the top 5–25 percent of people in his/her field.

A graduate student of mine, Rabecca Hall, wrote,

> Even if the pay for performance does motivate some teachers, it doesn't mean improvements will be made because they may not have the capacity or resources to bring about those improvements.
>
> I have personally been in a situation where early in my career I was motivated to improve my instruction, but lacked direction on how to do so. To be a better teacher we have to receive professional development, not money bonuses. (personal communication, July 30, 2012)

Campbell's Law of Performance Measurement is prescient. P4P not only doesn't work in improving test results but also corrupts the system, as we've found in health care, business, and government. We can conclude that the culture of education certainly has been changed, but not for the better.

Why are we rushing to implement another fraudulent fad?

REFERENCES AND RESOURCES

Anderson, N. (2012, September 22). Study undercuts teacher bonuses. *Washington Post*.

Danielson, C. (2007). *Enhancing professional practice: A framework for teaching*. Arlington, VA: Association for Supervision and Curriculum Development.

Eichenwald, K. (2012, July 3). Microsoft's downfall: Inside the executive e-mails and cannibalistic culture that felled a tech giant. *Vanity Fair*. www.vanityfair.com/online/daily/2012/07/microsoft-downfall-emails-steve-ballmer

Figlio, D. (2011, September 20). The debate over teacher merit pay: A Freakonomics quorum. *Freakonomics*. http://www.freakonomics.com/2011/09/20/the-debate-over-teacher-merit-pay-a-freakonomics-quorum/

Lewis, B. (2010, October 5). Pros and cons of merit pay for teachers. *About.com*. http://k6educators.about.com/od/assessmentandtesting/a/meritypay.htm

Marsh, J. (2011, September 20). The debate over teacher merit pay: A Freakonomics quorum. *Freakonomics*. http://www.freakonomics.com/2011/09/20/the-debate-over-teacher-merit-pay-a-freakonomics-quorum

Meyer, H. (1975, Winter). The pay-for-performance dilemma. *Organizational Dynamics*.

Rand, T. (1977). Diagnosing the valued reward orientations of employees. *Personnel Journal*.

Riddle, M. (2010, December). PISA: It's poverty not stupid. *The principal difference. Bridging research and policy to practice for school leaders*. [Web log post]. http://nasspblogs.org/principaldifference/2010/12/pisa_its_poverty_not_stupid_1.html

Rothstein, R. (2011, September 20). The debate over teacher merit pay: A Freakonomics quorum. *Freakonomics*. http://www.freakonomics.com/2011/09/20/the-debate-over-teacher-merit-pay-a-freakonomics-quorum

FOUR

Instead of Teacher Evaluation, Which Isn't Working—A Different Approach

When patterns are broken, new worlds can emerge.

—Tuli Kupferberg

INTRODUCTION AND ORGANIZATION

A major model of teacher evaluation presently being used in the United States due to NCLB is to test kids during or toward the end of the school year—and then attribute the results, whether scores are high or low, to the effectiveness of the teacher. Simplistic? A fantasy? Simplistic hardly begins to describe this evaluative model. Indeed, the preceding chapters pointed out the defects of this model, such as chapter 1 dealing with the unrealities of No Child Left Behind (one absurd requirement of which mandates that all students must be on proficiency levels by 2014—that is, *all kids must be average or above by 2014*).

Chapter 2 deals with the fantasy of developing Common Core State Standards for the tens of millions of kids in a country increasingly diverse with huge ranges of talents, abilities, academic interests, achievement, and poverty. Chapter 3 deals with attempts to develop merit pay for teachers, thereby running headlong into our self-concepts and destroying teacher morale and motivation in the process (probably not intended by the developers).

And this chapter notes that basing teacher evaluations on testing kids' academic gains rests on two entirely false assumptions: the first is that money increases the motivation of teachers to work harder, and the second is that teachers love to compete with their peers. Chapter 3 demolished these assumptions.

Interestingly, these three initiatives (NCLB, Common Core Standards, merit) all follow the free-enterprise paradigm, a fiction that focuses solely on the individual, who, struggling against great odds, eventually ends up succeeding. And they are based on the belief that we are individuals who work alone and who want to work alone and that we want to compete with others.

Alas, it is not that simple. We live in a society with social classes, with social classes that exert a huge impact on what kids bring to the classroom. We'll note that. We also will discuss the limits of evaluation and suggest looking at models of supervision and coaching for more effective approaches to helping teachers improve their teaching.

We'll also note that children (and the rest of us) learn in different ways, as Anthony Gregorc's model reveals, and that synthesizing models of teaching and learning makes sense. We'll also examine models of supervision and end with a summary, some conclusions, and even a few implications as grist for our thinking.

BUMPING INTO SOCIAL REALITIES

We are dealing with the American institution of education immersed within the American culture and dealing with such an immense impacting factor as social class. The social class structure of our society that delivers our kids into schools every morning exerts an enormous impact on them well before they run through the schoolhouse doors (Ladd & Fiske, 2011). Middle class kids generally do quite well when we look at how they achieve in the school setting, as the Program for International Student Achievement (PISA) scores reveal in chapter 1.

Since, as chapter 1 noted, we have the highest levels of poverty in the industrialized world, our kids coming from the social classes that bear the burden of poverty do not tend to do well at all. They rank among the lowest nations in the world, which have high levels of poverty on their PISA scores. As a matter of fact, as noted earlier, the PISA scores reveal that poverty and low scores are highly correlated. The greater the poverty, the worse the scores. Reviewing the scores in chapter 1 attests to that.

Why, then, do we pretend to use academic tests to rate teachers effectiveness? All we are doing by testing is to determine the socioeconomic levels of the schools—which we know already. (But the testing companies sure appreciate education's contribution to hugely increasing their profits.) That is, all the tests do is reveal the social class of the kids in the schools—certainly not the effectiveness of the teachers. (Again, note the individualized paradigm being used here.)

Using this individualized paradigm, the teacher, through his/her hard work, can overcome the years-long impact of poverty, and can generate test scores similar to middle-class kids in one or two years. Right.

Except, of course, this is a fantasy.

REALISTIC ALTERNATIVE APPROACHES: MOVING FROM EVALUATION TO MODELS OF SUPERVISION/COACHING

Since the evaluation model of annual testing being used is so out of whack with the realities of schools, it makes sense to change the individual model paradigm from evaluating teachers by testing their students to models for helping teachers and principals to improve their professional functioning. By doing this, we immediately change our thinking and actions to asking: How do we facilitate teachers and principals to improve their teaching and, presumably, kids' learning?

This switch in thinking then shifts efforts to improve teacher function through evaluation (which doesn't work, as we saw in chapter 3) to a variety of approaches in which we try to facilitate supporting and helping teachers improve their teaching. In short, this constitutes what some call a number of supervisory/coaching processes and approaches.

How to Pull This Off? Models for Change

I've found that when we start trying to make effective changes in an organization such as a school, it is useful to try to help the folks in the school understand their kids, themselves, their colleagues, and their administrators. This, essentially, takes a step back from the rivalries, jealousies, and interpersonal baggage that invariably get generated as people try to establish themselves, become accepted, develop influence and power, and function in an ongoing complex organization such as a school (Hensley, 1982).

What better way than to use an instrument that helps people to understand, and, maybe to accept others? I generally like to use the Gregorc personality style delineator (Gregorc, 1999) for this purpose, since it helps reveal behavior patterns and tendencies that people of each style tend to use in their everyday interaction with peers and kids. One of the understandings we try to develop is that these patterns of behavior are not meant to provoke others but tend to emerge simply because that is the way those with high levels of that particular style of behavior tend to act, for the most part.

Most people tend to like the workshop, which is nonjudgmental and generates understanding of oneself and acceptance of others' personality styles. The understandings also seem to last a long time, as people continue to think about the concepts and apply them. The next step in this workshop approach is to examine how each personality style tends to learn. Some of us are:

- visual learners
- audio learners
- tactile learners
- conceptual learners

How Each Style Learns

Visual learners generally tend to learn sequentially, linearly. They can become proficient with algebra, tend to see things more in black-and-white terms, and like to deal more with facts and details rather than the big picture. These folks consist of about a quarter of American learners. They often like to take charge of work. They would rather work alone, and they tend to be time driven. *Pilots, bookkeepers, travel agents.*

Audio learners tend to be more global, more intuitive. They go from the whole to the parts, are more random, prefer the arts and literature, and may be better at geometry than algebra. These folks tend to be the majority, or at least half, of learners. They vastly prefer to work with others but are not time driven, which means that they have a hard time finishing things on time unless they're in a group or team with a time-driven visual learner. They like to work with people. *Counselors, child care workers, elementary teachers, artists.*

Tactile learners tend to like active learning. They tend to be good mechanics, like hands-on activities, would rather be active learners, tend to be good problem solvers, and generally are pulled into a number of projects, often not finishing them. They are not generally time driven. They tend to be highly intuitive and creative and march to their own drummer. *Entrepreneurs, inventors, trouble-shooters, software developers.*

Conceptual learners, very few in number, tend to be big-picture learners. They like to work to see the whole, enjoy working with ideas and concepts, and naturally prefer to indulge in analyzing, comparing, and contrasting, needing to think about ideas and things before committing to a course of action. They need more wait time as they deliberate over questions asked by teachers. They like to research things before moving into action. Generally they like to hang out with people like themselves. *Professors, analysts, attorneys, policy wonks.*

Synthesizing Models of Learning and Models of Teaching

These understandings thus form the basis of the next step, examining the model or models of teaching the teacher is using and how each supports—or doesn't support—the various learning styles people use. Then, perhaps, we can figure out approaches to help people improve their approach (if that's needed).

What, then, could we note are some of the major models of teaching? There are a number of approaches. Here are a few:

- direct instruction
- behaviorism (ugh—see chapter 2)
- discovery learning
- cooperative learning
- constructivism—the new guy on the block
- using technology (Dr. Lynne Menard's study) to move into constructivism
- using simulations, role playing
- team teaching

Since this chapter is not a primer on teaching styles, it is not within our scope to delineate each model thoroughly. Rather, we can examine how each of these models deals with the learning styles to which Gregorc points. However, several questions can be raised to facilitate the analytic process:

How is the class organized?
What are the teacher's roles?
What are the kids' roles?
How is trust built?

Table 4.1 is very concise, even laconic, but it does point up how various teaching models impact and affect learners with different learning styles.

This table points out some interesting things. The visual learner would rather work alone, and so is better with direct instruction and technology and has a hard time with any of the teaching models requiring intuition and working with others. The audio learner, usually quite intuitive, is a natural for working with others, and so does very well with discovery and cooperative learning, constructivism, simulations, role play, and team teaching. As a matter of fact, if you want to try team teaching, you'd better have one such person on the team, since he or she will look out for the emotional health of the process and people involved. Generally, this person also will provide the necessary creativity.

The tactile learner usually will want to work alone, as this person tends to be a lone wolf and has issues of autonomy and independence, and so will dislike the pressure involved in direct instruction. He or she can accept most of the models and will add a strong dollop of creativity to the process. This person is often a troubleshooter. The conceptual learner will provide a big-picture aspect to any learning and will look for any conceptual underpinnings to any topic. This person perceives the relationships of ideas and phenomena to each other.

Fortunately, this analysis provides a natural segue into the next section, which deals briefly with facilitating teachers to help people with diverse learning styles do better with the teaching model or models they use professionally.

Table 4.1. Relationships among Models of Teaching and Models of Learning, Briefly

Teaching Model	Learning	Style	Models	
	Visual	*Audio*	*Tactile*	*Conceptual*
Direct instruction	A natural fit, since linear	Hates it	No fit	Despises it
Behaviorism	Mild fit	No fit	No fit	No fit
Discovery learning	Hard to do	Good at it	Good at it	Good at it
Cooperative learning	Hard to do, and to cooperate, since is a loner	Very good at it	Can do it	Not enthusiastic
Constructivism	Requires intuition, so difficult	Very good at it	Can do it	Can do it
Technology	Can do it	Can do it, better in groups	Very good	Can do it
Simulations/ role play	Hard to do	Loves it	Very good	Can do it
Team teaching	Hard to do	Loves it	Can do it	Hard to do

MODELS OF SUPERVISION

A Social Work Model

A very professional model of supervision is that practiced in the field of social work, which requires intensive, weekly meetings between supervisor and social worker. While I mention this, manifestly, it does not seem possible in education, given that a principal usually has a large number of teachers to "supervise." Nonetheless, the model is important because it reveals the intensive work needed to help people develop into competent professionals.

Necessary Ingredients

The model is based upon a social worker having a supervisor who is quite experienced and understands the practice of supervision and the work that the supervisee is doing with his or her various groups. Under normal circumstances, the supervisor has a good background in understanding how people behave and interact with each other, and the supervisor and supervisee have a relationship built on trust and acknowledgment that the expertise of the supervisor is being used to assist the supervisee in improving his or her professional practice.

The Process

As a group social worker, I would summarize briefly what happened with each of the eight groups I met with weekly or twice weekly. In addition, we focused on one additional group in terms of the social processes (acceptance/rejection, empowerment, conflict, trust, etc.) that occurred when the group met. The supervisor and I would analyze my behavior in terms of how I worked with the group and with individuals. What were my understandings of the group processes occurring, my understandings of the interactions among people? How could I improve on working with each person and each subgroup within the group? What were their needs and how could the group and I help meet them? What norms had developed in the culture of the group, and how could I impact them positively and help establish the norms and the culture?

We tried to understand the behavior of each person in the group— and, if both of us were not quite sure, we could make an appointment with a psychologist or psychiatrist to get a better handle on that person.

The implication for education is that teachers and administrators need to understand what makes different people tick—their motivations and their interests. We have pointed to that in our discussion of using the Gregorc personality style delineator to assist us in understanding the individual and his or her relationships with others. We also then pointed to the need to understand how different people learn, as is revealed further in the Gregorc system.

The next task is to understand better how groups function and grasp what group processes are and how to use them more effectively in working with groups within the class or faculty. And we had better be able to help construct the culture of the group (class or school) if we want to become ever more effective. Organizations (i.e., schools or classes) always develop a culture, whether or not we are paying attention to that process (Shapiro, 2009). We'll pick up on this shortly.

Supervisory Models in Education to Help Teachers Improve Their Teaching

A note on the use of instruments in evaluation and supervision in education: In education we have developed a large number of instruments to assist supervisors, evaluators, and administrators in their efforts to help teachers improve their instructional practices. Zepeda (2012, p. 15) notes:

> Observing teachers in action is the primary method of assessing teaching. Through formal and informal classroom observations, supervisors and coaches gain insights into classroom practices, instructional strate-

gies, learning activities, including performance assessments, the taught curriculum, and the types of teacher-student interactions that evolve throughout the course of instruction. Informal classroom observations are a part of the overall supervising program that promotes teacher development and growth, interaction between teacher and administrators, fault-free problem-solving, and building teacher capacity.

Zepeda has published a large number of instruments in her *Informal Classroom Observations on the Go: Feedback, Discussion and Reflection* (2012). Obviously, if using instruments to supervise/coach in education, it becomes important for those engaged in the supervisory process to utilize instruments that support their purposes. We will deal with that shortly.

Zepeda spends some time in her book laying out the conditions necessary to make sure that the supervisory/coaching process is effective, which requires positive relationships among supervisors/coaches and teachers. We'll deal with more of this in the next section on clinical supervision, and then we'll move on to problems generated in a district that was in a hurry to implement a system-wide evaluative program.

Clinical Supervision

Clinical supervision, as Glickman, Gordon, and Ross-Gordon (2009) note, "is both a concept and a structure" (p. 228). The five processes laid out are roughly similar to those in the social work process described above:

1. Preconference with each teacher
2. Observation of classroom
3. Analyzing and interpreting observation and then determining conference approach
4. Post conference with teacher
5. Critique of previous four steps (p. 228)

Obviously, this process assumes that the supervisor and teacher have a professional working relationship and a good degree of mutual trust. It assumes that the supervisor is an expert in instruction and that a good deal of preservice training, particularly focusing on observation techniques, precedes the observation. Since more than one supervisor may be involved in a school or district, such training has to be effective to ensure inter-rater reliability.

Unfortunately, as chapter 3 noted, a number of these requirements for effectiveness were by-passed in the rush to get the system up and going in a school district using the Danielson model. People who entered the class and came in as "evaluators" were strangers to the teachers. Also, teachers from the high school or the upper grades were asked to evaluate primary and kindergarten teachers, which stunned the teachers, who felt they had no comprehension of what quality elementary education was, which rendered the observations not only invalid but also insulting. Both of these missteps angered teachers and developed distrust.

The district apparently recognized these as missteps and tried to correct them. Evaluators were assigned to either one or several schools to permit faculty and evaluator to develop closer and more trusting relationships. The district is attempting to provide evaluators from the same rough grade levels as those with whom they are working, important steps to improve the process.

Notwithstanding the obvious pitfalls, clinical supervision, if properly conducted, can provide a major professional approach to improve instruction and learning. It also requires a number of competent supervisors who can meet somewhat regularly with teachers. A once-a-year visit is quite inadequate to improve instruction. People have to be able to establish relationships for this process to work, which requires more frequent interaction to build trust and rapport.

Another Model with a Group of Teachers and a Non-evaluative Analyzer

I was an assistant superintendent in the DeKalb, Illinois, Unified District 28, about sixty miles west of Chicago. We developed a model in which a group of about eight elementary teachers volunteered to work on improving their instruction. We hired a very nonthreatening university professor who understood elementary education to work with the teachers. Note the absence of the principal in this process. Each of them videotaped themselves teaching a short segment and then would view and analyze this segment at a group meeting.

They used a Flanders Interaction Analysis (1960) or matrix to analyze the classroom interaction. The Flanders model is fairly simple, but extremely useful in grasping who initiates interaction in the classroom. Simon and Boyer's *Mirrors for Behavior II* (1970) notes that the instrument can reveal "information about the social-emotional climate. Focusing on those teacher behaviors which encourage or discourage 'student freedom'" (p. 37).

Lambert, Goodwin, and Roberts (1965) describe the model as follows.

	1. Accepts Feelings
	2. Praises or Encourages
	3. Accepts or Uses Ideas of student
Teacher Talk	4. Asks Questions
	5. Lectures
	6. Gives Directions
	7. Criticizes or Justifies Authority

8. Response

Student Talk   9. Initiation

10. Silence or Confusion

Note the nonjudgmental nature of this process. People with this matrix can analyze the class interaction. Generally, every three seconds they record the behaviors and interactions of themselves and the students in the class.

The expanded Flanders matrix breaks down eight categories to add greater specificity to the instrument—for example, by splitting the praise category into superficial and more genuine praise sub-categories. The student silence category is split into "'non-constructive' versus 'constructive' use of time" (Simon & Boyer, 1970, p. 38). Obviously, numerous other models have been developed; however, we chose this system for several reasons, one of which was that it was relatively easy to use.

One of the participants in this process was a very experienced middle-aged woman with whom I had a pretty good relationship. The district had a bowling league, in which she and I participated. So I asked her after a few weeks how the process was going, and she responded, "Oh, I was not pleased when I realized I was talking about 75 percent of the time." I asked her what she wanted to do, and she responded, "I'm going to reduce that to 70 percent this week." I thought that was pretty reasonable, and said so.

Needless to say, this model was used in other schools, with results that teachers thought helpful.

Other Models Involving Groups as the Major Instrument Generating Change

A variation on the above model involves teachers meeting regularly and talking about issues about which they are concerned. Again, as is true of any team, trust, acceptance, and honesty become essential ingredients. My wife experienced this when she worked in Hawaii in an interdisciplinary team in a community college. She felt that she and her colleagues profited greatly from a noncritical, nonjudgmental, supportive, collegial approach, utilized to resolve problems and to learn from each other. The weekly meeting was set aside as a non-interrupt meeting that proved to be extremely helpful.

Team teaching can be an experience similar to that above, providing that levels of trust, acceptance, and collegial support develop. One necessary ingredient is that people generally have the same philosophy of education. As an assistant superintendent, one of whose functions was to hire people, I had no compunctions about selecting team members until a younger and good friend of mine told me that since I couldn't select spouses for teachers, I really had to delegate selection of teammates to the team. Obviously, she was right. Teams who selected their members based on common philosophies (such as instructional model, discipline) tended to be more successful.

More Instruments to Select, Depending upon One's Purposes

Zepeda's array of instruments is useful in stimulating the teacher and supervisor to make decisions regarding what aspect of instruction they want to focus upon. For example, does the teacher or team want to improve the conceptual level on which he or she is working with the kids? If so, Zepeda (2012) offers an instrument dealing with Bloom's taxonomy (1956) on pages 51–58 and 61–62. The latter pages deal with asking questions on various cognitive levels. Do the teacher and supervisor want to focus on developing an improved approach to wait time? (See Zepeda, pages 58–60.) Does the teacher want to improve his or her use of cooperative learning? (See pages 86–91.) Are we interested in improving our post-observational conferences? (See pages 105–108.)

Please see the section on professional learning communities (PLCs) in chapter 13.

SUMMARY, CONCLUSIONS, AND IMPLICATIONS

A quick look at the simplistic model of evaluating teachers by using their students' scores on tests turned out to be, well, simplistic. The way for a teacher to get high scores is to work with upper-middle-class kids—and then, with a straight face, take the credit. The unfortunate social reality, of course, is that large doses of poverty depress kids' test scores, so let's abandon that model of evaluating teachers and, instead, figure out approaches to improve teaching and learning.

We set the scene first by looking at how people learn, based on Anthony Gregorc's interesting personality styles delineator, discovering that people tend to be visual, audio, tactile, and conceptual learners. We then described in more detail how each style learns and then developed a table analyzing how each learning style works—or doesn't—using each model of learning. This, then, set the implications for describing and analyzing a variety of supervisory/coaching models from social work supervision to clinical supervision to other approaches. We also finished setting the table by analyzing the preconditions necessary to make such relationships work, such as a good deal of trust.

We discovered that presently educational supervisory models rest on using instruments, so we described and analyzed a number of these and found that selecting instruments depends upon the teacher's and supervisor's decisions about what they want to achieve—that is, their purposes. What do they want to achieve in the rather complex supervisor/supervisee relationship?

REFERENCES AND RESOURCES

Bloom, B. S. (1956). *Taxonomy of educational objectives, Handbook I: Cognitive domain.* New York: David McKay.

Flanders, N. A. (1960). *Interaction analysis in the classroom: A manual for observers.* Ann Arbor: University of Michigan School of Education.

Glickman, C. D., Gordon, S. P., & Ross-Gordon, J. M. (2009). *The basic guide to supervision and instructional leadership,* 2nd ed. Boston: Pearson.

Gregorc, A. (1999). *Gregorc Personality Style Delineator: A self-assessment instrument for adults. An adult's guide to style.* Columbia, CT: Gregorc Associates.

Hensley, R. (1982). Issues present when entering a system. In J. W. Pfeiffer & L. D. Goodstein (Eds.), *The 1982 annual for facilitators, trainers and consultants.* San Diego, CA: University Associates, 141–142.

Ladd, H. F., and Fiske, E. B. (2011, December 11). Class matters. Why won't we admit it? *New York Times.*

Lambert, P., Goodwin, W. L., & Roberts, R. F. (1965). A note on the use of Flanders Interaction Analysis. *Journal of Educational Research, 58*(5), 222–224.

Shapiro, A. (2009). *Making large schools work.* Lanham, MD: Rowman & Littlefield.

Simon, A., & Boyer, E. G. (Eds.). (1970). *Mirrors for behavior II: An anthology of observation instruments.* Vol. A. Philadelphia, PA: Classroom Interaction Newsletter in Cooperation with Research for Better Schools.

Zepeda, S. J. (2012). *Informal classroom observations on the go: Feedback, discussion and reflection,* 3rd ed. Larchmont, NY: Eye on Education.

FIVE

Evaluating Teachers by Using Value-Added Models (VAMs) (Whatever That Means)

Another Political Tool to Hold Schools Accountable

Beware of gifts from statisticians.

— Anonymous

Evaluating teachers based on students they don't teach is "kind of an invalid measure."
— Carol Cook, chairwoman, Pinellas County, Florida school board

Should schools be held accountable for significant effects of student background characteristics?
— Marcella Dianda and Denise McKeon

So, let's see if value-added models (VAMs) are, indeed, a gift.

But first a question: If VAMs are so good at evaluating teachers, why not use them to evaluate the performance of other professions, such as physicians, dentists, and attorneys (just to name a few)? Just pick a variable and rate them. For a dentist, for example, how about using the rate of cavities their patients get? Or how accurately mammograms were read and diagnosed? Each dentist and physician then should be rated on a scale with other such practitioners. The comparisons, as with teachers, should be published widely. How would that work? (W. S. Lang, personal communication, December 14, 2012).

The vast number of professions rest their evaluation on observations, as we used to use for helping teachers improve their practice. Now we're moving to complex algorithms, statistical models virtually none of us understand, to try to determine how well teachers are teaching, which represents quite a change in our thinking—and practicing.

ORGANIZATION

First, we'd better get a clear picture of what value-added models are and their supposed purposes. Next, we'll poke at the underlying assumptions (nothing like getting at the basis of people's beliefs about a concept or practice to see if they hold water). Since this is a scientific study, we'll examine them using such normal scientific approaches as assessing their validity, reliability, and stability.

If they don't measure up (as with the reforms analyzed in the preceding chapters), then the VAMs face a serious problem—namely, their validity becomes seriously flawed. And if they are invalid, why are we even thinking about using them?

We will provide a table just published concerning overall state scores and four schools districts' scores using the VAM model for the first time. If we see problems with the empirical evidence, we really have a problem. Then we can look at whether their use for evaluating the individual teacher's contribution to the kids' learning is feasible or if there are other factors that also contribute (such as poverty, the home, other teachers, and the school environment, to name a few).

We ask what are the socioeconomic factors involved, as well as the limits of tests and testing. Next to last, what unexpected results (the Law of Unexpected Consequences) have developed from VAM use? That is, we'll expose the enormous injustices and difficulties resulting from trying to use VAMs that seem inherent in their use.

We'll end with a summary, conclusions, and implications.

DEFINING VALUE-ADDED MODELS

A profound contribution to our thinking about the purpose of teacher evaluation is that "most current . . . systems do little to help teachers improve or to support personnel decision-making" (Darling-Hammond, Amrein-Beardsley, Haertel, & Rothstein, 2012, p. 8). This comment sets the purposes for VAMs or any evaluation system to exist, obviously, or else why waste time and effort to perform it?

Question: OK, what is value added all about?

Fortunately, before he died, *Phi Delta Kappan* columnist and evaluation guru Gerald Bracey (2007) wrote an article about this following a debate (sort of) with William Sanders, the agriculture biostatistician who founded the idea and process. Bracey, tongue-in-cheek, titled his article, "Value Subtracted: A Debate with William Sanders." He then clarified the value-added assessment (VAA) process as follows: "A value-added model tests students at the beginning of the year and at the end. The change in test scores over the year is the 'value' that has been added. The question then becomes: How much of this added value does the teacher account for—as opposed to what is added by parents, community, and so forth?" (p. 1)

OK, we've defined what VAMs are all about, so we can proceed.

VAMs seem to be used for two purposes. One purpose consists of trying to measure what an individual teacher contributes to kids' learning (if that's possible). The second casts a wider net, suggesting that VAMs can be useful in figuring out the "factors affecting achievement and measuring the effects of programs or interventions" (Darling-Hammond et al., p. 8). The authors state that VAMs can indeed be useful for such purposes. We'll deal with this briefly toward the end of the chapter.

ASSUMPTIONS UNDERLYING VAMS

Fortunately (or maybe unfortunately), we seem to have a sizeable number of assumptions underlying this rather complex process.

In fact, how do we measure this addition to value? As Alfie Kohn (2010) notes, "Test scores are accepted on faith as a proxy for quality, which means we can evaluate teachers on the basis of how much value they added—'value' meaning nothing more than higher scores" (p. 1). So addition to value really means how well the kids do on tests given toward the end of the year on a couple of days. The rest of the 178 days in the classroom, then, really don't count. So the major built-in assumption of value-added education is that kids are in school to take tests—and to do well on them over an extremely limited amount of time.

Other examples are raised by Bracey (2007), who notes that the model assumes

- teachers are independent actors;
- students are passive recipients of teacher "effects";
- educational tests form equal-interval scales; and
- students and teachers are randomly assigned to schools and classes.

Unfortunately, none of these are valid. Teachers are not independent actors, especially those involved in constructivism, collaboration, teaming, and interdisciplinary models. Second, students are not passive learners. Constructivist theory and practice informs us that students (even if they look passive) are active creators of their own knowledge. Third, educational tests do not form equal-interval scales (which means that the distance between each item is equal, or scale units are equal to each other), and, fourth, neither teachers nor kids are randomly assigned to classes and schools. In most districts, many parents make sure to choose both the school and class. Pretty obviously, veteran teachers usually exert a choice in what and whom they teach. That Sanders is oblivious to these realities is serious if we are to hold valid his flawed insights. What is sad, but terribly dangerous, is that Sanders doesn't know how schools work. How could he? He's a biostatistician who focused on agriculture.

Sanders's model *assumes causal connections* between a teacher's behavior and his or her kids' learning. In other words, Susie did well in Ms. Yuk's class because whatever Ms. Yuk did (that is, the value she added) caused Susie's improved performance. Therefore, Ms. Yuk is quite a good teacher. But if Susie's test scores decline, Ms. Yuk also caused the decline and must be a terrible teacher, and maybe she should be thrown under the bus (read: fired). But what if this assumption is invalid and the model *cannot make valid causal inferences* about individual teachers, as Diandra and McKeon (2004), as well as Bracey, insist?

So of what use is it for predicting? Obviously, none at all. If what Ms. Yuk does isn't the sole cause of Susie doing well—or not—why are we bothering with VAMs? Is it another unsupported fad? Another fraud?

Note to this point: We are measuring a teacher's effectiveness by how well his or her students do on a test. But we have just destroyed this causal relationship. VAMs cannot measure this cause and effect.

Darling-Hammond et al. (2012) add several assumptions to the above lot:

> Using VAMs for individual teacher evaluation is based on the belief that measured achievement gains for a specific teacher's students reflect that teacher's "effectiveness." This attribution, however, assumes that
>
> - student learning is measured well by a given test,
> - is influenced by the teacher alone, and
> - is independent from the growth of classmates and other aspects of the classroom context.
>
> None of these assumptions is well supported by current evidence. (p. 8)

Our conclusions so far? Every assumption is flushed down the drain.

LIMITATIONS OF THE VAMS ASSUMPTION THAT ONLY TEACHERS CAUSE GAINS

Darling-Hammond et al. (2012, p. 8) note that

> gains in student achievement are influenced by much more than any individual teacher. Other factors include:
>
> - School factors such as class sizes, curriculum materials, instructional time, availability of specialist and instructional tutors, and resources for learning (books, computers, science labs, and more);

- Home and community supports or challenges;
- Individual student needs and abilities, health, and attendance;
- Peer culture and achievement;
- Prior teachers and schooling, as well as other current teachers;
- Differential summer learning loss, which especially affects low-income children, and
- The specific tests used, which emphasize some kinds of learning and not others and which rarely measure achievement that is well above or below grade level.

To this list we can also add school size. Small learning communities (SLCs), also called house plans, exert a strong influence on student achievement, behavior, and a host of beneficial results (Shapiro, 2009).

The above Darling-Hammond et al. list plays hob with the assumption that the teacher is the sole cause of gains in whatever the test is supposed to measure. Apparently, educators are not so all-powerful. Let's take a look at the issues of validity, reliability, and stability in our pursuit of the value and use of VAMs.

VALIDITY, RELIABILITY, AND STABILITY OF TEST RESULTS — MAJOR ISSUES

Validity for an instrument of a test may be defined as whether it measures what it is supposed to measure. Does a water meter actually measure the water passing through the pipes?

Reliability may be illustrated as follows. If you measure your forearm with a rubber band that stretches out of shape and then you use the same rubber band, which is now larger, to remeasure your forearm, the results will not be reliable because your measuring device has changed. Instruments/tests have to be reliable for your results to have any validity.

Stability is similar to reliability in that if a test is supposed to measure something, when it is used again on similar subjects, it should give similar results. If not, it is not stable. (This will prove to be a huge problem for VAMs.)

The first major point about VAMs, as Bracey noted (2007), is that it is circular: "It defines effective teachers as those who raise test scores, then uses test score gain to determine who's an effective teacher" (p. 1).

I wondered whether different VAM models would provide different results. Fortunately, Darling-Hammond et al. (2012) have researched this. They note, "Teacher value-added scores differ significantly when different tests are used, even when these are within the same content areas" (p. 9). The lesson for teachers is that the VAM being used needs to fit what they are doing or teaching (assuming they are lucky). Otherwise, they might be flagged as underperforming or in need of further training — or whatever categories are used in that system to inform teachers that they're not up to snuff or are candidates to lose their jobs.

Bracey (2007) cites a study in which it was discovered "that, using a test that tests mathematical procedures, they could generate a list of effective teachers. Using a test of math problem solving they could generate a list of effective teachers. *But they weren't the same lists!*" Conclusion? We do not have stable results. And this is dangerous for teachers! What if VAMs are used that measure something entirely different from what the teacher is teaching? The teacher can be judged ineffective.

Darling-Hammond et al. cite a study of five school districts that absolutely demolishes the validity and credibility of VAMs:

> [The study] found, for example, that of teachers who scored on the bottom 20% of rankings in one year, only 20% to 30% had similar rankings the next year, while 25% to 45% of these teachers moved to the top part of the distribution, scoring well above average. . . . The same was true for those who scored at the top of the distribution in one year: A small minority stayed in the same rating band the following year, while most scores moved to other parts of the distribution. (p. 9)

Table 5.1 reveals the serious lack of stability using value-added models.

An independent study of teacher ranking in New York City found similar variability: "In math, about a quarter of the lowest-ranking teachers in 2007 ended up among the highest-ranked teachers in 2008. In English, most low performers in 2007 did not remain low performers the next year" (Otterman, 2010, p. 1).

Darling-Hammond et al. note that the VAMs of teachers are affected by the students assigned to them, with lower scores occurring if the students have English as a second language or are homeless or simply have difficult home lives. Researchers found considerable differences from class to class, year to year. And even after controlling for prior student test scores and student characteristics, researchers still found significant

Table 5.1.   Percent of Teachers Whose Effectiveness Rankings Change

	By 1 or more deciles*	By 2 or more deciles	By 3 or more deciles
Across models**	56–80%	12–33%	0–14%
Across courses***	85–100%	54–92%	39–54%
Across years***	74–93%	45–63%	19–41%

Note: * Deciles = units of 10
**Depending on pair of models compared
***Depending on the model used
Source: Newton, Darling-Hammond, Haertel, & Thomas (2010)

correlations between teacher ratings and students' race/ethnicity, income, language background, and parent education (p. 10).

The authors note that the idea of a stable "teacher effect" "that's a function of the teacher's teaching ability or effectiveness is called into question if the specific class or grade-level assignment is a stronger predictor of the value-added rating than the teacher" (p. 12).

The grading system for Florida reported the results in table 5.2 for the state as well as for four counties (Kreuger and Mitchell, 2012).

Please note that I have taught in this region (about twenty years for undergraduate courses and thirty years on the graduate level in the field of education). I did not perceive the considerable range of effectiveness as described by the above table. However, as a graduate student and evaluator in the county noted, "Not all teachers were educated in this region who work here. About 6 percent transfer from other areas or are added through other forms of certification tests to become teachers" (H. Holder, personal communication, January 29, 2013).

However, even though this was the first reporting year using the VAMs system, the great variability provides credence to the lack of stability in the structure and process of the system.

P. L. Thomas (2012) summarizes this section of our study by stating, "The relatively new but growing body of evidence on the validity and reliability of test-based teacher evaluations reveals that data are unstable; in other words, as the populations of students change or the school settings change, the rankings of the teachers fluctuate."

SOCIOECONOMIC EFFECTS, PLUS A FEW OTHERS

Question: Incidentally, what do *you* think about this? Do you think that socioeconomic (read: poverty) factors may have quite an impact on kids' testing results?

Table 5.2. Comparison of Value-Added Results for Four Districts and the State of Florida in Percentages

State or District	Highly Effective	Effective	Developing	Needs Improvement	Unsatisfactory
Florida	2.1	94.4	1.2*	2.1*	1.2*
District A	16.8	81.9	.6*	.7*	0
District B	41.5	55.9	.5*	1*	1.1*
District C	3.6	94.4	1*	1*	0*
District D	5.3	73.2	3.7	17.8	0

* = approximately

What about the quote at the beginning of this chapter: Should schools be held accountable for significant effects of student background characteristics? Can they?

McCaffrey, Lockwood, Koretz, Louis, and Hamilton (2004) point out that even after they controlled for free and reduced lunch, such eligibility predicted test scores. Tekwe et al. (2004, May) support this conclusion—namely, that when variables such as socioeconomic status and race/ethnicity are included (or even excluded), they affect the value-added estimate.

Additionally, missing test scores impact any value-added results, as will the fact that tests test different factors over the grades. For example, math tests in the third grade measure arithmetic skills, while by the eighth grade they shift to problem-solving, pre-algebra, and algebra skills. They test divergent phenomena, so results cannot be compared.

Raudenbush (2004) complicates things by stating that the models are best for estimating school practice, the school environment, and school demographics, about which we most obviously are fully aware. He calls this a "Type A" effect. Value-added models, he states, cannot isolate practice at the school or classroom levels from other demographic and school environmental factors, which he labels a "Type B" effect. So, his conclusion is that the quest for the Holy Grail of estimating each teacher's contribution to each student's learning will not and cannot work.

BUT THE LIMITS OF TESTS AND TESTING

First of all, you cannot test everything. Tests just sample some of the content supposedly studied, which the test-maker assumes is representative of the field studied. But what if the test maker is wrong and has selected items that do not represent the correct materials? Big problem, since with VAMs teachers can be fired.

Obviously, learning math and being competent in reading seems pretty essential in our modern society. But so are other goals or aims of education, such as wanting to learn, being curious, learning to make use of one's time, making wise decisions, being resourceful, being resilient, strongly supporting democratic values, valuing others, and being sympathetic and empathetic, to name just a few.

Question: What would you add? How about creativity?

A PARTIAL SUMMING UP

Dianda and McKeon (2004) simply destroy VAMs through the following analysis:

The use of value-added models is ill-advised because of the following key problems . . .

1. Given current statistical know-how, it is impossible to isolate the effects of teachers' and schools' practice from demographic and economic factors that also affect student achievement. . . .
2. When variables that tap student and school-level socioeconomic and demographic characteristics are excluded from the models, value-added estimates are biased against schools with an over representation of poor and minority students. But including these variables results in value-added measures that are biased against schools with an under representation of poor and minority students.
3. While value-added measures include complex statistical procedures, they are only as valid as the tests on which they are based. These tests vary in quality and in the degree to which they match the instruction teachers and the schools provide.
4. For a variety of technical and logical reasons, value-added models cannot work for the purpose for which they are intended—drawing causal inferences. (p. 9)

As the empirical evidence rolls in, it continues to be damning. Validity, reliability, and stability are all lacking.

But, as Darling-Hammond et al. discuss, perhaps VAMs could be employed on a much larger scale, rather than looking at individual teachers. For example, VAMs might be useful for examining how various teaching approaches can impact large groups of students. That might prove valuable if the research focuses on large-scale sampling.

Different models of teaching perhaps could be examined on a comparative basis, although this might prove fairly difficult, since people using different models behave quite differently in their teaching approaches. For example, a high school lecturer is quite different from a constructivist second-grade teacher, or, for that matter, a constructivist colleague next door.

And Horrendous Problems Generated by Unthinking Bureaucratic Use of VAMs

In an article titled "A 'Value-Added' Travesty for an Award-Winning Teacher," Valerie Strauss (2012) pointed out the unthinking use of VAMs for those who do not teach third grade and other grades in which kids are tested, such as physical education, art, and music teachers; counselors; kindergarten, first-, and second-grade teachers; and so on. In some Florida districts, they get graded on the basis of *school-wide outcomes*, not on *what their students have done*, because *their kids are not tested*. Note that the state legislature and governor set up a system based on kids' tests and administrator's evaluations—50 percent for each. Teachers can lose their jobs with unsatisfactory ratings, despite having tenure.

So, in a K–2 primary school, how did the system make decisions about how to use VAMs to evaluate the teachers? Easy. Strauss pointed out that teachers at a K–2 primary school were graded *on the basis of third graders at another school* (whom teachers never saw or taught). Most unfortunately, this school had a low socioeconomic population, so its achievement scores were quite low. In its evaluation process, this district uses the following percentages:

- A teacher's lesson—20 percent of the score
- The principal's evaluation—40 percent of the score
- The VAM data *from the other school*—40 percent of overall score

This allocation of percentiles does differ from district to district.

This led this teacher's scores and the scores of *all other teachers* in the school to be unsatisfactory. Although she was voted Teacher of the Year, state regulations indicate that if a teacher is evaluated as unsatisfactory two consecutive years or twice in three years, that teacher can be placed on an annual contract or terminated. Despite being tenured, having taught for twenty-five years, and being voted Teacher of the Year, she could lose her job.

Bureaucracy triumphs!

SUMMARY, CONCLUSIONS, AND IMPLICATIONS

In the end we have to ask: Are value-added models an appropriate accountability tool? (And how can the bureaucracy screw things up by using VAMs so foolishly and unthinkingly?) We asked why only teachers are being evaluated by VAMs and not other professions. We also analyzed what VAMs do, discovering that they try to parcel out the part that teachers add to a student's increase of knowledge over a year in his or her class.

Alas, we discover that the assumptions underpinning value turn out to be invalid, particularly assumptions that teachers are the major cause of any increase in test scores that kids generate at the end of the year, since other factors (home, size of class and school, maturation, culture of the school and class, etc.) are operating as well. We also dealt with the issues of validity, reliability, and stability of the VAMs and found them to be largely invalid, unreliable, and unstable. A teacher might well find herself one year in the top 20 percent and the next in the bottom 20 percent of peers. And she might also get considerably different scores on the same lesson depending on the VAM model being used and the socioeconomics of her students.

Socioeconomic factors, therefore, play a huge role, even when statisticians try to control for them, and the limits of tests and of testing play large roles in generating unexpected consequences as the use of VAMs metastasizes.

Another fraud makes its way into the educational scene on a massive, dysfunctional basis—and hurts people.

REFERENCES AND RESOURCES

Bracey, G. (2007, May 1). Value subtracted: A "debate" with William Sanders. *Huffington Post.* www.huffingtonpost.com/gerald-bracey/value-subtraced-a-debate-_b_ 47404.html

Darling-Hammond, L., Amrein-Beardsley, A., Haertel, E., & Rothstein, J. (2012, March). Evaluating teacher evaluation. *Phi Delta Kappan, 93*(6), 8–16.

Dianda, M., & McKeon, D. (2004, May). Value-added assessment. Special issue. *Journal of Educational and Behavioral Statistics: Of teacher and school performance, 29*(1).

Kohn, A. (2010, September). What passes for school reform: "Value-added teacher evaluation and other absurdities." *Huffington Post.*

Kreuger, C., & Mitchell, T. (2012, December 7). Most Florida teachers rated as effective. *Tampa Bay Times*, pp. 1A, 11A.

McCaffrey, D. F., Lockwood, J. R., Koretz, D., Louis, T. A., & Hamilton, L. (2004, May). Models for value-added modeling of teacher effects. *Journal of Educational and Behavioral Statistics, 49*(1).

Otterman, S. (2010, December 20). Hurdles emerge in rising effort to rate teachers. *New York Times.*

Raudenbush, S. (2004, Spring). What are value-added models estimating and what does this imply for statistical practice? *Journal of Educational and Behavioral Statistics: Of teacher and school performance, 29*(1).

Shapiro, A. (2009). *Making large schools work: The advantages of small schools.* Lanham, MD: Rowman & Littlefield.

Strauss, V. (2012, December 3). A "value added" travesty for an award-winning teacher. *Washington Post.*

Tekwe, W. E., Carter, R. L., Chang-Xing Ma, Algina, J., Lucas, M., Roth, J., Ariet, M., Fisher, T., & Resnick, M. B. (2004, May). An empirical comparison of statistical models for value-added assessment of school performance. *Journal of Educational and Behavioral Statistics, 49*(1).

Thomas, P. L. (2012, June 20). Test-based teacher evaluation earns an F, again. *Daily Kos.* www.dailykos.com/story/2012/06/20/1101670/-test-based-teacher-evaluation-earns-an-f-again.

SIX

Failing Kids—Still a Failure

Actually, grade retention is one of the most powerful predictors of high school drop out.
> —Shane R. Jimerson (retention guru), Sara M. Woehr, and
> Amber M. Kaufman

So, let's put this more forcefully—if you want to make sure a kid drops out—just fail him.
> —Arthur Shapiro

Ironically, the No Child Left Behind Act . . . has determined that no child should be left behind, yet, when students are retained, there is a possibility that they are left behind.
> —Kelley Stapleton and Rebecca A. Robles-Piña,
> Sam Houston State University

We all are considerably more than a fistful of academic talents.
> —Arthur Shapiro

INTRODUCTION AND ORGANIZATION

As noted in the preface, ideas can generate consequences. For retaining (read: failing) kids, the era of standards and accountability seem to be driving the uncommonly high failure rates in the United States even higher. But first, let's back up to the organization of this chapter, and deal with each of these:

- The extent of failure is startling—it's an epidemic.
- The research is virtually unanimous that the impact on kids is exceedingly harmful.
- No Child Left Behind, by its requirements, mandates increasing failure.

63

- We'll reflect on why we're so persistent about such a harmful practice. Some rationale or rationales must be lurking behind what
  we're doing, so let's see what they might be. The emergence of
  standards and accountability, our attitudes toward hard work, and
  persistently positive attitudes about punishment enter into the
  equation.
- We'll point to other purposes of education aside from high test
  scores in math and English and the pernicious impact of poverty on
  kids' education.
- Next to last, we'll end with a number of tried and true approaches
  to reduce retention, such as decentralizing into small schools, continuous progress, key elements of Finland's system, plus more.
- We'll end with a summary, and a few conclusions and implications.

THE EXTENT

The research has been clear—unequivocal for a century—that no child
should be left behind. But we're still doing it. In spades.

How much?

We retain about 2.4 million kids a year, costing over $14 billion per
year. This also costs each student an extra year of his or her life if he or
she is retained just once. That means about 10 percent of kids have been
retained (National Center for Educational Statistics, 1988). Holmes (2006)
notes that U.S. elementary retention rates are 15 percent, which is similar
to rates in undeveloped countries such as Congo, Togo, and Chad. Japan
and Sweden retain no one, 0 percent, as their national policy (Holmes,
2006). Nor does Norway.

But if you're an African American child, you have a 17 percent probability of being retained (11 percent if you're Hispanic). Males, as well as
younger, smaller, and more immature kids, are retained more than others. So are kids from lower socioeconomic groups, those who have behavior problems, and learning-disabled kids (Karweit, 1991).

As we mentioned earlier, in Florida, the first year NCLB kicked into
life, over 44,000 third graders were slated to fail, with almost 29,000 actually being retained. And the Florida legislature and former governor Jeb
Bush decided that if a kid didn't pass the Florida Comprehensive Assessment Test (FCAT for short) the second time, he or she would be retained
again. So, almost 10,000 kids were now two years older than their peers
in grade 4. So when they hit eighth grade at age sixteen, they'll be able to
drive there. In Texas, 208,876 K–12 students were retained in 2005–2006
(Lee & Roska, 2007).

THE RESEARCH

Retention means being held back in the same grade while peers are moving into the next grade. Interestingly, the practice continues although the research almost uniformly points to its harmful impact on kids. The rationale for retention seems to be *based on popular belief, not research*:

- It supposedly prevents failure.
- Students may be immature—"nativists" believe that learning is sequential, linear, and that kids develop in stages, so they have to be ready, as opposed to remediationists (to be explained shortly).
- The student achieves at a low level.
- The student is younger, smaller, or more immature.
- According to NCLB mandates, a student has to pass exams (unless a way can be found around it).

"Thus, student failure is not deemed a failure of the educational system, but of the student" (Karweit, 1991).

Results of Retention

- Retention is the number one predictor of dropping out: dropout rates show that *69.18 percent of kids retained once* drop out; if a student is retained twice, there is a *93.75 percent probability* of dropping out—a disaster.
- Retention does not improve achievement.
- Students perform more poorly when they reach the next grade.
- Kids feel stigmatized, stressed (pressure even felt down to kindergarten), and shamed (the single most stressful life event [Anderson, Whipple, & Jimerson, 2001]).
- Students spend a year more in school (if they don't drop out), thereby losing a year of their lives.
- Retention costs the state 8 percent more for failing kids once. In Texas, the 1986 cost was $16.89 billion.
- Retained students are 40 percent more likely to be on governmental assistance.
- They are also more likely to be unemployed, and eight times more likely to be incarcerated.
- They experience lowered socio-emotional outcomes, including lower self-concept, poorer attendance, and more aggressiveness (probably not the intention).

These consequences are extremely serious. Retaining kids results in a huge increase of dropouts. Obviously, kids are sensitive to other kids. They stay behind while their friends move on to the next grade. Equally obviously, they feel ashamed. And they are stigmatized—even if only retained once. If twice, generally they're ruined socially. What normal sixteen- or seventeen-year-old girl wants her friends to ask why she's dating that stupid boy in her class who is two years older than she is? It's social suicide for her—and for him. They both know it.

Want an illustration of schools stigmatizing kids? I was a director of secondary education, so, naturally, I hung around the secondary schools. Before I could act in my first couple of months, we had a school that divided kids into A-, B-, or C-level classes. (Guess which was considered the "best"?) I watched a couple of seventeen-year-olds (or so I thought) walk toward their classes. She was heading toward her A class. As the boy stopped by his C class, I heard him say, "I'm so embarrassed to be shoved into this class."

That became a major priority of mine, although the principal and the guidance counselors didn't seem to perceive this as a problem. I also had to discuss with the guidance counselors the nature of their role regarding whether they should place the kids' interests first or the administrative value of efficiency. Also, this school seemed to fall squarely on the meritocracy side of education rather than on the democratic. (Again, more on that later.)

WHY ARE WE PERSISTING IN DOING THIS?

Several reasons come to mind.

Nativists vs. Remediationists—That Is, Interventionists

Question: Do you think that teachers favoring one of these alternatives can play a role in retaining or promoting a child? Read on.

Remember, in the first paragraph of this chapter, we noted that ideas and beliefs can generate consequences, some unforeseen. The unforeseen, or unexpected, can be termed the Law of Unexpected Consequences (LUC). Let's see how the beliefs in this section play out and impact retention as we consider nativist and remediationist held beliefs by teachers (Smith & Shepard, 1987). Nativists believe that kids develop in a series of unfolding stages, which seems to be governed by an internal time table, a sort of time clock. When the clock goes off, he or she will be able to do a certain task. According to this view, the teacher can do little to help the child. This belief supports retaining children, since teachers believe nothing can be done until that kid's clock turns on.

Remediationists, however, believe that a child is open to learning and development and that the job of the teacher is to help the "unready" child. Such teachers believe that they can intervene and stimulate and help the child pull off a task. They view all kids as able to learn (and certainly not developing in absolute, linear stages).

The implications of these viewpoints are immediate. Schools with high numbers of nativist teachers tend to have high retention rates, while low retaining schools have a high proportion of remediationist teachers. Those kids who might be retained in a nativist school probably would not be in the other school. Aristotle famously noted that chance plays an important part in human affairs. In this case, chance can play quite a role in determining whether your kid or mine is — or is not — promoted.

This proves very discomforting, doesn't it?

The Emergence of Standards and Accountability

We dealt with the rise of accountability and standards in chapters 1 and 2, respectively. Accountability raised its specter under the guise of No Child Left Behind, and standards were picked apart in chapter 2 dealing with Common Core State Standards. Both are quite recent and perceived as drivers of educational reform. But, as we noted above, ideas can generate consequences — some foreseen, others quite unexpected. Let's see how the Law of Unexpected Consequences seems to be operating here.

As we find in many states a drive to increase accountability and to raise the bar (read: increase standards), what do we expect is the result? Obviously, increased failure. While it is satisfying for policymakers to stress that they are getting tough by increasing standards, kids struggling to meet existent standards face more failure.

So, No Child Left Behind "basically puts a stop to social promotion by stating that all children will meet state standards in order to move into the next grade . . . [rendering] social promotion more of an obsolete term. Consequently, the act encourages educational administrators to retain low-achieving students who do not meet the prerequisites to go onto the next grade" (Stapleton & Robles-Piña, 2009).

It is important to remember that kids go to school for 180 days and take NCLB exams for one or two of those days. Consequently, kids recognize clearly that everything rests on doing well on the tests (which are usually given in February or March). Thus, the rest of the year really doesn't matter — not a strong motivator to continue working hard for the three months or so following the tests.

Additionally, up to now, NCLB has been quite narrow, focusing only on math and English, although it is expanding into testing science. Again, the message to kids is quite clear — these are the only subjects that count. Of course, the fact that kids with problems get a double dose of reading and math considerably reduces the amount of time spent in history, social studies, science, art, music, physical education, and the like. Sometimes those classes are taught only a couple of times a week. Sometimes they are eliminated, sending another message about adults' values: these subjects really don't count (nor does recess for the younger ones).

Another impact of standards and accountability on teachers is that teachers obviously realize that their kids will be tested toward the end of the school year. This makes them antsy about who comes in their door in August or September. They tend to ask whether the kids who show up have reading, writing, and behavior skills that will support the curriculum and the goals teachers have forged for their own success.

So they're not too thrilled with kids who enter with "deficits," since they think it will affect their ability to reach their goals. Note that with current models of reward systems discussed in chapter 3 regarding merit, this can negatively affect their pocketbooks. So, in this case, again, students are being whipsawed by the bureaucratic needs of the system, so that the student is being blamed, rather than the system being considered too rigid.

Michael Katz (1975) used a metaphor of the school as a factory to describe what we are analyzing above. Note the increased bureaucratization such as a standardized curriculum, rigorous "performance standards reinforced by periodic testing for accountability" (Smith & Shepard, 1987, p. 133).

Our Cultural Attitudes toward Hard Work

Our cultural heritage of Puritanism sometimes raises its head in the most interesting places. In this case, we'll focus on the schools. Actually, we all believe that we should be hard-working. And we all say that. Hardly anyone of us would brag about goofing off when at work—even when we do. We all talk about working very hard on our jobs, despite the fact that many executives regularly take off for an afternoon of golf, and many others take long lunches. Despite this, we believe that we work hard.

Now, for kids.

Virtually everyone in our society believes that kids should work hard—*very* hard—in schools. If kids have problems, NCLB has after-school tutoring, which is absolutely free to the kids and their parents, to work hard after school, or on Saturdays. This is obviously very attractive to kids struggling to do at least average work in school. The message is this: "Welcome to tutoring. Come here so you can work really hard after school under very close adult supervision, since you didn't do too well during the day."

It's a very attractive, motivating message—to which kids are responding by staying away in droves. See chapter 1 for details (if you need them). Obviously, a lot of kids have internalized this cultural imperative and do work hard. These mostly are the ones who do well in school. But not everyone feels successful in school—and thus becomes less motivated to work hard. This group usually includes kids who are retained.

But many kids see through the hypocrisy of adults wanting kids to work hard. Want an illustration? My son, in third grade, had a physical education teacher who asked the kids to do a daily "fun run" of about three hundred yards in her class. After the third or fourth day, I detected a somewhat different attitude in him. So, of course, I inquired. He responded, "My friends and I realized it's not so much fun to run that far. She thought she fooled us."

Our Cultural Attitude Regarding Punishment—and Our Assumption That It Motivates Us

Former Florida governor Jeb Bush stated this most articulately. When faced with more than 44,000 third graders facing retention after the first year of NCLB testing, he asserted, "That breaks my heart. But if we don't deal with it now, going forward there are going to be a whole lot of shattered dreams." This attitude bespeaks the notion of "tough love," which "may be good for us"—or not.

The American culture does have an established attitude toward punishment, which is most clear when we look at our attitudes toward law breakers. We have 5 percent of the world's population and 25 percent of the world's prisoners, far more than Russia and other less democratic nations. What drives this extraordinary practice? Is it our view that we have to punish people severely, and that this will motivate them (and others) to behave better?

Is it a result of our politics? So that politicians can claim that they're tough on crime in order to establish their bona fide credentials for reelection? (That certainly is one driver.) We've been persistent regarding this for several decades, as the "three strikes and you're out" laws (actually, it means three strikes and you're in—forever) indicate. Such laws have overpopulated our bulging prisons virtually to equal the budgets of education in some states, resulting in diminishing our resources to support our schools, infrastructures, and other public institutions.

How does this play out in the schools? Do some of us fail kids to punish them? Do some of us, like former governor Jeb Bush, actually feel "that it's good for them"? Do we believe that failure as a punishment will motivate kids? Or that punishment is a motivator? We know that punishment does cause fear in many people, which obviously includes kids. A grad student of mine, when we were talking about fear, once said, "You know, fear is the greatest inhibitor."

If, indeed, fear is such an inhibitor, it is almost self-defeating. Because punishment can paralyze people, it also generates anger, feelings that it is unfair, motivation to strike back and to get even, and a host of other negative results. So punishment not only appears to be quite self-defeating but also hardly qualifies as a motivator (certainly not for schools).

We actually took a hard look at motivation in chapter 3 on merit pay and discovered that punishment is not mentioned by any serious literature on the subject. So, although this seems to be a theme in school administration, it is *not* in motivational thinking. It's, once again, moving into popular beliefs rather than using good theoretical/research bases.

Aims That Conflict: The Ying-Yang of Merit vs. Democratic Values —
How They Play Out

The school I referenced above when I was director of secondary education with A, B, and C classes pretty clearly sat in the meritocracy side of values. I couldn't figure out why some kids were in A classes when their math and English scores were below those in the B classes. Mel Warren, my director of elementary education colleague, a longtime resident of the community, sniffed at my comment: "Look at their addresses."

The kids in the A classes tended to reside in the upscale section of town. Working with the faculty to move into a house plan and teams served to end this disgraceful practice.

Actually, moving schools toward a meritocracy is fully consistent with performance testing. The secondary school referred to was using homogeneous grouping to achieve its values. If we want to emphasize democratic values, we have to forego homogeneous grouping.

WHAT DO YOU WANT FOR *YOUR KIDS* THAT IS MISSING IN THE RESEARCH?

Aren't we more than just math and reading scores? Isn't there more to education than reading and math? Like other *goals*?

- Don't we want our kids to appreciate life?
- To be kind and thoughtful?
- To respect others?
- To be able to think critically, to become skeptical and to recognize flimflam?
- To enjoy life?
- To be resilient when they face the inevitable obstacles and frustrations that arise?

What about other *areas of knowledge* besides reading and math?

- What about being good, participating citizens?
- How about having a base of great literature and appreciating it?
- Understanding the culture around them?
- Being able to write well, maybe even with insight and skill?
- Knowing how to think scientifically, and to recognize the history of our country and world, with its trends and major developments?

- What about knowing something about the arts, music? Or playing an instrument, singing in a choir?

OK, what about other *talents* than math and reading, as Calvin Taylor proposes (1968)?

- How about being able to communicate effectively?
- How about being able to organize?
- What about being creative in one or more fields?
- What about being a good analyst?
- Don't we want our kids to develop good human talents of empathy and insight?
- How about good decision-making talents?
- How about artistic talents?
- And what about physical talents, including dance?

Question: What *do you want* to add to these talents, skills, and areas of knowledge?

The sole emphasis on math and reading is absurdly limiting when we talk about what we want for our kids to call them educated. And note that even in reading, since it's too hard to test oral presentations (which are integral in English classes), we just omit that area in testing. Surely, we want our kids to be able to speak thoughtfully, clearly, and with insight. That certainly is not being tested in the reading tests we shove into our kids' faces.

Obviously, we have developed a testing culture that is driving far too much, exerting far too much influence in our schools and in our public's perceptions of evaluating schools and their purposes. We now evaluate schools solely by scores in math and reading that our kids produce.

William Benjamin (1989), in a prescient article, predicted that the curriculum will be driven by our increasing mania for testing. Alas, he was on target. We are testing crazed (our thanks to Gerald Bracey, who called that one early in the last decade), and it sure is dominating education—for much the worse.

POVERTY AND ITS IMPACT ON KIDS— AND *EDUCATIONAL EQUITY*

The problem of low student performance is not going to be fixed by working harder or by developing charters or vouchers in the vain hope that we'll discover some magical beans that will grow bigger, heartier student minds. *The problem is the pervasive poverty in the United States*, far exceeding the rest of the industrialized world.

David Berliner (2009) notes that the blame for the achievement gap in schools is misplaced. The eight-hundred-pound gorilla affecting our kids' achievement scores (and lots of other issues) is poverty. This report indicates that out-of-school factors are the real culprits and that it makes no sense to blame the schools for factors that lie largely outside of their influence.

Berliner then lists six factors underlying poverty, all cultural and outside of schools' control:

- birth weight and nongenetic parental influences
- medical care
- food insecurity
- environmental pollution
- family breakdown and stress
- neighborhood norms and conditions

He adds some initiatives that schools can implement, which could help mitigate the destructive effects of poverty:

- extended learning opportunities in the form of summer programs
- after-school programs
- preschool programs

Obviously, other reforms can be suggested from other sources, as we will see below in this chapter and in chapter 13, "Major Reforms That Really Work."

These are heavy-duty deprivations. While schools feed low-income children breakfast and lunch, do the kids have anything to eat at night? What about weekends? I co-taught college classes with a young woman who dumpster-dived after school in her middle school and high school career every day and on weekends to find something to eat. She wasn't too enthusiastic about the non-role her father played in this poverty. Such deprivation marks people permanently. (It sure did for her.) It is noteworthy that over 22 percent of our kids' families live in poverty in this, the richest country on earth. Of that 22 percent, 50 percent are living at poverty levels that are actually half of the top levels of poverty. That is, if $22,000 is the level at which the federal government says a family of four is living in poverty, half of those in poverty are making $11,000 or less.

Such poverty essentially generates the problems youngsters face in achieving in school. Until we fix the conditions of poverty, it becomes quite difficult for kids to achieve at levels that their middle-class peers more readily are able to pull off.

SOME PRACTICES TO FINESSE FAILURE

Organizational/Structural

Size of Schools

We deal with this more fully in chapter 13. Here are a few points that directly apply to reducing failure.

- Decentralizing schools into small learning communities (SLCs), also called house plans, schools-within-schools, or halls is one model that provides very useful strategies in resolving this problem (Shapiro, 2009).
- SLCs serve to personalize a school, since everyone knows everyone in a school of 350–600, which is possible when we decentralize a large school.
- Teachers advocate for "their" kids (as I discovered when we decentralized a formerly dysfunctional junior high into a middle school).
- Because everyone knows everyone, toxic environments usually do not form.
- Kids with problems usually do not fall through the cracks, since adults (and other kids) can step in to help.

Obviously, the above points refer to facilitating increasing kids' achievement, thereby finessing the issue of retention. We note also that retained kids and kids who do not achieve well tend to participate much less in school activities. Barker and Gump (1964), in a pioneer study, found that kids in smaller schools participated from three to twenty times more in such activities.

We know that human beings have many other talents than those used in math and reading, such as physical and artistic talents, organizing and planning talents, creative and human relationships talents, and communication talents, among others (Taylor, 1968). Smaller schools can meet peoples' need more adequately than much larger schools, which may have quite an impact on the issue of retaining kids. We are all considerably more than just a fistful of academic talents.

OK, that's enough on this issue to indicate that decentralization can exert considerable positive influence on the retention issue. It is more fully laid out in the final chapter.

Continuous Progress, Non-Grading/Multi-Aged Grading

Want to finesse failing kids? Continuous progress, or non-grading, can serve as another tool to finesse the retention issue. If you ungrade — that is, multi-grade a school (say K–2, or 2–4, or any other model) — a kid doesn't need to be retained. He or she just moves in terms of his or her own needs and abilities. Many school systems have used this and have sent their retention rates plummeting. Another neat outcome often results: since such classrooms have a wide range of abilities and ages, continuous progress allows students to take responsibility for their own learning to a greater extent.

Staffing Each Child

When I arrived at a northern Illinois school system as assistant superintendent, the superintendent, Ronald Simcox, had designed a model of staffing, these days called wrap-around, that was a doozy. Every other Wednesday morning I would chair a process in which every kid who was recommended by any faculty member would have his or her case analyzed and evaluated by the professionals on the staff (Shapiro, 2003, pp. 305–311).

Essentially, we called this a Pupil Personnel Services Council. We always had the teacher, two local pediatricians, and whatever special services were called for, such as social workers, psychologists, speech therapists, special education teachers, the counselor, parents (if indicated), and sometimes the student. We would work out a prescription for the child and then monitor his or her progress. This procedure was so successful, for the most part, that we employed the same process for a neighboring district that asked for help. The prescription often called for different instructional approaches, which led to in-service work to facilitate personnel to be able to deliver the services.

The prescription might include:

- Work with a speech therapist
- Treatment for a medical condition
- Referral to a psychiatrist
- Referral to a psychologist
- Placement in a gifted or other special education program
- Placement in a co-op work program
- Placement in a variety of academic, business, or vocational programs
- A workshop for psychologists, social workers, or other personnel with a psychiatrist or other specialists according to the needs of one or more cases, and the education of personnel (Shapiro, 2003, pp. 366–367)

Manifestly, this was a complex, sophisticated affair that was deemed effective and was publicized by local papers.

A Recognition Program

Sometimes, it's worthwhile to stop and think a bit. Since I'm a constructivist teacher, I like to apply some theory to improve my teaching. So, years ago, I discovered Maslow (1954), whose hierarchy of human needs seems pretty useful, even to me today. His levels, each of which has to be satisfied before we can move to a higher level, are as follows:

- physiological
- safety
- social
- esteem
- self-actualization

Taking Maslow at his word, as I've worked with schools, we've established a recognition committee, whose task is to set up a system in which *everyone* in the school—be it the custodian, principal, food service worker, secretary, student, or teacher—who does anything, gets recognized. Usually, we set it up in the most trafficked area in the school, often by the administrative center. As the clippings and photos go up, people cluster around the area. This becomes an important, central part of the school, since most of us appreciate being recognized.

Other Organizational Models

Developing quality preschools would be enormously helpful. It took the French seventeen years to develop a fully professional national system. It's about time that the much wealthier United States takes this up as an educational priority.

Summer schools do not have to be boring repetitions of the regular year. What about science camps based on activities, such as nature camps? How about immersion foreign language camps? We had one in a high school where I was principal, which did wonders for every kid involved. What about arts and creative writing summer camps?

Question: What would *you* recommend?

When I worked at the high school of the Laboratory School of the University of Chicago, we set up a tutorial program, but we made a common error in our thinking. We thought that asking the top students to assist kids who needed help was the way to go, but it didn't work too well. We listened to the kids' suggestion: that kids who knew somewhat more than what they knew but weren't way ahead was the model to use. It worked. We learned to ask kids for perceptions and input, a pretty radical idea.

Looping, having a teacher stay with the same class for two or three years, is an excellent idea, since it gives teachers and kids two or more years to be together. The Danes have a class teacher who stays with the class for a number of years, which they believe is helpful in the very complex teaching-learning process.

Finland's System for Quality Education

The Finns in about three decades have pulled off quite a feat, moving from a backwater nation educationally to one of the top. They've also established a system to counter educational differences among social classes. J. Norton Grubb (2007) investigated Finland's organizational structure and system to find out how they managed to deal with this problem.

Their system consists of the following:

- Well-prepared, highly educated teachers, who earn the equivalent of a master's degree and work in teaching internships for four years—no shortcuts for certification
- A thoughtful, high-quality curriculum
- Universal free preschool, including "preventive measures to identify possible learning and development issues before children start school" (Sahlberg, 2011, p. 48)
- A highly educated classroom teacher whose responsibility is to immediately pick up on any kid who falls behind. He or she works one-on-one or with groups of two to four kids.
- A teacher's assistant who can work one-on-one with kids who fall behind
- A special-needs teacher, a specialist in learning problems and in special education, providing immediate systematic attention to children with special education needs in the classroom
- A multidisciplinary team consisting of the teacher, the special needs teacher, the counselor, the social worker, and representatives from other special services (health, housing), all of whom are fully funded throughout the country.

These are consistent patterns of immediate assistance to the teacher and student in contrast to the "grab-bag of after-school programs and tutoring efforts, randomly distributed by grade levels and subjects" in the United States (Grubb, p. 108). In other words, the Finns have developed a *consistent system* that they apply immediately.

Incidentally, Finns do not have a word for accountability. But they are professional (as is obvious).

- Finns have built a system that immediately picks a kid up who is having problems.
- They do not retain kids.
- They do not use standardized tests—feedback is in narrative form from their teacher, describing their progress (we've done that, with considerable parental approval).

- All children are given the same opportunity to learn.
- Teachers have great autonomy.
- Teachers are fully trusted.

Classes are small (sixteen to eighteen) and so are schools, running about two to three hundred, so that everyone knows all the students. They also use "looping," which keeps teacher and team together with students for two to six years.

The Finns are strongly interested in greater equity. They do "not rely on excessive amounts of low-level testing or on draconian accountability systems" (Grubb, p. 109).

Quite a difference from the model we've slid into, with its "standardization of the curriculum enforced by external testing, narrowing of the curriculum to basic skills in reading and mathematics, reduced use of innovative teaching strategies, adoption of educational ideas from external sources (often not educators), rather than development of local internal capacity for innovation and problem-solving, and adoption of high-stakes accountability policies, featuring rewards and sanctions for student, teachers, and schools" (Darling-Hammond, 2010, p. 33).

Different Instructional Approaches

How about asking kids what they've learned?

Social scientists have found that asking people about their opinions (sometimes asking what their friends think) is a pretty good way to find what people know. So, I always ask toward the end of a class, "Today, I learned . . . ?" It's a summary, a time for reflection, which often is skipped over in our anxiety about making sure that kids get what we want them to get. It actually forces time for reflection regarding what they've learned in the class.

At the end of a course I always ask people to present their most significant learning in the class to others, which often generates some pretty creative presentations. Obviously, this represents a constructivist approach to teaching and classroom management. Other approaches to enrich the armamentarium of instructional tools teachers can dip into consist of developing projects, writing and carrying out simulations, pulling off role playing, and developing classroom newspapers, journals, and the like as vehicles to expand creative writing by kids. Writing and acting out plays are other creative activities.

Tribes, Positive Behavioral Interventions and Support (PBIS), and Promoting Alternative Thinking Strategies (PATHS)

Stapleton and Robles-Piña (2009) suggest Tribes and Positive Behavioral Interventions and Support (PBIS) as useful for student advance-

ment. They cite Gibbs (2001), who "describes . . . *Tribes* as an excellent
and integrative program that is designed to create a warm culture where
students can work together cooperatively and experience success and
appreciation" (p. 13). They also state that PBIS is an empirically based
character development program that can reach all elementary and secondary students.

Many other programs have been developed to help kids learn new
skills. PATHS (Promoting Alternative Thinking Strategies) focuses on
helping kids learn to work together to learn cooperative approaches. Jimerson and Ferguson (2007) also note that such a program may increase
self-esteem, thus, hopefully improving achievement.

Another approach is to enrich the academic and activities programs,
rather than reduce them. Children need to be able to express themselves
in the arts, including dance and theater. Not everyone blooms only academically, as suggested above in talking about talents. We can reach kids
through other means.

Question: What additional approaches can *you* think of?

SUMMARY, CONCLUSIONS, AND IMPLICATIONS

Pretty obviously, we regard retention as a disaster for everyone, from the
child to teachers to the schools to society. We've found that No Child Left
Behind is an even greater disaster than chapter 1 portrays because it
mandates retaining kids. We've also reflected on some of the reasons we
Americans tend to fail so many kids and have suggested a number of
rationales, some evident, some more obscure.

These include nativist vs. remediationist perceptions of how children
learn, the emergence of the accountability movement with its emphasis
on standards, and our cultural attitudes toward working very hard. We
also looked at our cultural ideas about punishment and the belief by
some that it can serve as a motivator (fortunately, not valid). We also
considered the results of teacher belief in merit vs. a democratic approach
and its impact on retention.

We'll also indicate that while reading and math are important, so are
other essential goals of schooling, such as thinking critically and respecting others, as well as other academic fields (you know, like literature,
history, science, the social sciences), and other absolutely essential crucial
talents such as being able to communicate well, to organize, to make
decisions in order to live more effectively in our complex society and
culture. Unfortunately, in our single-minded haste to improve our test
scores, these crucial educational goals, academic areas, and talents are
being overlooked—really, bulldozed.

We further dealt with the enormous impact of poverty on kids and
our society, noting that it destroys freedom of choice, ruins educational

equity and social cohesion, and damages productive efficiency. In all the hullabaloo over testing only for math and reading, we took a quick look at the eight-hundred-pound gorilla crushing so many of our kids — *poverty* — that our culture wants to ignore

We then analyzed some practices designed to finesse failing kids, starting with organizational and structural approaches. These included decentralizing schools into small learning communities (SLCs) in order to improve achievement, among other positive results. We also pointed to continuous progress, or non-grading/multi-grading, and other organizational models, such as developing quality preschools on a national level, as all European nations have done.

We also described some ideas about summer school programs and the necessity of school activities programs. We also described and analyzed a Pupil Personnel Services Council to help us help kids with personal and educational problems and issues. We then briefly described how a recognition program based on Maslow's hierarchy of human needs would work in a school.

We described and analyzed at length the key features of the system established by the Finns and what we could learn from them (much of our teaching techniques were borrowed from expert colleagues who were kind enough to help us out). We concluded with some ideas about instructional approaches and even suggested a system of asking kids what their most significant learning was toward the end of each class and at the end of a semester.

It seems to me that we've laid out a lot of options to try to finesse our use of failure as an institution in our schools. Hopefully, you will think about some of these and even try them slowly where you can.

Question: What else would you suggest?

REFERENCES AND RESOURCES

Anderson, G. E., Whipple, A. D., & Jimerson, S. R. (2001). Grade retention: Achievement and mental health. National Association of School Psychologists. www.cdl.org/resource-library/articles/grade_retention.php

Barker, R. G., & Gump, P. V. (1964). *Big school, small school*. Stanford, CA: Stanford University Press.

Benjamin, W. F. (1989, Spring). From the curriculum editor: The test-driven curriculum. *Florida ASCD Journal, 5*, 2–5.

Berliner, D. (2009, March 9). Blame for achievement gap misplaced. National Education Policy Center, School of Education, University of Colorado at Boulder, http://nepc.colorado.edu/newsletter/2009/03/blame-school-achievement-gap-misplaced

Darling-Hammond, L. (2010, October–November). They're number one. *NEAToday Magazine*.

Gibbs, J. (2001). *Reaching all by creating tribes learning communities*. Windsor, CA: Center Source Systems, LLC.

Grubb, J. N. (2007, October). Dynamic inequality and intervention: Lessons from a small country. *Phi Delta Kappan, 89*(2), 105–114.

Holmes, C. T. (2006). Grade level retention efforts: A meta-analysis of research studies. In L. A. Shepard & M. L. Smith (Eds.), *Flunking grades: Research and policies on retention*. London: Falmer.

Jimerson, S., & Ferguson, P. (2007). A longitudinal study of grade retention: Academic and behavioral outcomes of retained students through adolescence. *School Psychology Quarterly, 22*, 314–319.

Karweit, N. (1991, May). *Repeating a grade—time to grow or denial of opportunity?* Report No. 16. Baltimore, MD: Center for Research on Effective Schooling for Disadvantaged Students.

Katz, M. (1975). *Class, bureaucracy and schools*. New York: Praeger.

Lee, S. W., & Roska, L. (2007). Grade level retention in Texas Public Schools, 2005–2006. Division of Accountability Research, Department of Assessment, Accountability and Data Quality, *Texas Education Agency (TEA)*. Retrieved July 2, 2008, from http://www.tea.state.tx.us/research/pdfs/retention_2005-06.pdf

Maslow, A. (1954). *Motivation and personality*. New York: Harper & Row.

National Center for Educational Statistics. (1988). National education longitudinal study. U.S. Department of Education. Retrieved December 7, 2008, from http://nces.ed.gov/surveys/nels88/pdf/05_f2_dropout.pdf

Sahlberg, P. (2011). *Finnish lessons*. New York: Teachers College Press.

Shapiro, A. (2003). *Case studies in constructivist leadership and teaching*. Lanham, MD: Scarecrow.

Shapiro, A. (2009). *Making large schools work: The advantages of small schools*. Lanham, MD: Rowman & Littlefield.

Smith, M. L., & Shepard, L. A. (1987, October). What doesn't work: Explaining policies of retention in the early grades. *Phi Delta Kappan, 69*(2), 129–134.

Stapleton, K., & Robles-Piña, R. A. (2009, Fall). Grade retention: Good or bad? A review of the literature. www.shsu.edu/~piic/Fall2009/Robles-pina.html

Taylor, C. (1968, February). Nearly all students are talented—let's teach them! *Utah Parent-Teacher*, 9–10.

SEVEN

Evaluating vs. Grading
(Really *Rating*) Schools

No nation with successful schools ignores everything but basic skills and testing.

— Diane Ravitch

Grading a school A–F is a very expensive way to determine its socioeconomic level.

— Anonymous

INTRODUCTION AND ORGANIZATION

When I was a young lad teaching in a somewhat upscale suburb northwest of Chicago, we had an English department chair, Dr. Charles Ruggles, who deservedly was being paid more than the principal (and both of them knew it). From some far-off galaxy came a proposal to bring a consultant in to take a look at the department, at which time I exclaimed to the chair that this presented considerable danger. (Incidentally, I was in the social studies department.)

Dr. Ruggles disagreed, stating that it would be a godsend because it provided a vehicle for constructive change for the department. He told me that it presented an opportunity for him to present issues objectively that he thought needed attention, and if the consultant and department members agreed, the department would benefit considerably. The chair enthusiastically welcomed this possibility. His strategy was to take advantage of an exterior event for his purposes, which, I learned, was a brilliant strategy. It became an important arrow in my quiver of change models.

I began to learn a great deal from this extraordinary man—about long-range strategies, thinking strategically, and looking for opportunity where others might see danger lurking. About developing a vision. About taking advantage of external and internal events that occur to translate them into opportunities for action.

I present this vignette to signify that evaluating an organization can be quite beneficial *if* it is done to improve it. But if ulterior motivation enters, the process can be poison.

With this caveat, let's compare and contrast the present drive to grade schools with the process and criteria used by the regional accrediting associations, such as the North Central Association of Colleges and Schools, or the Southern Association of Colleges and Schools. We can also look at the process and results when organizations (in this case, schools) use a consultant or consultant team to deal with issues or concerns or problems. We can compare and contrast the processes and the results and evaluate their worth.

Question: Do you think rating a school counts as a change strategy?

Essentially, we are comparing and contrasting three models that ostensibly are focused on improving schools:

- Grading schools (the model used by NCLB)
- Assessment by a regional accrediting agency
- Using a consultant or a consultant team

We might emerge with some conclusions about the NCLB model, which directly rates schools on test scores of kids (ostensibly, of course, to improve them). Our conclusions may be provocative to some, although not to some of us who tend to err on the side of skepticism.

GRADING SCHOOLS—PURPOSE AND OUTCOMES

Rating schools with a letter grade started in Florida and several other states recently. It provides the teachers, students, and community a snapshot of the school's—what? Standing? Performance?

Question: What do you think letter grades reveal?

Berliner (2006), of course, provides us with an answer. He and a number of others note that it reveals the school's and community's socioeconomic status. In other words, it usually portrays the level of poverty or affluence of the school.

In chapter 1, we found that poverty is the key to understanding kids' test scores. The higher the level of poverty (measured in the U.S. by free and reduced-lunch percentages), the lower the Program for International Student Assessment (PISA) scores and, presumably, the letter scores. Our affluent schools rate with the top nations in the world on PISA scores. Our high levels of poverty schools, at 75 percent or more, rate about the same as those of Mexico, where their levels of poverty are comparable. Poverty speaks—in a *very* loud voice.

Letter grades for schools are determined by the kids' test scores on state end-of-year tests, which many states now give, courtesy of No Child Left Behind. Massachusetts gives the Massachusetts Comprehensive Assessment System (MCAS) and Texas uses the Texas Assessment of Knowledge Skills (TAKS). Florida tortures its kids with the Florida Comprehensive Assessment Test (FCAT).

A school's scores in comparison with those of other schools in the state are used to rate the school from A to F. Thus, *a school's test scores serve as the basis* for getting their letter grade.

Question: How would *you* rate a model that rates an entire school based only on one factor?

But there's another major piece embedded in NCLB—the Annual Yearly Progress (AYP) statistic. AYP works like this: All the school's minority populations are considered as separate categories (such as African American, Hispanic, Asian, English as a second language, and various subcategories of special education, including emotionally handicapped, physically handicapped, and so on). Each of these categories must include at least 95 percent of the kids in them taking the tests and they must pass the state minimums in each subject. If only *one category* fails to include 95 percent of these kids, or they don't pass the state levels in the exam, the school is labeled as failing. If a kid who just arrived that same day from another country and cannot speak a word of English takes the test, he or she had better pass it—or the school is labeled as failing.

This has led to some extremely interesting results, such as about 70 percent of Minnesota's schools, recognized nationally as quite good, failing AYP. New Trier Township High School in Chicago's elite North Shore community, recognized internationally as one of the best high schools in the nation, was failing AYP.

Since this bar is set so high, schools are failing it in droves. In small school districts, if a school is deemed an AYP failure, there are few other schools to which kids might be able to transfer. The same condition applies to larger districts, since schools with high poverty levels—that is, Title I schools—usually cannot pass AYP, resulting in the majority of high poverty schools being deemed failures. Chapter 1 on NCLB discusses this more fully.

We'll return after the next section to try to figure out the reasons for such a simplistic approach being used nationally.

AN ASSESSMENT/EVALUATION BY
A REGIONAL ACCREDITING AGENCY

If you want a stimulating, exciting, and highly educating experience, try being on an evaluation team for a regional accrediting association. First of all, it takes at least two and a half (or more) days. Second, you will find yourself hobnobbing with some people with real expertise in areas you will learn a great deal about. People come into the schools and focus on such areas as:

- philosophy and purpose
- structure and organization
- administration
- the faculty—their expertise and credentials
- the professional support personnel—credentials
- business and other support personnel
- the student body—age structure, socioeconomic nature, and so on
- the program and curriculum
- special education program
- innovative and creative aspects of curriculum
- extracurricular activities
- fiscal and business structure and provisions
- physical structure and conditions

We're talking about twenty people who work hard inspecting records, interviewing people in order to develop a precise sense of each of their areas, writing it up, and synthesizing it with the other specialties so that the entire body provides a written document with their recommendations for improvement to the governing board and administration at the end of the visit. Note that no grade is attached to the process.

The key for the visiting team is that the school's or district's philosophy and purpose drive the entire process. Every part of the organization is evaluated in terms of the stated philosophy, which is utilized to develop recommendations to improve the operation of the school to achieve that purpose and philosophy. Note that this is not utilized to evaluate the school.

During the process, one can develop long-term relationships with very interesting, talented people. This provides a big picture, as well as a very detailed portrait, of the complex organization that is any school. It is a gratifying, educational experience.

USING A CONSULTANT OR CONSULTANT TEAM

Similar to the process noted above, a consultant or team can study an entire school or district, or focus on more narrow purposes, such as the following:

- working on a board of education plan to develop long-range goals
- developing a change strategy to achieve goals
- conducting a school study of the district or a single school to improve the curriculum
- proposing a plan to remodel a part of or an entire building
- developing an alternative organization to accomplish stated goals
- improving the reading program
- developing a K–8 mathematics program
- developing a coherent social studies program
- developing a middle school humanities program

Consultant teams can be of considerable help for any number of areas. Again, note that no grade is attached, no evaluation is made—just a plan and strategy to make recommendations to solve issues or concerns, or to accomplish some goal.

COMPARING THE NCLB MODEL WITH THE OTHERS— ITS VALIDITY

Clearly, the accrediting association and the consultant models can provide professionally competent recommendations to improve the school or district. Using student tests to grade a school is an extremely narrow approach to getting a sense of the school. It really tells us what we already know about the school if we're aware of its socioeconomic status. But the testing companies sure appreciate it. And tests certainly soak up a lot of money, energy, and time.

Two basic questions: How useful is it? For what purpose?

If the test forms the basis for NCLB, then the whole effort rests on the validity of the testing movement. Dan Laitsch (2006), notes, "The current high-stakes system assumes that it is self-evident that all schools should pursue increased test scores as their dominant goal and that these scores offer the most reliable evidence of how well the school is performing."

Is that what American education should be about? Don't we want our kids to develop other goals in addition to scoring well in math and English? How about such goals as those listed below:

- critical thinking
- working well with other people
- being literate

- becoming a good, responsible citizen (the most important purpose of American schools [Rose & Gallup, 2000])
- communicating and listening effectively
- respecting and accepting others in our diverse society
- developing talents such as creativity, organizing, problem solving, analyzing, and decision-making

Question: What would *you* add?

And what if this testing basis is shaky? What if they turn out to have problems of validity? What if the tests do not lead to increased achievement? If so, we have another fad that's a fraud. So, let's investigate and look at the empirical evidence, not hopes or wishes or opinions, or those with vested interests, such as many politicians interested in making a name for themselves as "the education governor/senator."

What do some of our very best thinkers (not politicians who might have ulterior motivations) think about this testing mania expressed in NCLB running education for the last decade or so? The answer—to paraphrase Gerald Bracey—is not very much.

As early as the beginning of the 2000s, Bracey referred to the testing craze as the test mania. He was right. And the mania not only has not subsided, but it has actually increased. And the validity? James Popham (2000), one of our testing gurus, wrote:

> The test being used (in Florida) is the Florida Comprehensive Assessment Test (FCAT), a test that's supposed to measure students' achievement of knowledge and skills contained in the Sunshine State Standards. . . . What if the FCAT is, instead, measuring what students bring to school, not what they learn there?
>
> If the FCAT is simply assessing students' socioeconomic status, for example, then to use students' test scores as the chief determiner of a school staff's grade is patently absurd. . . . The correlations between students' test scores and their socioeconomic status are staggeringly high. (Section D)

Let's take another gander at the validity of testing, this time from a former employee of Pearson, a major testing company (you'll love this):

> In my experience, the for-profit test-scoring industry could produce results on demand. There was no statistic that couldn't be doctored, no number that couldn't be fudged. No figure that couldn't be bent to our collective will. Once, when a state Department of Education (it wasn't Florida's) didn't like the distribution of essay scores we'd been producing over the first two weeks of a project, we simply followed its instructions to give more upper level scores. "More 3's" became our battle cry on that project, even if randomly giving more 3's was fundamentally unfair to all the students whose essays had been assessed differently in the days before.

In the end, I guess I'm saying that you probably needn't worry too much about this year's falling FCAT scores, because they're only a number. If you want a different number next year, just ask; surely Pearson will just make more. (Farley, 2012)

To this, we can add Diane Ravitch's (2011) analysis. She notes that the National Research Council of the National Academies of Education has just published a nine-year review of incentives and test-based accountability: "The panel . . . concluded that tying incentives to test scores has not improved education in the United States. The gains have been small to none, and the negative consequences include inflated test scores and gaming the system."

Sparks (2011) likewise reports, "Nearly a decade of America's test-based accountability systems, from 'adequate yearly progress' to high school exit exams, has shown little to no positive effect overall on learning and insufficient safeguards against gaming the system, a blue ribbon committee of the National Academies of Science concludes in a new report."

A Couple of Conclusions, One Obvious, One Bizarre

Obviously, the testing movement does not provide a valid base to evaluate the schools. Tests seem to evaluate the socioeconomic status of the kids entering the doors. Farley frankly considers the testing industry too corrupt to trust, since they'll give the state governments what they want.

What absolutely astounds me is that *people actually believe these school letter grades have meaning.* Teachers and administrators will say this or that school is an "A" school or another is a "D" school. And they'll act as if it's true, as if it really measures the quality of the school, when usually it's a measure of the social class of the kids. We can have a school that's quite good at meetings kids' needs and broader educational goals even if the kids are experiencing a lot of poverty, as a section below will demonstrate.

The extent of this widespread belief that the letter grades are a measure of the quality of the school was evidenced when a high school with which I had been working to decentralize into small learning communities (SLCs) received a high "C," up from its former low "D." What did the school do? Advertised its higher score on its sign outside.

How Are Scores Set?

In Florida, a statewide committee was pulled together to establish cutting points for each letter grade. That is, what bottom score gets an A, what is scored as a B, and so forth? This committee reported to the commissioner of education and also to the former governor. When they sent their recommendations, these were returned for adjusting—they thought by the governor. One of my former students reported that even then these scores were adjusted further (some thought by the former governor).

If a governor wants to be known as "the education governor," it makes sense for him or her to be able to show in election years that kids' test scores went up and that it was because of his/her wonderful educational policies. Surprised? This whole process reeks of politics. We've come down a long road to politicize schools when just a few years ago they were exempt.

PURPOSES OF RATING SCHOOLS—NOT SO HIDDEN

Berliner and Biddle (1995) recognized the attack on the public schools very early and published a book that called this heavy criticism of the schools *The Manufactured Crisis: Myths, Fraud, and the Attack on America's Public Schools*.

Is the purpose of the whole movement of giving schools grades an attempt to shame the schools? After all, the message is that schools scoring average and below average grades pretty obviously aren't doing too well. Can schools scoring average or below average on writing and math tests be meeting their kids' needs? Obviously, they can and do.

We have to attack this by looking at the broader picture regarding what we think are the purposes of education in our democracy. So, let's answer this by using Maslow's hierarchy of human needs (1954). We meet their physiological needs when we feed breakfast and lunch to kids who need it (Maslow's first level). Kids usually feel safe in schools. In fact, for some kids school functions as a haven. Teachers and administrators can diminish much bullying if they become aware of it. Safety is Maslow's second level.

As a matter of fact, many homeless kids try to make sure that they get to school. It's part of normalcy that their lives may not provide under homeless conditions. My wife was teaching in a school where the faculty finally figured out after months that a teen was homeless, although he showed up every day for school looking normal. They discovered that he housed himself in the baseball practice area, sleeping in the dugout, coming to school, showering in the physical education facilities, and arriving for class daily. Obviously, school was of primary importance for him.

What is your conclusion regarding the purpose of the school for this youngster?

Kids certainly can get their social and esteem needs met (Maslow's third and fourth levels), especially if teachers organize their classes so that kids can work in groups. Kids can learn a great deal even if their poverty levels diminish their test scores. For example, they can learn leadership roles, they can learn to think creatively, and they can learn to value that. They can learn that people develop different viewpoints and that those views may be as valid as theirs.

They can learn that many interpretations can be constructed of literary works and about historical periods and events and that this is hardly a black-and-white world, even though some may insist that it is. They may learn that people develop a wide variety of talents (such as being fine organizers and/or planners, writing creatively, developing artistic talents including dance, musical skills, predictive talents, and others), and that these are at least as valuable as any academic skills that the schools test.

Now, the $64,000 Question: Why the Attack on the Public Schools?

This movement appears to have started about three decades ago with the publication of *A Nation at Risk* in 1983. We have to speak frankly in this book—and, hopefully, in public to address this attack. The present attack on the public schools seems to come from politically conservative sources that recently have begun to focus criticism on public higher education. The strategy seems to be driven by defunding it—and privatizing it (as is being carried out in the K–12 schools).

The privatization movement described in chapter 8 is strongly supportive of vouchers and charters, but also of privatizing numerous other governmental functions, including prisons, bookstores in the universities, and other functions. This strategy generally emanates from the conservative and, occasionally, the libertarian movements. (More on this is in chapters 8, 9, and 10.)

The strategy can be seen in the litany of attacks, depreciations, and put-downs toward teachers, which have become widespread. These have included claims that teachers make too much money (this has been spoofed by Jon Stewart on *The Daily Show*), that they get too generous pensions, that teacher unions protect poor teachers, that some teachers are lazy and not working hard, and so on. Some of the interest in grading schools and using value-added models (VAMs) (discussed in chapter 5) and evaluating teachers to get rid of so-called "bad teachers" (chapter 4) gets its motivation from this conservative movement.

Note that this litany of teacher bashing seems to have subsided after the Sandy Hook elementary school massacre in Newtown, Connecticut, when we found out that teachers and administrators courageously tried to protect their kids, a number of them getting killed in the process.

SUMMARY, CONCLUSIONS, IMPLICATIONS— AND A FINAL QUESTION

The attempt to improve schools by testing kids and then rating schools hasn't improved the schools. But this process of rating schools is impacting them enormously because people *actually believe* that the letter scores are real, that they mean something about the quality of the schools.

In contrast, we've seen that the process of assessing schools via regional accreditation agencies and using consultants can improve schools. These comprise professionally driven reform models. We then compared the NCLB model with these professional models and found the former wanting inasmuch as it depends entirely on testing math and English, which completely overlooks other critical subjects, educational goals, and human talents. And we looked at the validity of testing and found it quite limited and even subjective, as Farley, an insider in the testing industry, noted in his critique of that industry.

Unfortunately, the litany of propaganda-style criticism of the public schools has led to widespread belief that they are failing, opening the door to privatizing schemes such as vouchers and charters, supposedly to improve the public schools.

Since the testing model hasn't improved the schools and the tests have serious problems with validity, why, then, are we continuing this foolish line of action? It is merely telling us what we already know—namely, the socioeconomic levels of the kids in the schools.

Why continue to attack the public schools? Well, of course, it depreciates them, opening up opportunities for businesses to profit in an entirely new market—public education. Our admonition in the preface was to "follow the money." It seems to be a factor in the efforts to reform our schools. Let's see how it plays out in the following chapters.

REFERENCES AND RESOURCES

Berliner, D. (2006, January 31). Fixing school isn't everything. *NEA Today*.

Berliner, D. C., & Biddle, B. J. (1995). *The manufactured crisis: Myths, frauds, and the attack on America's public schools*. Reading, MA: Addison-Wesley.

Farley, T. (2012, May 20). Standardized testing industry can't be trusted. *Tampa Bay Times*.

Laitsch, D. (2006, November 27). Unintended consequences of high stakes assessment undermine education reform, report finds. http://epsl.asu.edu/epru/documents/EPSL-0611-222-EPRU.pdf

Maslow, A. H. (1954). *Motivation and personality*. New York: Harper & Row.

National Committee on Excellence in Education. (1983). *A nation at risk: The imperative for reform*. A report to the Nation and the Secretary of Education. Washington, DC: United States Department of Education.

Popham, W. J. (2000, June 4). Florida's school-grading program is a fraud. *St. Petersburg Times*, Section D, 1, 8.

Ravitch, D. (2011, June 11). A standardized path to school ruin. *St. Petersburg Times*.

Rose, L. C., & Gallup, A. M. (2000). The 32nd annual Phi Delta Kappa/Gallup poll of the public's attitudes toward the public schools. *Phi Delta Kappan, 82*(1), 41–58.

Sparks, S. D. (2011, May 24). Panel finds few gains from testing movement. *Education Week.*

EIGHT

Privatization: Fad, Fraud, Fantasy and/or Fiction?

The fundamental question we must answer: Does privatizing improve education?

—Henry Levin

The hidden assumption underlying privatization is that people who know nothing about education can do a better job than experts. It's absurd. We don't do that in any other profession. We don't choose a businessman to be our physician or dentist or attorney. We're not that crazy.

—Arthur Shapiro

At the more than 5,500 charter schools nationwide, private management companies—some of them for-profit—are in full control of running public schools with public dollars. "I look around the world and I don't see any country doing this but us," Ravitch said. "Why is this?"
—Stephanie Simon, *Privatizing Public Schools*

ORGANIZATION AND INTRODUCTION

First, we'd better get a grip on what privatization is all about, particularly its several forms. Then we might take a quick glance at how the idea of privatization got started: with Nobel Prize–winning economist Milton Friedman asserting that since the free market is useful for business and industry, theoretically it should be useful for improving education.

This, of course, has led to some unexpected consequences (the Law of Unexpected Consequences, or LUC, rears its not-so-beautiful head), such as stratification and segregation, as well as large profits for some owners running for-profit schools. We'll point to the emergence of ideology in this area, which, unfortunately, is eclipsing research findings, even from think tanks. Henry Levin (2013) established four critical criteria to analyze the phenomenon of privatization and said that achieving balance among two or three of these might be quite difficult.

Then we'll take a look at how some extremely successful propaganda has convinced many of us into believing that the *public school sky really is falling*. We'll take a quick look at the propagandizing process that is still going on that fooled much of the public into actually becoming convinced that the public schools are failing (when, obviously, they're not).

We'll take a look at how free enterprise ideology is now driving the argument, trumping and actually ignoring contradictory research findings and data. We'll also point out the destructive consequences on the traditional role of local citizens' involvement and control of public school education through their school boards. In other words, as the privatization movement gathers steam, it has resulted in school boards being shoved aside and replaced by for-profit corporation management.

We next look at some unanticipated consequences of privatizing with charters and vouchers, discovering that segregation and stratification are emerging. These strategies thus fail to meet Levin's criterion of equity, a serious flaw undermining the whole notion of privatizing. We also illustrate the impact of ideology on our behavior as food for thought.

The Philadelphia case study analyzed later in this chapter ends with a postscript—that after five years of for-profit educational management organizations trying to improve the schools, the schools were no better off.

And we add another postscript—an example of the extreme extent to which privatizing can develop in legislation in the case of the Michigan legislature and governor in late 2012. They have been trying to establish a complete, separate charter school system statewide responsible only to the governor. This by conservatives who turn livid at the idea of "big government."

We end with a summary, conclusions, implications, and a very *pithy* summing up by Henry Levin about the success of this movement.

AN EXTREMELY BRIEF PRIMER ON PRIVATIZATION

Recently, January 5, 2013, to be precise, Henry Levin, who heads up the neutral National Center for the Study of Privatization of Education (NCSPE) noted that privatization comes in several forms:

- private funding of education
- private operation of government schools
- government funding for private schools
- government funding for nonpublic schools in which the district pays the school to educate students

However, Levin noted that residential location is a primary form of school choice, since those who can afford to do so live in upscale residential areas, presumably with more zingy (read: effective) schools. Levin estimates that about half of American families use this form of school choice. Other forms of school choice within districts include magnet schools (largely formed since the late 1960s) and open enrollment, which Levin estimates at about 10 percent of U.S. enrollment in more than thirty states (Shaughnessy, 2008, p. 3).

He notes that private schools enroll about 10 percent of U.S. kids and charters about 2 percent; about another 2 percent are home schooled. Obviously those people with lower incomes, less parental education, and those who are minorities suffer housing discrimination and can develop fewer options, as we will see later, resulting in segregation and stratification.

In 1955, Milton Friedman proposed that because the private market is superior in producing goods, we should extend this market-based approach to the schools.

Question: If the free market is such a boon to mankind, why does the U.S. government have to regulate business and industry to prevent them from forming monopolies to rip us off?

Second question: Have you noted that lack of banking regulation led to the crash of 2008?

Friedman thought that the government should fund basic education, but that vouchers should be available. That is, the government should fund vouchers. Thus entered the concept of school choice into the American consciousness.

Moving On

Early voucher programs, such as Milwaukee's in 1990, were constructed to try to improve education for disadvantaged and minority populations. Vouchers will be a focus of chapter 10.

Also, a prevailing concern, to put it baldly, is that private organizations will try to grab profit off our tax dollars, which to some extent has occurred. This is particularly true of online "virtual charter schools," which have successfully generated large profits since they do not have to have school facilities or teaching and other personnel, thus considerably reducing their costs (Levin, in Shaughnessy, 2008). Chapter 11 deals with this phenomenon.

Some charter schools have enriched their owners considerably, as well. Simon (2012) quotes Diane Ravitch: "The bottom line is that they're seeking profit first." To add gasoline to the fire, Simon also quotes John Katzman, an education entrepreneur: "How do we use technology so that we require fewer highly qualified teachers?" Katzman founded the

Princeton Review test-prep company and is presently interested in online learning.

And since these online virtual charter school students often do not take required NCLB tests, they evade accountability requirements, an interesting illustration of the Law of Unexpected Consequences. So, in this instance, the immense effort to accomplish privatization and thereby increase accountability ironically is used to finesse the very accountability mandates for which it was developed and loudly trumpeted.

Levin (2013) developed four categories or criteria to evaluate privatization approaches or models. He noted that achieving balance among the four was problematic:

1. Freedom of choice—increased for parents because increased range of choices was developed
2. Productive efficiency—maximization of educational results for any given resource (Levin)

    • Limited to test scores on math and reading only—far too limited, since education has multiple goals, not just jacking up test scores
    • No evidence on non-cognitive outcomes
    • Mixed results on achievement, but parents' satisfaction with their opportunity for choice is higher
    • Weak studies for adjusting for infrastructure costs, which affects the other three criteria

3. Equity—fairness, a major goal in our democracy

    • Increased stratification has resulted, which leads to different educational experiences for kids
    • More funds are available in higher socioeconomic areas, which permits them to attract teachers and principals with better qualifications, which negatively impacts equity

4. Social cohesion—How does an educational reform affect participation in social, political, and economic processes? (Levin, 2002). We need to prepare kids for democracy to support a diverse society; however, there is little direct evidence available from research.

Difficult question: How do we achieve balance?

The problem of achieving balance becomes evident as we focus on two of these criteria because we can see the trade-offs and conflicts. For example, if schools develop a common curriculum, they will improve social cohesion, but will reduce freedom of choice. If the school attracts the support of philanthropists and/or increases fees, it reduces the criterion of equity because poorer kids are shut out.

In Europe, which is facing immigration on a large scale, social cohesion and equity are important, so that is where they have focused on developing balance. If a school supports transporting kids, they incur much higher costs and may reduce choice. Increasing the range of choices depends on the subsidies and fees a school can attract and develop. What do they sacrifice with that choice?

Since only 5–10 percent of Americans have freedom of choice, if equity and cohesion are vital, Levin notes, we have generated a fraud. Most of the rest of the population are denied equity.

Levin's four criteria seem to generate a great deal of thought.

Question: What are your thoughts regarding balancing these criteria? What would *you* sacrifice?

The Process That Convinced Many (But Not All) That the Sky Is Falling

This analysis, with gratitude, follows somewhat the line of thought of John Weathers of the University of Colorado at Colorado Springs (2007). He notes that we see in the United States a remarkable propaganda success by strongly conservative business interests that wish to convince us that American schools are failing and, therefore, we have a great crisis. We constantly hear the phrase "the schools are failing." Or else "the failed schools."

If we fall for this, we are set up to ask, "What is causing this failure?"

The very simplistic conservative answer is that this failure is due to the schools being run by the government because you can only get mediocrity from such a monopoly:

Government = monopoly = bureaucracy = mediocrity

This simple-minded model being peddled completely ignores the huge number of schools with middle- and upper-middle-class kids that are as good as any in the world. This is particularly true of suburban and exurban communities, small cities, and other areas with such populations. We described this in chapter 1 when we looked at how our middle-class and upper–middle-class schools with very low poverty compare on the international PISA tests. Lo and behold, our kids do as well as the top nations in the world. And, interestingly, most of us like and value our local public schools.

The critics, ignoring this outstanding success, then insist that we must do something immediately or another generation of kids will see more failure. They cry, like Chicken Little, that the sky is falling, so immediate action is imperative. Now! (Notice that the focus early on was on the impoverished city schools.)

We're pushed to ask, "What is this something that we must do immediately?"

Why, of course, we must privatize—and establish systems of choice. And what are the vehicles to do that? Charter schools, vouchers, and online schools, despite the fact that research simply does not bear out the supposed higher quality of these nostrums.

And what are the vehicles to demonstrate that the heretofore well-respected public schools are utter failures? Why, of course, rating schools with letter grades A–F and implementing No Child Left Behind's Annual Yearly Progress (AYP), which is carefully crafted (as chapter 1 lays out) to make sure that lots and lots of schools are labeled as failing.

Voilà! Look how bad our public schools are. Boy, are they failing!

Question: How are conservative interests pulling this scam off despite the major values of American education being "that public schools should be:

- Open to all students;
- Public institutions run by the government whose affairs should be determined by a democratically elected body of representatives from the local school district;
- And non-profit.
- In addition, it has become part of our enacted social policy that public school money should not be used to pay the tuition of private or parochial schools" (Weathers, 2007).

OK, we've established the setting (or groundwork). The rest of this chapter deals with the clever process involved in pulling off this fraud, some analyses of privatization claims, and what privatization means for each district's local control of education and for the role of citizens in a democracy. I'll give you a heads-up: it wrecks this function, which has governed public schools since the start of the republic more than two centuries ago.

TAKING A HARD LOOK AT THIS PROPAGANDA SCHEME

First, let's back up a bit and analyze this very recent and successful process of extreme criticism of our schools that has gotten such traction. How did they manage to pull this off?

Two fundamental questions:

As we operate daily, how do we construct meaning?

And second, how do we develop or construct our understanding, our grasp of what is real?

We construct meanings for things and ideas by *interacting* with others and in this process, using language.

Let's illustrate this process. We name things (table, smile, pabulum) for little kids so that they can learn what they are, which then enables them to communicate about the things. We do the same process for ideas, which helps kids to understand such concepts as fairness, kindness, being truthful, voting, and so on.

In trying to establish meanings on a national scale, we talk of generating norms—that is, customs. We saw recent discussions in the United States during the last election about the importance of voting. Australians *have* to vote, so they hear little about this need. U.S. elections often do not even have a majority voting. So we talk a lot about the importance of our role as citizens to vote. To illustrate another norm, as a nation we constantly talk about the importance of accepting everyone regardless of sex, their so-called race, and ethnicity. Obviously, we communicate about all these ideas to build up a shared culture of meanings as expressed in norms and customs.

Somewhat recently, the idea of privatizing some aspects of government has been carried out under the assumption that we can save money using such a strategy. As illustrations, some prisons have been privatized, as have bookstores in some colleges and universities. The federal government has jumped into this trend. As we may recall, large numbers of private contractors were and are involved in our wars in Iraq and Afghanistan, many for quite legitimate reasons. But the costs have been ferocious. In Iraq, for example, it has cost us $800,000 per year for every one of the 160,000 troops we had there.

Now, this venture of privatization is being expanded to include public education. How did conservative forces manage to pull that off?

Easy. Create a crisis. Claim *very, very loudly* that our schools are failing. And claim that they are failing because of the big, bad government (despite the fact that most are doing quite well *if* their poverty levels are low—that is, if the school has middle-class kids with low poverty).

Unfortunately, the propaganda that our schools are failing is now widely believed, even by those in the teaching profession, despite being invalid, as we laid out in chapter 1. There we said that middle-class schools with low poverty levels score with those of the best countries in the world on the PISA international tests.

But now we face the problem of how to refute these misleading, phony claims.

We Face a Complication—Ideology: What It Is and How It Works

Weathers notes, "Ideologies are constructions of practices from particular perspectives (and in that sense 'one-sided') which 'iron out' the contradictions, dilemmas and antagonisms of practices in ways which accord with the interests and projects of domination. . . . So ideologies are domination-related constructions" (p. 76). He goes on to say that if we are able to "have control over ideology construction, [it] means having control over how people view the world. The struggle over control of the symbols . . . is typically indirect, conducted through the various forms of media, most notably print, radio, and television news and news analysis programs. Many forms of news media attempt some semblance of objectivity, but . . . various outlets have a clearly discernible political slant" (Weathers, p. 76).

We are all quite aware of illustrations of control of the media, such as those in the Nazi depiction of Jewish citizens. Constant repetitions of an anti-Semitic ideology swung German perceptions into supporting their wholesale murder. Repetitions of ideology can do wonders, or, as easily, they can destroy.

Question: So, how are conservatives selling simplistic ideas of free-market business ideology applied to education?

"Being able to define the situation as a crisis is the first and one of the most vital moves in the struggle over control of the discourse in the symbolic realm where market discourse and more traditional education discourse meet" (Weathers, p. 78).

The conservative cause has been mightily aided by the publication of *A Nation at Risk* (1983) by the nation's governors, a study that pointed out that schools were not fulfilling their purpose of educating our kids. Interestingly, David Berliner and Bruce Biddle (1995) picked up on this false criticism of the public schools as a scam and published their book claiming that the conservatives have manufactured a phony crisis to develop control over the public schools. They actually called the claim a myth and a fraud.

Weathers then analyzes the process that privatized parts of the Philadelphia schools to reveal the strategy used by the conservatives in accomplishing their goal. First, a report was generated trumpeting well-known findings that the city schools with huge amounts of poverty were doing a poor job educating the city's kids. The simplistic model they continually used was that government schools created a monopoly that led to mediocrity, as explained earlier.

They succeeded in constructing a crisis, which parts of the public and the press fell for, and which the governor bought into. He then dismissed the elected school board and appointed what we today call a "czar," a businessman to run the schools, who (unsurprisingly) also bought into the crisis.

Every other factor involved in depressing achievement scores on the very narrow focus of math and reading was conveniently ignored, most importantly the fact documented by Levin that "family background (language, parental education, family income) is the most important indicator of how much education a child attains and student achievement" (Shaughnessy, 2008). They also ignored the actual increases in test scores in the city schools; huge amounts of poverty, which led to a declining tax base (which could be addressed, but was ignored); and the need for equal funding for all Pennsylvania schools. People who questioned this crisis model were marginalized and criticized for supposedly not caring for the kids: it was the public schools' fault that the kids "were failing," so blame the schools for the socioeconomic condition of a major city.

Pretty clever, if you can pull this off—and they did, resulting in a number of schools being run by private companies.

The Role of Ideology in Refusing to Accept Research Results

An example of ideology taking front and center stage despite research can be seen in our present debate about guns and gun control. Even after the horrific murders of first graders at Sandy Hook Elementary School, the National Rifle Association's solution was that armed police should be in the halls of every single school in America.

They would not countenance discussion regarding the prevalence of guns in the United States, or eliminating military assault-type guns available virtually to anyone, or demanding background checks in order to purchase a gun. Note that even background checks failed to be approved in the United States Senate. That's an example of ideology—in spades.

Similarly, the role of free-market business ideology remains a paramount driver in our discussion of privatizing education (and in a lot of other governmental sectors), even with many think tanks refusing to look objectively at the research. Paul Thomas (2011) notes the strong role ideology plays in this arena despite the fact that "the growing body of research on choice, competition and market forces as tools for education reform *shows that the hypothesis fails in reality* [emphasis added]. . . . A close look at think tanks reveals that market-force advocacy is both powerful and resistant to evidence" (p. 1).

Thomas further notes that "the reality is that think tanks remain ideology-driven, not evidence-based" (p. 1). Thomas then provides us with an illustration of this with a report from the Wisconsin Policy Research Institute (WPRI), a free-market think tank, on Milwaukee's public school choice program. Thomas notes that WPRI fellow David Dodenhoff concluded in 2007, "Taken as a whole, these numbers indicate significant limits on the capacity of public school choice and parental involvement to improve school quality and student performance within MPS [Milwaukee Public Schools]. Parents simply do not appear sufficiently engaged in available choice opportunities or their children's educational activities to ensure the desired outcomes."

But then, Thomas notes, despite the contradictory research findings that his own study found, Dodenhoff surprisingly concludes, "Given the high stakes involved, district parents should insist on nothing less" (p. 2).

Question: OK, what is he saying? He's actually contending that even though the evidence says that choice and the free market really do not work to change the schools through parent involvement, he is going to ignore it and keep on trucking.

Thomas subsequently observes that the media picked up the report and noted the lack of evidence to support parental choice and market forces as levers to reform the public schools. Thomas points out that, indeed, in a report preceding Dodenhoff's study, titled "Report from the Senior Fellow," George Lightbourne supports the negative findings, stating, "The report you are reading did not yield the results we had hoped to find. . . . [Dodenhoff] discovered that there are realistic limits on the degree to which parental involvement can drive market-based reform in Milwaukee" (p. 2).

In other words, we really believe in the market forces despite the evidence, so come hell or high water, we'll keep on going. Then Lightbourne declares the exact reverse of the evidence: "The message from the study is that educational leaders and policy makers must continue to strive to increase parental choice and involvement" (p. 2).

Thomas then states, "In short, *regardless of the evidence* (my emphasis), think tanks have advocacy agendas that are unwavering; they have a constituency that they *must speak to* and not confront" (p. 2). He notes that many of the think tanks he is writing about perceive that they will achieve school reform using market-based policy approaches. Therefore, he further states that this sector of school reform is strongly biased in the direction of market-based policies "that are supported by ideology—but not the body of evidence" (p. 2).

Thomas notes that these patterns of ideologically driven results in contradiction to evidence "are reflected in dozens and dozens of studies."

Thomas cites other areas of school reform subject to this misrepresentation and ideologically driven literature, such as corporate charter school advocates still driven by business market values. He also notes that the "miracles," such as the "Texas Miracle" (exposed in chapter 1), the "Chicago Miracle," and the "Harlem Miracle," all proved to be flawed, if not outright frauds—all driven by ideology. Similarly, "Waiting for Superman" proved as illusory as the rest noted above. Luckily for you (our short-suffering reader), we'll have some fun with these supposed miracles in chapter 12. We'll also throw in the "New Orleans Miracle" as a bonus.

The Law of Unanticipated Consequences (LUC) Strikes Again— Stratification and Segregation

Question: Well, with all these songs and dances about the wonders of the market improving our educational lives, want some evidence about the underbelly of choice?

Thomas points out that choice increases stratification of schools socioeconomically, but without improving academic performance of the student body. Interestingly, Levin reported in 2013 that Sweden, which moved into trying out vouchers as early as 1992, reported that such practices increased segregation—that is, stratification—in the schools. Elacqua (2010) in a Chilean study confirms this result, stating,

> Critics . . . are worried about whether disadvantaged parents have enough information to make good choices and whether parental preferences will lead families to select schools based on the race or class composition of their student bodies and not on their academic quality. Critics also fear that in order to remain competitive and save costs, private schools will have incentives to skim off the highest performing students who are usually least demanding in terms of resources. Most evidence in Chile confirms skeptics' concerns. Researchers have found that Chile's unrestricted flat per-pupil voucher program has [led] to increased stratification across public and private schools.

Indeed, if one merely reflects, such a result is almost inevitable as people of the same socioeconomic levels often will tend to cluster into the same schools. However, this unfortunate result is rarely mentioned in the literature extolling the virtues of choice and the market.

A Brief Conclusion

Thomas concludes, "Like medicine, then, education and educational reform will continue to fail if placed inside the corrosive dynamics of market forces" (p. 5).

Want Some Further Illustrations about the Impact of Ideology on Our Behavior?

Because we as a nation are so committed to our ideology of democracy, we want to export it to other nations with far different belief systems. So, we've tried to implant it in such countries as Iraq and Afghanistan, with little success. Democratic values and norms depend upon agreement about human rights being accorded to all people in a culture. So even our extension of rights in our republic's early days were limited only to men, and only to those who were Caucasian. But now almost everyone shares in these rights of voting, of not being discriminated against, of accepting all religions as worthy (well, sort of).

Why do we expect that cultures with a long history of repressing other religions, minorities, and women will provide rich soil for implementing democratic institutions? Most Middle Eastern nations have no wall separating church and state, which took England centuries to accomplish. It's too far a stretch to expect that countries where dictators or kings make the rules, where women cannot even drive, will morph into democracies in rig jig time. Actually, it's a fantasy.

Another area in which ideology manifestly drives behavior is religion. This motivates our behavior of going to church, or temple, or mosque. It certainly has something to do with our contributing to these organizations, participating in services and in their governance.

Even now we have Americans who are so enamored of their religious ideology that they want to break down that wall separating church and state and infuse religious practices into our schools and other public institutions. Usually, that's because they believe they're in the majority. So their religious ideology in that case seems to trump their democratic ideology. Would they want Wiccan customs to be practiced in the schools?

Undemocratic Consequences of the Philadelphia Case Study

In replacing an elected school board with an outsider or with a private not-for-profit or a for-profit corporation, the governor of Pennsylvania removed actual accountability, which actually lies with the citizens of a school district. This constitutes a violation of the social compact—that the schools belong to the citizenry. By giving the parents "choice," the school community's role was abrogated, eliminated, in favor of a businessman who was supposed to improve education. One of his moves was to present a number of schools to two private corporations to operate.

Thus, our recently very strong insistence on accountability for schools and teachers has been overruled by this form of privatization. That is, the local community no longer is accountable for the schools, since they're being run by out-of-district corporations who have primary responsibility to their stockholders (if for-profit organizations) or to their board of directors (if nonprofit in nature).

This change of responsibility is a stunning reversal of our two-centuries-long basis of responsibility for education in the local citizenry. It constitutes a *revolution* in shifting accountability and responsibility from local citizens to an unaccountable nonlocal corporation. Even if the organization is nonprofit, this still holds true, unless the organization is essentially local. Even then, the organization is not responsible to the local citizens who still are taxed to pay for the school(s).

A Last Word from Henry Levin

Remember at the beginning of this chapter, we cited Henry Levin's insightful question: Does privatization improve education? Levin summed up the effectiveness of privatizing schools as follows: "The view is that choice and privatization have had very small educational impacts, both positive or negative. There are individual cases of great success and great failure, but small differences on average" (Shaughnessy, p. 2). However, this analysis indicates the actual (and damaging) major change to our democratic governance structure illustrated by Weathers's case study of Philadelphia.

A POSTSCRIPT TO THE PHILADELPHIA CASE STUDY

After all the efforts to depreciate public education (the failing schools myth) in the eyes of the Pennsylvania public and to make the case that privatization will improve public education, what is the result?

A longitudinal study of "mathematics and reading achievement scores gains from fifth to eighth grade for students in EMO (Educational Management Organizations) were not larger than those for students in schools managed by the district" (Mac Iver & Mac Iver, 2007).

This seems somewhat like a stake driven into the heart of a vampire, doesn't it?

A RADICAL PRIVATIZING PLAN FROM MICHIGAN

The extreme extent to which privatizing has become an ideology is illustrated in Michigan, where the very conservative Michigan legislature and governor have pushed hard to privatize big chunks of the state's public education. Their vehicle to pull this off is to set up a *system of schools independent of the state board of education and state superintendent of public instruction* and run by an education achievement authority.

This organization would be able to create new forms of charter schools that would be exempt from the laws governing schools and would also not be governed by local school boards. This is obviously a radical change undercutting our centuries-long tradition of local school board control and management of public schools (Savage & Savage, 2012; Strauss, 2011, p. 25).

SUMMARY, CONCLUSIONS, AND IMPLICATIONS

This chapter briefly pointed out that privatization has several different forms, that schools could be funded privately or run by private interests or that we could develop public funding for private or nonpublic schools. Privatization also exists in some form through families choosing (if they can afford it) their residential location, as Levin notes.

The modern privatization movement started with Milton Friedman's idea that because the market worked so well in business, it could do the same for education. He proposed developing and funding vouchers with tax funds for kids to go to private schools. He seems to have ignored the fact that since we cannot trust business and the banking industries, we have to regulate them or they may tend to run wild, as seen in the recent crash of our and the world's economy. We also noted that the privatization movement may entice some to focus on profit rather than educating kids, a sobering warning.

We cited Henry Levin's four criteria or categories of privatization:

- freedom of choice
- productive efficiency
- equity
- social cohesion

We dealt briefly with the problems of balancing each of these with the others. And the problems are intrinsic to each value. As an illustration, if we want to develop a common curriculum for schools like Common Core Standards, we immediately may increase social cohesion, but will decrease choice. If we want to increase fees to provide an improved curriculum, it will negatively impact equity. Balance proves to be interesting, but difficult. Each choice impacts the other values.

We then described how conservative interests have convinced many of us that our schools are failing, despite the fact that they certainly are not, particularly if middle- and upper-middle-class people are involved. Our burden of over 20 percent of our kids in poverty is the eight-hundred-pound gorilla devastating their achievement (although a good deal of the positive does occur in our high-poverty schools). By convincing people that the sky (oops, the school) is falling, a crisis was created opening up private interests to take over operation of public schools, as we noted in the case study of Philadelphia.

We also noted the heavy impact of ideology in the privatization movement, with the ideologues quite unwilling to accept the conclusions that the evidence is negative for the general educational effectiveness of various programs. Strangely, even with evidence that the supposed nostrums of privatization (parental choice, for example) are not working, the think tanks persist. Apparently their adopted mission is more important than scientific evidence.

Just to exemplify some additional areas where ideology exerts a great deal of impact, we looked at how our democratic ideology leads to trying to export it to Iraq and Afghanistan. We seem to have been quite unsuccessful in this enterprise, despite the sacrifice of American lives and billions of dollars, and yet we persevere. We also noted very briefly the impact on human behavior of religious ideologies as another example of beliefs leading to behavior.

We found that the Philadelphia case study gives us insight into the potential revolutionary change in our democratic educational institutions and practices that the privatization movement has developed, in that responsibility is being shifted from citizen-elected boards of education to unelected for-profit corporations and nonprofit organizations. Thus, the bedrock principle of American education—that is, local accountability and responsibility—is eliminated under the guise of increasing choice. How does that square with our democratic ideology for education?

And we found in a study of Philadelphia math and reading scores that the private management organizations' results were no different from those of the public schools.

Alas, another fantasy.

Even worse, an extremely radical plan is being proposed by conservative legislators and the governor to privatize huge chunks of public school education in Michigan, to the tune of establishing a separate system independent of local and state control. It will greatly expand the charters in the state, substantially reducing local control (Savage & Savage, 2012; Strauss, 2011).

A PITHY SUMMARY

We cited Henry Levin's fundamental question at the beginning of this chapter: "Does privatizing improve education?"

After all the hullabaloo about improving education through increasing choice, after all the immense effort by the privatizers expended supposedly in reforming education through using market-based approaches, and after years of manipulating and propagandizing to convince us *that this is the only way to the Promised Land*, privatization guru Henry Levin summarizes the results: "Choice and privatization have had very small educational impacts" (Shaughnessy, p. 2).

REFERENCES AND RESOURCES

Berliner, D. C., & Biddle, B. J. (1995). *The manufactured crisis: Myths, frauds, and the attack on the public schools.* Reading, MA: Addison-Wesley.

Elacqua, G. (2010, May). *The impact of school choice and public policy on segregation: Evidence from Chile.* New York: National Center for the Study of Privatization in Education. Teachers College, Columbia University. http://ncspe.org/readrel.php?set=pub&cat=243

Levin, H. M. (2002, Fall). A comprehensive framework for evaluating educational vouchers. *Educational Evaluation and Policy Analysis, 24*(3), 159–174.

Levin, H. (2013, Jan. 5). Lecture on privatization. Annual conference, International Congress for School Effectiveness and Improvement (ICSEI), Santiago, Chile.

Mac Iver, M. A., & Mac Iver, D. J. (2007). *Are education management organizations improving student achievement?* New York: National Center for the Study of Privatization in Education, Teachers College, Columbia University.

National Commission on Excellence in Education. (1983, April). *A nation at risk: The imperative for educational reform.* Washington, DC: United States Department of Education.

Savage, C., & Savage, A. C. (2012, November 29). Michigan Republicans move to privatize public education under the guise of "reform." *Eclectablog.* http://www.eclectablog.com/2012/11/michigan-republicans-move-to-privatize-public-education-under-the-guise-of-reform.html

Shaughnessy, M. F. (2008, April 8). An interview with Henry Levin: About privatization. *Education News.*

Simon, S. (2012, August 2). Privatizing public schools: Big firms eying profits from U.S. K–12 market. *Huffington Post: Education.*

Strauss, V. (2011, November 25). Michigan's embarrassing school reform legislation. *The Answer Sheet.* www.washingtonpost.com/blogs/answer-sheet/post/michigans-embarrassing-school-reform-legislation/2011/11/22/gIQAwaQNwN_blog.html

Thomas, P. (2011, April 8). Why advocacy and market forces fail education reform. *Truthout.* http://truth-out.org/news/item/618:why-advocacy-and-market-forces-fail-education-reform

Weathers, J. (2007). Privatizing schools: The struggle over how we define democracy and the role of public institutions. *Working Papers in Educational Linguistics, 22*(2), 67–93.

NINE

Charter Schools: A Form of Privatization

How do we use technology so that we require fewer highly qualified teachers?
—John Katzman, founder of Princeton Review, a test-prep company

Absolutely key question: Are charters more effective than public schools in improving education? If not, what's the hullabaloo all about? Why bother? Or is it ideology?

INTRODUCTION AND ORGANIZATION

In the United States, charter schools are a relatively recent occurrence— an offspring of the privatization movement. That started with Milton Friedman's previously mentioned notion in 1955 that since the free market was so effective in both business and industry, it would perform a similar function for education. Little did he know that he had opened Pandora's box.

We'll examine the nature and stated four purposes of charters and their unstated, but real underlying purpose. Then we'll very briefly revisit Henry Levin's four criteria to assess or evaluate the impact of charters in order to be able to analyze them more effectively. Levin's criteria, as stated in the previous chapter, include the following:

- freedom of choice—greatly increased with a range of options for parents
- productive efficiency—maximization of educational results for any given resource, limited to math and reading tests scores only for charters
- equity—fairness, a major goal in our democracy

- social cohesion—how educational reform affects participation in social, political, and economic processes

Next, we will describe what charter education is all about, its four *stated* purposes, and its obvious relationship to expanding the ideology of privatization. We will delve into the various ways charters are governed. Then we'll take a look at the extensive research on this concept, which will lead us to conclusions about the effectiveness of charters in relationship to standard public schools. We will utilize Levin's four criteria to evaluate the effectiveness of the charters.

We'll also discuss research on those four purposes to determine if, indeed, we are achieving these purposes nationally, also using Levin's criteria. Oddly, we'll find not too much research on a couple of the purposes. Then we'll see how our pursuit of privatization in the form of charters has generated unexpected issues and problems (remember, the Law of Unexpected Consequences [LUC] seems to be lurking around the corner for this initiative). We'll find that, unfortunately, charters have a tendency to segregate, negatively impacting Levin's criterion of equity. They also reduce funds for the public schools and have other serious negative results.

In addition, we'll mention the finding that reducing school size into small learning communities improves achievement and participation. We'll also note how a radical expansion of charters and privatization is being considered in Michigan, to the point of replacing our public education system.

Last, we'll develop a summary and draw some conclusions and even implications.

THE NATURE AND PURPOSES OF CHARTER SCHOOLING

Charter schools are funded with public money, but are operated privately. They can be run by a board of local citizens or by a management company that is either nonprofit or for-profit. They are free from most states' normal public school (read: bureaucratic) rules and rarely have a union representing the teaching staff. Thus, they are granted a good deal of autonomy over their operations. Charters are supposed to provide families with options so that the parents can choose the school that suits their kids best.

Question: Why can't we do that for all public schools?

Often, they are granted a contract or charter (hence the name *charter schools*) with the state, which normally states the conditions under which it can operate. In some states, these are set for five years. Usually, the state or district wants the charter to improve student performance, which generally means getting higher test scores—a rather limited goal, don't you think?

Charters started in 1991 in Minnesota with two pioneer schools, and by 2012 they numbered 5,500 in over forty states. So, we can conclude that they constitute a social movement, also driven by the privatization ideology, regardless of the findings of research. This is clearly seen in many states that strongly support charters, such as New Mexico, Florida, Michigan, and Texas. For example, when Florida school district boards of education appeared to be a bit tough on granting approval to proposals, or when they tried to hold charters that were not doing a good job accountable, the state intervened, ruling that a charter could appeal to the state to overrule a local district that wanted to close down an existing school.

Conclusion: Levin's first criterion, that charter schools provide freedom of choice, certainly has been attained.

The extent of charters can be seen in Florida, where more than 150 for-profit management corporations exist. The state in 2011 spent over $1 billion on charters. In contrast, the state, while reducing $1.3 billion to K–12 schools two years ago and only restoring $1 billion the succeeding year, still found $30 million to help subsidize new charter creation. In addition, while no funds were allocated to public schools for construction that year, $55 million were made available to charters only, indicating a bias in the state legislature and executive branches. In 2013, the state increased that to $91 million (Solocheck, 2013).

Michigan, which has been at the center of charter growth, has increased from 138 in 1998–1999 to 280 in 2012, and has lifted caps on their expansion to become effective in 2015.

Charters as a concept have been exported to other countries as well, as has the privatization movement, including nations as disparate as New Zealand, Sweden, Chile, the United Kingdom, and a host of other countries.

Major *stated* purposes of charters were and are as follows:

- to provide parents with public school options
- to provide competition for the public schools (obviously, to improve them)
- to build models that public schools can emulate to improve themselves; in other words, some original thinking was that they could provide laboratories for reform that would develop alternative creative approaches and models that could be adopted by local schools and districts
- to develop creative curricula to meet the individual needs of kids locally

Question: Since we have for-profit corporations opening up large numbers of schools, how were they able to develop locally built and designed curricula, which involves a great deal of time and effort from a number of people? (Just thought I'd ask.)

But *underlying the stated purposes* of charters lies the real and unstated reality—that charter and other privatization approaches, such as vouchers, are meant *to replace public education.*

That is what chapter 8 on privatization found. That is why public education is being propagandized as failing. That is the message that is emerging in the extremism of Michigan's legislature's attempt to privatize Michigan's public schools by establishing a statewide separate school district independent of the public school system's board of education and state superintendent (Savage & Savage, 2012). (More on this later.)

We'll see how well these purposes have fared shortly, partly by using Henry Levin's benchmark criteria and looking at the research.

Governance

State laws and regulations dealing with charter school governance vary widely. While *public schools* are headed by a locally elected board (or, in the case of large cities, an appointed board recommended by a blue-ribbon advisory committee to the mayor), charters can diverge from this arrangement. If it is a locally run operation, the board can be selected from those interested in the school. If it is a for-profit educational management organization, this is not always the case.

Numerous for-profit management organizations have sprung up nationwide and have been successful in developing large numbers of schools, even across state lines. Some states, such as New York, Tennessee, and New Mexico, will not permit for-profit management companies to open schools. Depending on the state, they do not need to have local residents sit on the board, if they even have one. Some states, including Connecticut, Virginia and Washington, require that teachers, parents, and local district representatives sit on the boards, while others do not require such local representation. Florida's exemplary required qualifications for a board member are that he or she cannot have a criminal record.

Most charter school boards require little training, if any at all, and thus, offer minimal support to the school or schools. For example, "Florida's 'governance training' for new board members lasts four hours, can be completed online, and needs renewal only once every three years" (Harwell, 2012, pp. 1A, 8A).

Depending on the state, regulations can be tight or virtually nonexistent. States with loose restrictions include Arizona and Florida. Obviously, this can and does generate interesting problems and conflicts, often including financial problems.

WHAT DOES THE RESEARCH TELL US?

Diane Ravitch (2010), as usual, sums up the research succinctly:

> Most studies have found that charters, on average, are no better than public schools. On the National Assessment of Educational Progress, from 2003 to 2009, charters have never outperformed public schools. Nor have black and Latino students in charter schools performed better than their counterparts in public schools. (p. 1)

The CREDO Study

A Stanford Center for Research in Educational Outcomes (CREDO) study found that 37 percent of charter schools performed "significantly below" their local public counterparts. Seventeen percent performed better than their matched local public schools, while the rest, 47 percent, scored about the same (CREDO, 2009).

The CREDO report discovered some additional interesting variations. When we deal with large numbers of subjects, people, statistics, tests, or what have you, we almost always find a good deal of variation. So, let's see what the CREDO study found, and not be too surprised. The researchers found that "English Language Learner students reported significantly better gains in charter schools, while special education students showed similar results to their traditional public school peers" (p. 2).

The CREDO study found some differences in achievement among the various states. For example, some states and cities reported higher gains in math and reading for charters than their public school counterparts. These included Arkansas; Denver, Colorado; Chicago, Illinois; Louisiana; and Missouri. States with reading and math gains that were about the same as the public schools included California; Washington, D.C.; Georgia; and North Carolina. States whose reading and math scores were significantly below their counterparts in the public schools included Arizona, Florida, Minnesota, New Mexico, Ohio, and Texas.

So, what are we to conclude so far? Some states have done better than others, some about the same, some worse.

The Philadelphia Case Study

It is worth repeating the longitudinal study of educational reforms in Philadelphia that we used as a case study in the previous chapter to reveal the trickery and propagandizing that privatization advocates employed to manipulate the public into believing that "their schools were failing the kids." So the local school board was junked and a businessman was appointed to head up the schools, and he entered into contracts with at least two for-profit management companies to run a good number of the public schools.

And the results?

"Overall, the longitudinal mathematics and reading achievement gains from fifth to eighth grades for students in EMO-managed schools were not larger than those for students in schools managed by the district" (Mac Iver & Mac Iver, 2007).

Alas, the Philadelphia miracle never occurred.

Derringer (2012) notes test results in Michigan were at or below state averages:

> In fourth grade reading, math and writing tests, the statewide averages for traditional-school students ranked as meeting or "exceeding" standards were 84.8 percent, 91.8 percent and 48.2 percent, respectively. Charter-school students scored 76.8 percent, 87.6 percent and 37.7 percent on the same tests.
>
> In eighth grade reading, math and science, traditional-school students meeting or exceeding standards were 82.3 percent, 78.8 percent and 78.9 percent, while charter students were at 77.6, 67.8 and 68.7 percent. (pp. 2–3)

Derringer quotes Miron, who testified before the Michigan legislature: "There have been close to eighty different studies now, and [those results] have been pretty consistent" (Derringer, p. 3).

CREDO's study on Michigan released in January 2013 was a doozy. It found that 80 percent of charters scored below the fiftieth percentile nationally of reading achievement. In math, 84 percent score below the fiftieth percentile nationally. The National Association of Charter School Authorizers reported that 26 percent of Michigan's charters scored in the bottom 15 percent of the state's schools in eighth-grade math. As for reading, 21 percent fall into the bottom 15 percent.

Conclusion Regarding Levin's Benchmark/Criterion of Productive Efficiency

So far, results for charters are inferior to public schools.

These studies indicate similar results: "In the past five years, compared with traditional public schools, charters have consistently shown lower rates of A's and higher rates of F's, [Florida] state records show. Last year, charters accounted for 10 percent of Florida's public schools but 50 percent of its F's" (Harwell, 2012, p. 8A).

Imberman (2007) reported that when kids returned to public schools from charters, he found few long-term benefits. Mathematica (2012) conducted a study of charters. They, too, concluded "that, on the average, charter schools had no significant impacts on student achievement in math and reading."

Stanley Smith, a Florida finance professor, examined the performance of charters, plus the effects of poverty and being in a minority status. He notes, "The numbers tell us that we should question the state's increasing emphasis on charter schools because as a group they underperform traditional public schools" (2012). In his study, after controlling for income level, minorities performed better than did nonminorities, an unusual finding needing replication.

Smith then added 147 charters to his study, again controlling for poverty and minority characteristics. He found that the average charter performed significantly lower than the average traditional public school.

Chile

Elacqua (2009) studied the effects of privatization in Chile, which moved heavily into vouchers and charters to the tune of 46 percent of kids in public schools, 31 percent in for-profit voucher schools, 16 percent in nonprofit (religious and secular voucher) schools, and 7 percent in private non-voucher schools. This comprises a huge base for research, obviously. He reports mixed results:

> Initial results indicate that non-profits have a small advantage over for-profit and public schools and for-profit school students have slightly higher test scores than comparable public school students at fourth grade, once student and peer attributes and selection bias are controlled for. There is no significant difference in achievement between for-profit and public eighth grade students. . . . There is not a consistent statistically significant difference between for-profit independent and public schools. (p. 2)

More Results

Hill and Weluch (2008) found that for-profit charter schools developed lower math test scores in their Michigan sample than not-for-profit charters.

A study was made by Esposito and Cobb (2008) "to match choice schools—magnet, technical and charter—with non-choice schools to estimate school level effects of choice schools on academic achievement. In general, performance was not significantly different between the matched choice and non-choice schools."

Conclusion Regarding Levin's Criterion/Benchmark of Equity

In this case, equity is diminished for the kids in charter schools. They do not perform as well. Basing their research on National Assessment of Educational Progress (NAEP) results in 2003, Lubienski and Lubienski (2006) noted that findings between public and private school, after being controlled for demographic differences, reveal that public school students generally score better than their private school peers. They also reported mixed results, with fourth graders in charters being outscored by public schoolers, but eighth-grade charter kids outscoring their public school counterparts.

Buddin and Zimmer (2006) asked if charters are closing the performance gap in two major urban districts in California. Unfortunately, they found that achievement scores in the charters were keeping pace, but they were not exceeding scores in traditional public schools. They also found that "the charter effect does not vary systematically with the race/ethnicity or English proficiency status of students."

The Knowledge Is Power Program (KIPP) Charters

KIPP schools have received a good deal of positive coverage suggesting they serve as models. The study by Miron, Urschel, and Saxton (2011) looked at their attrition and finance and found that "it serves fewer students with disabilities and students classified as English language learners. The study finds high levels of attrition in KIPP schools." The study points to the fact that this is common for high-poverty schools. However, the study found that African American males were substantially more likely to leave KIPP schools.

The study also found that KIPP schools received $6,500 more per pupil than local districts, and concluded that with such higher levels of attrition as well as higher levels of funding, the model might not be replicated as readily in traditional public schools.

But also note the conclusion regarding Levin's criterion of equity: With such a large funding discrepancy between public and KIPP schools, they really cannot be compared. Nor can they be used as exemplary models, as some literature claims.

Demographics

Corcoran and Stoddard (2009) found that low student achievement was predictive of greater charter support across school districts. Therefore, predictably, people residing in districts with more highly qualified teachers and greater local spending were less likely to be supportive of charters, as were districts with high teacher union membership. One could predict with this that affluent suburban districts would develop less demand for charters, since they would be quite satisfied with their local schools. However, areas with higher concentrations of Republican voters were much more likely to vote strongly for charters.

Conclusion: Levin's criterion of equity obviously applies here, in that equity is violated.

THE FOUR PURPOSES OF CHARTERS—ACHIEVED, OR NOT?

Purpose 1: Providing More Options

Obviously, the first purpose, providing parents with more options certainly has been achieved. Studies generally find that parents are quite satisfied in being able to choose.

Conclusion: Levin's first criterion of choice seems more than satisfied.

Purpose 2: Generating Competition

Research regarding the second purpose of generating competition for the public schools, ostensibly to improve them, has only one positive finding, and that is for Canada. Thomson (2008) reported that Alberta's fourteen charter schools have stimulated competitive responses from local school districts in the form of developing new choice programs. Thomson reports that the idea of choice appears very important to Albertans, noting that this appears rooted in the notions of social services delivery in the Canadian beliefs about government, supporting Levin's first criterion of increased choice.

In an interesting study in Michigan (2007), Ni states,

> This tests the hypothesis that competition from charter schools improves the efficiency of traditional public schools. . . . The results from three alternative estimation strategies consistently show that charter competition has a negative impact on student achievement and school efficiency in Michigan's traditional public schools. The effect is small or negligible in the short run, but becomes more substantial in the long run, which are consistent with the conception of choice triggering a downward spiral in the most heavily impacted public schools.

Two U.S. studies are contradictory, one indicating that competition may have impacted local public schools and the other finding an odd negative result. First, Rouse, Hannaway, Goldhaber, and Figlio (2008) state that schools in Florida "facing accountability pressures changed their instructional practices in meaningful ways. In addition, we present . . . medium-run evidence of the effects of school accountability on student test scores and [we] find that a significant portion of these test score gains can likely be attributed to the change in school policies and practices that we uncover in our surveys."

Question: Does this support the impact of competition or, rather, the impact of the state's efforts to create pressures for accountability?

Carr and Ritter (2007) found an impact, all right, but it was negative. Their study found that

> charter school competition has a consistently small but significant negative effect on the proficiency passage rates of nearby traditional public

schools. This finding may be due to a compositional selection effect from charter schools (as charter schools draw higher performing students, the passage rates at the traditional public schools decrease), or a direct negative impact on the quality of the education provided in the nearby traditional public schools (most likely due to decreased resources).

Buddin and Zimmer's (2006) survey found that California principals had little sense of competition from charters. Interestingly, they found that student achievement analysis revealed that charter competition had no impact in improving traditional public schools' performance.

Conclusion: Levin's productive efficiency and equity apply here.

If competition stifles public school effectiveness, it is quite a negative, although Buddin and Zimmer's (2006) study seems to make sense to me, in that I find little competitive pressure on principals.

Purpose 3: Building Models for Public Schools to Latch Onto

As for the third purpose, building models to improve the public schools, it is quite difficult to locate any research to support or deny this contention. This puzzlement may be due to Henry Levin's summing up of the impact of privatization and choice: "very small educational impacts, both positive and negative" (Shaughnessy, 2008, p. 2).

Since building models to improve the schools is a strongly asserted goal and we cannot find any evidence that this has been or is occurring, we probably can conclude that it isn't happening.

Conclusion for Levin's criterion of social cohesion: We find little evidence to support charters increasing social cohesion.

Purpose 4: Developing Creative Curriculum to Meet the Kids' Needs

The fourth purpose asserts that the charters would develop creative curriculum to meet the needs of children in the local schools. We might as well give this a decent burial—quickly, at least for the management chains. It takes a considerable effort to develop the curriculum for one course, let alone a whole curriculum for a number of fields for several grades. Perhaps a mom-and-pop charter could pull this off, but the chains do not even pretend that they're going to do this. They use their own curriculum, disparagingly termed a "cookie cutter" approach by critics, regardless of whether it fits the local population.

The effort referred to above would take several people working about four weeks in the summer over two summers to develop the curriculum for one course, after having the purposes and objectives laid out during the year. Developing the learning experiences and locating and printing the resources to support each of the objectives comprises a time-sapping effort, as does getting agreement on all the facets and components necessary from the committee members. I've run many such projects, have been elbow deep in the projects, and can testify to the generalization that this is complex, and greatly stimulating, but not easy and quick.

Conclusion for the criterion of productive efficiency: It is not happening.

THE LAW OF UNEXPECTED CONSEQUENCES (LUC)

The Morality of Profiting from Public Schools' and the Public's Taxes

I believe that this is an absolutely major issue.

Question: Should our tax dollars be used by education for-profit corporations for their profit?

Obviously, many companies provide services to schools, such as supplying food for cafeterias, supplies for custodians. We are not referring to that. We are focusing on the morality of profiting from privatizing the public schools. If opportunities for considerable profit did not exist, why would for-profits be so aggressive in pursuing opening new schools?

Stephanie Simon's (2012) article, "Privatizing Public Schools: Big Firms Eyeing Profits from U.S. K–12 Market," says it all. All of a sudden, the public schools' finances can provide a source for profits.

Question: Is the profit motive trumping quality in some management organizations? It certainly did in the case of the Life Force School in Dunedin, Florida, as will be seen shortly. How does that impact social cohesion? Does it ignore it?

Stratification

A major issue seems to be that stratification, that is, a process of segregation caused by school choice and privatization, seems to be well documented. Levin (2013) noted this occurring in Sweden as a negative outcome, as did Elacqua in Chile (2009).

The study by Bifulco, Ladd, and Ross (2009) found this to be occurring. They found that schools in Durham, North Carolina, "are more segregated by race and class as a result of school choice programs than they would be if all students attended their geographically assigned schools. In addition, we find that the effects of choice on segregation by class are larger than the effects on segregation by race."

Thomas (2011) also mentions that charters generate equity and stratification problems (p. 4). D'Entremont and Gulosino (2008), consistent with previous research studies, also found increased racial segregation. They pointed out that charters in New Jersey located just outside of predominantly African American communities are actually "encircling the residential location of the students they are most likely to enroll."

Another study by Booker, Zimmer, and Buddin (2006) found the same forces operating. That is, black students in California and Texas were more apt to move to charters and to move to charters with higher concentrations of such minorities than in their local public schools. They also discovered that those students who moved performed on the average lower than their peers in the public schools they left.

This is a problem.

Conclusion for equity and social cohesion: These are negatively impacted by segregation forces.

Financial Mismanagement

One in four Florida charters has closed, a number for financial mismanagement, some for outright stealing. One charter, the Life Force School, saw its founder put $100,000 in her business accounts and enter into bankruptcy to prevent the school district from stopping her and closing her down. Another charter, Imagine Schools, "came under fire for paying up to $750,000 a year in rent to its own subsidiary" (Harwell, 2012, p. 8).

Obviously, in some cases, this is a problem, impacting equity and productive efficiency.

Reducing Funds for Public Schools

This point refers to funding being transferred to charter schools, yet infrastructure costs are hardly reduced with the loss of students, negatively impacting equity, social cohesion, and productive efficiency.

An Odd Impact—Reducing Enrollment in Private Schools

Yep, it's occurring. Chakrabarti and Roy (2011) found robust evidence of a decline in private school enrollment as an impact of charter schools being able to increase their ranks. However, they found the effect was only modest in size. They did not find that enrollments in Catholic schools and other religious schools declined more relative to those in nonreligious schools. The nonreligious schools, in other words, took the brunt of the decline.

Similarly, a study found that 20 percent of enrollment came from private schools in Michigan, confirming the findings above (Toma, Zimmer, & Jones, 2006). Obviously, some parents saw the advantages of reducing their tuition to zero when they transferred to a charter.

Conclusions for equity, social cohesion, and productive efficiency: These are all negatively impacted by poverty.

School Size

One factor that Berliner did not mention is school size. Shapiro (2009) noted that research on smaller schools by Bickel and Howley (2002) indicates that small school size, such as small learning communities (SLCs), can reduce the impact of poverty by up to 80–90 percent. But I have not found anyone even considering this as a factor in research on privatization.

Yet one of the advantages of privatization is that charters generally are smaller than their public school counterparts, but this fact is virtually entirely ignored in the literature and research. Another finding regarding small school size is the much greater participation in activities in schools that smaller size generates, from 3 to 20 percent more (Barker & Gump, 1964).

Another conclusion for productive efficiency, equity, and social cohesion: These three criteria are strongly supported by decentralizing schools into small learning communities.

Michigan's example of pushing privatization to extreme lengths by a highly conservative legislature and governor may lead to a duplicate charter system being established free of local school board governance. It has other features with huge implications for funding, and so on. This is being vigorously pressed by people who state that they are strongly opposed to big government.

SUMMARY, CONCLUSIONS, AND IMPLICATIONS

Clearly, the emergence of charter schooling is driven by the free-market ideology of privatization, which insists that privatizing will lead to the "Promised Land." The evidence? From nothing in 1991 to 5,500 schools today.

But, as we find in virtually all the studies, *charters generally have generated inferior results* to the public schools. The CREDO study told us that about 17 percent do better than their matched public schools, 37 percent performed worse, and about 47 percent scored approximately the same.

Why all the bother when results consistently underperform the public schools in spite of the fact that many charters can pick their students and do not bother to deal with equal numbers of English learners and special education kids?

The answer? *The movement is driven by ideology, not scientific research.*
The four purposes of charters are clear.

- Providing more options—successful.
- Generating competition for the public schools—found in Canada, but generally not in the United States.

- Building models for public schools to use in improving themselves—a total failure.
- Developing creative curriculum to meet each community's needs—does not occur with for-profit management companies.

Plus the unstated but nevertheless real purpose—replacing the public schools, especially exemplified in Michigan.

We also used Levin's four criteria or benchmarks to evaluate charters:

- Freedom of choice has been expanded prodigiously by privatization and charters—for those kids who are accepted.
- Productive efficiency—inferior to public schools, as exemplified by Florida's charters comprising 10 percent of the state's school kids but getting 50 percent of the "F's." Productive efficiency is low since curriculum is not generated.
- Equity—diminished. Charters tend to generate segregation and stratification in the U.S. and internationally.
- Social cohesion—little evidence that charters increase it. May negatively affect it because of the segregation resulting from charters being implemented.

We raised the morality issue of profiting from the public's tax dollars going to corporations, instead of being spent in educating our kids.

We noted the positive impact of small school size on achievement and participation, which suggests a reform model for all schools and school systems. Last, we noted that the privatization movement has been stretched to its ultimate extent, with the Michigan legislature and governor attempting to replace public education with charters and other approaches.

REFERENCES AND RESOURCES

Barker, R. G., & Gump, P. V. (1964). *Big school, small school*. Stanford, CA: Stanford University Press.

Bickel, R., & Howley, C. B. (2002). The influence of scale. *The American School Board Journal, 189*(3), 28–30.

Bifulco, R., Ladd, H. F., & Ross, S. (2009). *Public school choice and integration: Evidence from Durham, North Carolina*. New York: National Center for the Study of Privatization in Education, Teachers College, Columbia University.

Booker, K., Zimmer, R., & Buddin, R. (2006). *The effect of charter schools on school peer composition*. New York: National Center for the Study of Privatization in Education, Teachers College, Columbia University.

Buddin, R., & Zimmer, R. (2006). *Is charter school competition in California improving the performance of traditional public schools?* New York: National Center for the Study of Privatization in Education, Teachers College, Columbia University.

Carr, M., & Ritter, G. (2007). *Measuring the cumulative effect of charter schools on student achievement in Ohio's traditional public schools*. New York: National Center for the Study of Privatization in Education, Teachers College, Columbia University.

Chakrabarti, R., & Roy, J. (2011). *Do charter schools crowd out private school enrollment? Evidence from Michigan.* New York: National Center for the Study of Privatization in Education, Teachers College, Columbia University.

Corcoran, S. P., & Stoddard, C. (2009). *Local demand for school choice: Evidence from the Washington Charter School Referenda.* New York: National Center for the Study of Privatization in Education, Teachers College, Columbia University.

CREDO. (2009, June 15). New Stanford report finds serious quality challenge in national school charter sector. Press release. Stanford, CA: Center for Research on Education Outcomes (CREDO), Stanford University.

D'Entremont, C., & Gulosino, V. (2008). *Circles of influence: How neighborhood demographics and charter school locations influence student enrollments.* New York: National Center for the Study of Privatization in Education, Teachers College, Columbia University.

Derringer, N. (2012, March 13). In Michigan charter schools, results no better than other public schools. *Bridge Magazine.*

Elacqua, G. (2009). *For-profit schooling and the politics of education reform in Chile: When ideology trumps evidence.* New York: National Center for the Study of Privatization in Education, Teachers College, Columbia University.

Esposito, C. L., & Cobb, C. D. (2008). *Estimating the school level effects of choice on academic achievement in Connecticut's magnet, technical and charter schools.* New York: National Center for the Study of Privatization in Education, Teachers College, Columbia University.

Harwell, D. (2012, June 17). Life Force Charter School in Dunedin closed now, but how did it get so bad? *Tampa Bay Times,* 1A, 8A.

Hill, C. D., & Welsch, D. M. (2008). *Is there a difference between for-profit versus not-for-profit charter schools?* Working Paper 08-02. New York: National Center for the Study of Privatization in Education, Teachers College, Columbia University.

Imberman, S. A. (2007). *Achievement and behavior in charter schools: Drawing a more complete picture.* New York: National Center for the Study of Privatization in Education, Teachers College, Columbia University.

Levin, H. M. (2013, January 5). Does privatization improve education? Keynote speech at International Congress for School Effectiveness and Improvement (ICSEI), Santiago, Chile.

Lubienski, C., & Lubienski, S. T. (2006). *Charter, private, public schools and academic achievements: New evidence from NAEP mathematics data.* New York: National Center for the Study of Privatization in Education, Teachers College, Columbia University.

Mac Iver, M. A., & Mac Iver, D. J. (2007). *Are education management organizations improving student achievement?* National Center for the Study of Privatization in Education, Teachers College, Columbia University.

Mathematica. (2012). Charter schools: Are they effective? *Mathematica Policy Research.* www.mathematica-mpr.com/education/charterschools.asp

Miron, G., Urschel, J. L., & Saxton, N. (2011, March). *What makes KIPP work? A study of student characteristics, attrition, and school finance.* New York: National Center for the Study of Privatization in Education, Teachers College, Columbia University.

Ni, Y. (2007). *The impact of charter schools on the efficiency of traditional public schools: Evidence from Michigan.* New York: National Center for the Study of Privatization in Education, Teachers College, Columbia University.

Ravitch, D. (2010, March 28). Privatization is bad policy for education. *Los Angeles Times.*

Rouse, C. E., Hannaway, J., Goldhaber, D., & Figlio, D. (2008). *Feeling the Florida heat? How low-performing schools respond to voucher and accountability pressure.* New York: National Center for the Study of Privatization in Education, Teachers College, Columbia University.

Savage, A., & Savage, C. (2012, November 29). Michigan Republicans move to privatize public education under the guise of "reform." *Eclectablog.* www.eclectablog.

com/2012/11/michigan-republicans-move-to-privatize-public-education-under-the-guise-of-reform.html

Shapiro, A. (2009). *Making large schools work: The advantages of small schools.* Lanham, MD: Rowman & Littlefield.

Shaughnessy, M. F. (2008, April 8). An interview with Henry Levin: About privatization. *Education News.*

Simon, S. (2012, August 2). Privatizing public schools: Big firms eyeing profits from U.S. K–12 market. *Huffington Post: Education.* http://www.huffingtonpost.com/2012/08/02/private-firms-eyeing-prof_n_1732856.html

Smith, S. D. (2012, November 25). Charter schools underperform. *Tampa Bay Times.*

Solocheck, J. S. (2013, May 7). Florida educational news: Charter school funding, parent trigger, high school diplomas, and more. *Tampa Bay Times.*

Thomas, P. (2011, April 22). Why advocacy and market forces fail education reform. *Truthout.* http://truth-out.org/news/item/618:why-advocacy-and-market-forces-fail-education-reform

Thomson, K. (2008). *An evaluation of the charter school movement in Alberta, Canada.* New York: National Center for the Study of Privatization in Education, Teachers College, Columbia University.

Toma, E. F., Zimmer, R., & Jones, J. T. (2006). *Beyond achievement: Enrollment consequences of charter schools in Michigan.* New York: National Center for the Study of Privatization in Education, Teachers College, Columbia University.

TEN

Vouchers: Another Form of Privatization

Increasingly it has become apparent that the search for evidence on the educational effectiveness of vouchers is a charade that will not settle the debate. . . . Different political groups . . . oppose or favor vouchers largely on the basis of their ideologies rather than evidence of effectiveness.
> —Henry M. Levin and Clive R. Belfield, *Vouchers and Public Policy*

For nearly 150 years public education in the United States has been recognized as a fundamental public good. That recognition is now under attack.
> —Bob Lowe, *The Hollow Promise of School Vouchers*

Like medicine, then, education and educational reform will continue to fail if placed inside the corrosive dynamics of market forces.
> —Paul Thomas, *Truthout*

INTRODUCTION AND ORGANIZATION

Since privatization guru Henry Levin unequivocally states in the quote above that ideology trumps evidence when considering the value of vouchers, we seem to have fallen into a thicket. Hopefully, it will not be too thorny. So, our first task is to examine the two ideological main viewpoints Levin cites: the libertarian vs. the social contract positions.

Then a brief rebuttal to the hidden and false assumption that private schools are superior to public schools, which is driving public perceptions—and actions.

Next, we'll figure out where the idea of vouchers came from and what they are all about, including their proposed purposes. Then we'll identify some of the various forms into which they've evolved. After that, we'll identify the four insightful criteria or benchmarks that Levin developed to evaluate the whole privatization movement (you'll remember that we laid these criteria out in chapters 8 and 9).

Before we get too far in our review of research findings, we'd better present relevant court results, some of which have ended vouchers in their respective states. We'll also lay out a few myths about vouchers that evaporate in the face of reality. It is important to frame research results, so we've done exactly that with three questions posed by Patrick Wolf to guide our thinking and to make it more efficient and focused.

We'll then review various research findings on vouchers, starting with the example of Chile as the ultimate *completely national example of a voucher system*, which has generated some serious unanticipated negative consequences. We'll also be applying Levin's four criteria to the research results, which may prove exceedingly insightful about their consequences. Note that Levin takes no sides on the issue in his National Center for the Study of Privatization in Education—nor should we. We'll follow with research on U.S. vouchers studies.

We'll review very briefly attempts to expand vouchers prodigiously in some states, followed by an attempt to see what research has discovered about the impact of vouchers on broader social issues and concerns. Luckily, Wolf's three questions and Levin's four criteria provide us with a gold standard for the last section. We'll draw some conclusions, and even some implications regarding what the research on vouchers tells us. Would it surprise you that there should be a few?

IDEOLOGY VS. EVIDENCE: LIBERTARIAN VS. SOCIAL CONTRACT POSITIONS

Libertarians place their highest value on freedom of choice. That is, education should be guided primarily by private values and goals, which is precisely the position of the Friedman Foundation for Educational Choice. Libertarians, according to Levin and Belfield, assume "that choice will promote greater efficiency (and possibly) equity" (2004, p. 13).

This position focuses on liberty and, thus, holds parents' views on choices of education as vital and supreme. That is, *parents should be the unit to decide* where their kids should be educated, and not the local school district. Several Supreme Court decisions, such as *Zelman v. Simmons-Harris* (2002), emphasize freedom of choice in their decisions. The libertarian point of view is silent on how educational vouchers will be able to influence Levin's criterion of social cohesion, which we will address later. They view such vital components of schooling as admissions, curriculum, and the culture of the school as red tape and a threat to promoting freedom of choice.

In contrast to the libertarian viewpoint, social contract supporters tend to focus on participation in social, political, and economic life as students and as citizens. Student participation in extracurricular activities certainly would be encouraged by social contract supporters. Concerns about parity—that is, equity for students across class, race, and gender—are vital, as is a desire for bilingual and special education. The focus is on establishing a constructive social order as a public good. Another goal is becoming a productive member of a classroom, of a school, and of society. This clearly means a concern for establishing and improving the culture of the class, school, and society. It means participating actively in society, which is the reason civics was added to the curriculum in 1918 as one of the cardinal principles of secondary education.

We will see how this is played out when we look at research support for vouchers.

A HIDDEN AND *FALSE* ASSUMPTION UNDERLYING PRIVATIZATION, CHARTERS, AND VOUCHERS—THAT PUBLIC SCHOOLS ARE INFERIOR TO PRIVATE SCHOOLS

Underlying the entire discussion of privatization, of charters, and of vouchers is the hidden, and unspoken, assumption that private schools are superior to public schools. My experience ranges over inner-city, suburban, exurban, and rural schools, and I find this assertion astounding. Interestingly, in the Midwest with its numerous world-class suburban school systems, most private schools are considered inferior to the public schools.

While it should be noted that a good number of excellent private schools do exist, most people in that region, when told a kid is going to a private school, ask what the problem is. All other regions in the United States obviously have fine public schools as well, as we've mentioned in chapter 1 regarding the success of our upper-middle- and middle-class kids on the PISA tests.

Note that the PISA scores referred to in chapter 1 support this. Those schools' scores are equal to or better than the schools in the top nations in the world.

The bad press our public schools are getting comes from those with high poverty, usually in the inner cities, although, to be sure, poverty-stricken rural schools face similar dilemmas. The bad press, as chapter 8 notes, is propaganda from some privatization supporters that has been so successful in convincing the public that it has taken hold in the nation and is now widely believed.

But this is patently false.

BEGINNINGS

Like all things privatized in education, they start with the Nobel laureate, economist Milton Friedman, who thought that the market should apply to education to improve it. As a matter of fact, Friedman founded the Friedman Foundation for Educational Choice in 1996 (which he modestly named after himself) as a vehicle to advance the cause of providing more options for parents and students.

The Varieties of Vouchers

The Friedman Foundation (n.d.) lists a number of alternatives, including the following:

- School vouchers
- Charter schools
- Tax-credit scholarships, in which individuals or corporations receive a tax credit from state taxes for donating to nonprofits, which can use the funds to pay private school tuition; some states call these opportunity scholarships and permit students to use them to attend private religious schools
- Individual tax credits and deductions from state taxes for the costs involved in students attending private schools; this means that private school costs can be tax deductible, if the state permits it, even if the private school is religious
- Education savings accounts—parents withdraw their child from a public district or charter school and receive a payment into a savings account with restricted uses; parents can use the funds for private school tuition, virtual education programs, and so on
- Home schooling
- Online schools and digital learning (online schools and charters will be the focus of chapter 11)

Question: Seeing this list, would you conclude that these are attempts to replace public education?

Levin's criteria/benchmarks—useful for evaluating vouchers:

- Freedom of choice—heavy emphasis on private benefits of education
- Productive efficiency—involves maximization of educational results for any resource—that is, getting the most out of school
- Equity—fairness in access to educational opportunities
- Social cohesion—how an educational reform affects participation in social, political, and economic processes: "a common educational experience [should] orient all students [to become] full participants

in the social, political, and economic institutions of our society" (Levin, 2002, p. 5)

THE COURTS AND VOUCHERS

In Louisiana, a state district judge in November 2012 ruled that using vouchers for private religious schools was unconstitutional, much to the consternation of privatization advocates. In Florida in 2006, the State Supreme Court ruled that using public funds for supporting private religious education was unconstitutional. This essentially knocked out vouchers in the state, although heavily backed by the conservatives. In 2012, Floridians, by a considerable margin, turned down an attempt to change the state constitution to permit public moneys to support private religious education.

Similarly, in Colorado a state judge ruled that the Douglas County School District, a relatively wealthy district, violated the state constitution by sending state funds to private schools that infused religion into the curriculum. In Utah, a relatively conservative state, a universal school voucher proposal was defeated in a 2012 election.

However, in the case of Ohio, which does not have a constitutional provision forbidding the use of public funds for religious schools, the U.S. Supreme Court ruled that such action was constitutional. The Supreme Court has ruled that public funds can be used to transport kids to parochial schools.

BACK TO VOUCHERS

Myths about Vouchers

One myth is that vouchers are a way for disadvantaged students to attend a private school. Unfortunately, if a child has a disability, many private schools become disinterested in that student's attendance. In Milwaukee, for example, 42 percent of voucher schools offer no programs for special-needs kids.

Another myth is that you can attend almost any private school. Unfortunately, not quite. In Washington, D.C., for example, the maximum $7,500 voucher covers the tuition of only three high schools, and only one of these is not a Catholic school. It is important to note that people wanting to enroll their kids in a private school must take into account hidden costs, such as uniforms, books, transportation, and other charges, including fees for extracurricular activities.

In addition, many private schools do not want to accept kids by lottery, since they wish to preserve the composition of their student body

(Strauss, 2003). Accepting the results of a lottery-style selection process almost inevitably would affect that texture.

Another myth is that vouchers have accountability built into them. Much of the ideology surrounding privatization is that it will force public schools to become more accountable. Yet private schools are not required to administer standardized tests to their student body. Thus, voucher schools are essentially accountable to no one, unless they have functioning school boards with authority. So establishing vouchers undermines privatization claims of supporting accountability. Accountability is certainly supported—for public schools.

A myth is that vouchers will improve public education because of competition. We've addressed this in chapter 8 and found that most U.S. schools seem to respond to voucher private schools by shrugging—as if they do not matter. However, countering that notion is Hoxby's (2001) analysis of the impact of competition in Milwaukee's and Michigan's schools, revealing that research shows "public schools responding favorably to competition" (p. 74), although she noted that creaming (that is, skimming better students and funds) did occur in Milwaukee. As we noted earlier, this research is suspect, since it was not peer reviewed, a normal process for ensuring the validity of research.

A final myth is that private schools are run more efficiently than public schools. Levin noted that Milwaukee's private schools cost almost $1,000 more per student than their public school peers.

Here are three questions to guide our thinking (courtesy of Patrick Wolf, 2008, p. 415):

1. Do voucher programs primarily serve disadvantaged students?
2. Do parents like voucher programs?
3. Do students benefit academically from voucher programs? (Note the limits of this question.)

And what does the research tell us?

First, the Chilean Experience

First, we'll look at the example of a nation jumping headfirst into essentially an experiment in changing their *entire system of education* into the market-based model that Friedman envisioned. And that nation is Chile.

While Sweden has participated in privatization, according to Pons (2012), "Chile represents the purest example of a Friedman-designed education voucher system in the world" (p. 2). That, of course, is partly due to the fact that "In 1980, Friedman created and helped implement a system to try out the education voucher theory he first proposed in 1955" (p. 2). The Chilean system saw two major changes. First, responsibility was shifted from the federal government to the cities and *every student was given a voucher* for a public or a private school.

This generated huge impacts. Private school enrollment jumped from 13 percent in 1980 to half of all students by 2012. Funding for all schools also dropped precipitously, from 5.4 percent of GDP in 1980 to 3.7 percent in 1990, a drop of 31.5 percent. It has risen now to 4.4 percent of GDP in 2012, an increase of 19 percent. Pons states that voucher proponents note that the students score higher on international tests than other Latin American countries, but only slightly higher than Mexico and Uruguay, and rank about as high as other nations that have a comparable level of investment, such as Russia and Bulgaria. However, in 2013, at an international conference, the minister of education noted that half of Chilean kids cannot read.

Pons notes that the achievement gap is growing and that there is an increase in stratification. (Incidentally, at the same conference Levin noted that the Swedes were quite concerned about the stratification resulting from their voucher system.) Pons states that about three-fourths of Chilean public school enrollment consist of kids from the lower 40 percent of family income. Only 10 percent of lower income kids attend private schools, with the other 90 percent of kids in private schools coming from the upper 60 percent in income.

Upper-middle-income families have reaped the benefits of this system change, while the disadvantaged and disabled are more prone to be in the public schools. Much of the Chilean nation has begun demanding free public schools to the tune of one million out of a national population of seventeen million demonstrating on a single day.

Elacqua (2010) weighs in on these issues, noting that Chile's unrestricted flat per-pupil vouchers have led to increased stratification across public and private schools with the public schools serving the more disadvantaged students. He adds that public schools tend to be more diverse both in terms of ethnicity and socioeconomic status than are private voucher schools. He found that school tuition is an important variable to explain segregation patterns between and among public and for-profit and non-profit religious and secular voucher schools.

As for Patrick Wolf's three questions:

1. Do vouchers primarily serve disadvantaged students? Chile's vouchers were supposed to serve all students, but fail in that bid. They seem to be serving the middle and upper classes predominantly.
2. Do parents like the voucher programs? The more well-to-do obviously do, while the less well-to-do are literally marching in droves against them.
3. Do students benefit academically? We seem to be unable to respond to that unequivocally. Looks like it hasn't worked.

Question: Shouldn't we ask if students are benefiting, period?
Let's bring in Levin's four criteria.

1. Freedom of choice—works for the middle and upper classes, not for the disadvantaged
2. Productive efficiency—probably not, but, oddly, not enough data
3. Equity—not
4. Social cohesion—vouchers seem to be tearing the society apart

Vouchers do not seem to be achieving the purposes of improving education for all, and particularly for the disadvantaged in Chile. This is a major failure.

The United States

Vouchers were Friedman's choice—his vehicle—to implement market-based reforms in education.The voucher movement took flight in Milwaukee in 1991, essentially as a vehicle to improve education for inner-city minorities, supposedly by providing better choices than the schools to which the kids were going. By June 2012, nineteen states had developed voucher legislation and plans (Altaschuler, 2012).

But most voucher plans, except for Milwaukee, are relatively small. Even Milwaukee's plan was not big originally, starting with 337 kids in 1991 but reaching 20,189 out of about 100,000 kids in 2010–2011. Test scores comparing Milwaukee students in math and reading do not give an advantage to the voucher schools. Voucher schools in math score 34.4 percent proficient or above in comparison to public schools' score of 47.8 percent. Similarly, vouchers in reading scored 55.2 percent vs. 59 percent. The achievement gap has not closed, although it is a bit reduced.

Although such disparities have been consistent in the program for the past twenty years, ideology still drives voucher expansion decisions, with the Wisconsin governor pressing to expand the voucher program.

(Actually, reducing the achievement gap will be addressed in chapter 13, "Major Reforms That Really Work.")

Levin

Let's turn now to Levin's 2004 analysis of research. Remember his insistence that ideology drives contentions about research? Levin notes several reasons for the rise of ideology as a driving force in American education. The first is that vouchers have been pronounced legal by the Supreme Court. A second is that vouchers open up the possibility of financial gains (all we have to do is to refer to the large number of for-profit companies eager to provide tutoring mandated by No Child Left Behind, and the large number of for-profit charters springing up).

Levin points to a third reason—that scaling up the present small programs can profoundly, even radically, affect the control of education. And, actually, a fourth reason has developed: the profound social movement (Blumer, 1946) that has been developed by conservative members of our society to reform education to their philosophy of government and society.

Where before virtually everyone supported education as a public good, a sizable proportion of people now want to abandon the public schools and implement private education. This is seen in a number of states, such as Michigan, Louisiana, and Tennessee, which are attempting to expand charters prodigiously. This social movement evinces an immense change in attitudes toward the public schools.

Regarding vouchers' success, Levin and Belfield note "that the evidence has been extremely contentious. Despite a sizeable research effort, the evidence on vouchers does not provide clear guidance" (Levin & Belfield, 2004, p. 19). They point out that the Milwaukee "evaluations . . . have not established clearly whether students gain from participation" (p. 19) and that since 1995, no information has been available because testing on a common instrument was not required. Levin and Belfield then conclude, "There is no evidence, at present, that voucher programs make a *large* difference in educational outcomes for participating students" (p. 20).

An earlier paper by Levin (1998) says that the evidence shows that educational choice leads to greater socioeconomic and racial segregation of students and does not support the contention that costs of private schools are considerably lower than those of public schools.

However, more recently, Wolf (2008), contends that of "ten separate analyses of data from 'gold standard' experimental studies . . . nine conclude that some or all of the participants benefitted academically from using a voucher to attend a private school" (p. 416). Wolf cites a great many studies, some of which showed no statistically significant gains, while others do.

Sometimes, researchers report no gains for the first or second year and some for the third year. Wolf noted the variability in the research by indicating that "none of the experimental analyses of voucher effects on student achievement reports exactly the same results" (p. 443).

He added that some students are helped academically by vouchers, but noted, "More high quality experimental research is needed before we can close the books on the participant effects of school vouchers, but the results so far are promising" (p. 445). He found more achievement gains in math than in reading because he asserts that math achievement is more a result of instruction than reading.

Wolf concludes "that the effect of vouchers on student achievement tends to be positive; however, achievement impacts are not statistically significant for all students in all studies and they tend to require several years to materialize" (p. 446).

So, for question 3, *do* students benefit academically from vouchers? The answer is that some do and some do not. Wolf maintains that properly randomized studies account for parental bias in choosing to send their kids to voucher programs. However, even the best experiments can suffer from ailments such as attrition and other factors that reduce the theoretical perfection of such statistical operations.

In another study, Wolf, Gutmann, Puma, Kisida, Rizzo, and Eissa (2010) found that the Washington, D.C., Opportunity Scholarship Program improved reading, but not math achievement overall and for 5 of 10 subgroups (p. 1). They also found that the group considered the highest priority by Congress, those students coming from schools in need of improvement, did not develop increased achievement.

Wolf et al. (2010) stated there was "no conclusive evidence that the Opportunity Scholarship Program affected student achievement" (p. xv). However, they did note that the program significantly improved students' chances of graduating high school.

Previously, we noted that research indicated that while some Canadian schools were sensitive to competition exerted by charters, their American counterparts were indifferent to this pressure. Hoxby (2001), on the other hand, found that competition improved the public schools in Arizona, Michigan, and Milwaukee. So, again, we find mixed results. However, remember that Hoxby's research has been criticized for not being peer reviewed.

Rouse and Barrow (2008) note that the best research to this time finds relatively small gains in achievement for students utilizing vouchers. However, they state, most of these gains are not different statistically from zero.

Belfield in 2006 evaluated the Cleveland voucher program and found that demand for private school vouchers was based on religion, race, and family education levels. But, contrary to Wolf, who strongly supported the effectiveness of vouchers in what he called the "gold standard" studies, Belfield found no overall advantages for people who used vouchers. He found, in fact, that voucher users performed slightly worse in mathematics.

He also found that the vouchers were not differentially more effective for African American students, although other studies do claim more effectiveness for this population. For example, Howell (2001) studied vouchers in Dayton, Ohio, and found no statistically significant achievement gains for voucher groups in years one and two, but did find statistically significant achievement gains for the African American subgroup. Again, Howell, Peterson, Wolf, and Campbell (2006) found voucher gains in the second year by African American students in combined reading and math achievement.

Several states with conservative governors and legislatures have begun considering large-scale voucher programs, including Tennessee, Indiana, and Michigan. It will be interesting to see how they fare. As mentioned earlier, Utah voters turned down such a large scale expansion.

IMPACT OF VOUCHERS ON BROADER SOCIAL ISSUES AND CONCERNS

D'Entremont and Huerta (2007) expand the narrow focus of vouchers on achievement on tests in math and reading to concerns of local school governance. They note that voucher advocates have focused on building support for vouchers among marginalized populations who have become frustrated with their local public schools. The authors are concerned that these strategies may offend middle-class and suburban voters who may perceive these policies as attempts to undermine local school board authority.

They may also perceive such policies as potential lines of action to redistribute local school resources to other areas. The authors note that vouchers have the potential to erase municipal boundaries, negatively affect the local neighborhood social contract, affect housing patterns and prices, and alter student enrollments. Some recent initiatives in Michigan come to mind as examples of those possibilities, especially because of the libertarian thrust that Levin has noted, as described earlier.

Fundamental question: Will developing a market of competitive choices exert an impact on the basic governance structure of American education—that is, the local school district and its governance body, the local school board? The reason I ask this is that it *changes fundamentally* the source of decision-making in the local district *from the school board to the individual family*. Suddenly, each family makes its decisions as to where its children become educated.

This is called *Balkanization*—because each family becomes its own decision-making entity, just as the many little enclaves and ethnic centers have done in the Balkans (formerly Yugoslavia). Note that they've now split into numerous smaller states—and they continue to do so. Is this what could happen to our educational system? If so, it means an immense, radical change. And it absolutely affects the social cohesion factor that Levin uses to evaluate vouchers and charters!

The segregation reported in other nations and our own experience with vouchers constitutes a serious impact upon our educational system. It, too, has a deleterious impact upon the social cohesion and equity criteria Levin uses to evaluate privatization efforts. If we value daily interaction among all our classes, races, and ethnic groups, the segregation developed by vouchers limits this, negatively impacting both the social cohesion and equity criteria.

It is obvious that we have to move from the very narrow and limited focus on achievement measured by a couple of yearly tests in math and reading to much wider factors, which should include behavioral phenomena, some of which were mentioned in chapter 9 on charters. These would include such areas as major educational aims and goals (thinking critically, respecting others, becoming resilient), other knowledge areas (how about participating as citizens, learning about great literature, thinking scientifically), and developing other essential talents (communicating effectively, being able to analyze ideas, artistic talents).

You know, the really important things in life.

What relationship do vouchers have to other educational innovations, such as magnet schools and the small schools movement? This would seem important to think about if we want to reform our educational institutions.

SUMMARY, CONCLUSIONS, AND IMPLICATIONS

Clearly, since ideology is driving public response to and even the research on vouchers, Levin's summary of that research seems plausible — that it is a charade because different groups take sides on the issue depending upon whether they are libertarians or social contract–focused. Wolf, however, writing four years later in 2008, cites some studies that show some gains, and others showing little or no gain.

We explored both libertarian and social contract positions, followed by questioning the fallacious belief that private schools are superior to public schools. We than cited Friedman's list of different kinds of vouchers, followed by Henry Levin's four criteria to evaluate vouchers, and now discuss some conclusions this chapter has developed for each:

- Freedom of choice—parents very pleased with the options, because they have a choice.
- Productive efficiency—depends on whether the research supports vouchers. Levin states that research on vouchers is a charade, but Wolf and some others disagree. Yet Wolf's research on Washington, D.C.'s voucher initiative came up negative, with no difference developing for vouchers and non-vouchers kids' achievement.
- Equity—if vouchers generate segregated results, equity is destroyed. They do—and it is.
- Social cohesion—in Chile vouchers are tearing the society apart. Similarly, depending upon one's libertarian vs. social contact beliefs, we find the same result. Social cohesion is suffering when vouchers kick in.

We also briefly cited various court decisions limiting and supporting vouchers, and treated myths about vouchers to clarify major issues. We then cited Wolf's three questions.

1. Do voucher programs primarily serve disadvantaged students? In the United States they are "designed to serve exclusively students with various disadvantages" (Wolf, 2008, p. 419). The mind-set developed in constructing the Milwaukee model around trying to improve education for the disadvantaged, even the highly disadvantaged, seems to have taken root. Wolf points out that the twelve programs in the United States do exactly that. They serve disadvantaged kids.
2. Do parents like voucher programs? They certainly do, in part because they are involved in making a choice.
3. Do students benefit academically from voucher programs? The response regarding that is mixed, partly, as Levin and Belfield (2004) note, depending on one's ideological position. We will add more shortly.

We subsequently reviewed the Chilean experience and found the Law of Unanticipated Consequences (LUC) kicking in, with huge public negative responses and heavy segregating effects of this universal voucher experiment. Sweden also has found the same results from voucherizing. We also observed that evaluating schools and innovations with such limited tools that test only math and reading almost inevitably generate inadequate results and, thus, measures.

We need to expand our instruments to focus on much broader behavioral and attitudinal outcomes to develop a better handle on the very core of our educational system. We're much more than reading and math scores. Education is way beyond this.

We also saw mixed research results from studies asking whether competition from vouchers would put pressure on the public schools. More mixed results.

We seem to be witnessing a social movement that has emerged in the past two decades, which Levin characterizes as expressing a libertarian point of view, and which this chapter and those dealing with privatization and charters consider strongly conservative in nature. Thus, Levin characterizes various publics' responses to the evidence regarding privatization, charters, and vouchers as depending upon the prism through which one views the world, as well as the educational world. Thus, people will view the same evidence and emerge with radically differing conclusions and interpretations.

Such viewpoints generate radically divergent consequences if put into action regarding schools, since if one espouses libertarian or strongly conservative views and wants to privatize schools, then the basic governance unit becomes the family. This represents an immense shift from the former governance structure of the local school district governed by the locally elected school board. That is, a market of competitive choices made by the family inevitably will undermine and supplant local governance. It inevitably results in Balkanizing education, so that the great glue that the local school has provided in our society for the past two hundred years, that social cohesion, will be lost.

Last, despite all the posturing and claims about privatization, Henry Levin's (Shaughnessy, 2008) summary statement that choice and privatization have had very small educational impacts, both positive or negative, seems to ring true.

REFERENCES AND RESOURCES

Altaschuler, G. (2012, October 19). U.S. elections: Do school vouchers work? *The Conversation*.

Belfield, C. (2006). *The evidence on education vouchers: An application to the Cleveland Scholarship and Tutoring Program*. New York: National Center for the Study of Privatization in Education, Teachers College, Columbia University.

Blumer, H. (1946). Collective behavior. In A. M. Lee (Ed.), *Principles of sociology*. New York: Barnes & Noble, pp. 199–220.

D'Entremont, C., & Huerta, L. A. (2007). *Irreconcilable differences? Education vouchers and the suburban response*. New York: National Center for the Study of Privatization in Education, Teachers College, Columbia University.

Elacqua, G. (2010). *The impact of school choice and public policy on segregation: Evidence for Chile*. New York: National Center for the Study of Privatization in Education, Teachers College, Columbia University.

Friedman, M. (1955). *The role of government in education: Economics and the public interest*. Indianapolis, IN: Milton and Rose D. Friedman Foundation.

Friedman Foundation for Educational Choice. (n.d.). Types of School Choice. www.edchoice.org/School-Choice/Types-of-School-Choice.aspx

Howell, W. G. (2001). Vouchers in New York, Dayton, and D.C. *Educational Matters, 2*, 48–54.

Howell, W. G., Peterson, P. E., with Wolf, P. J., & Campbell, D. E. (2006). *The education gap: Vouchers and urban schools*. Rev. ed. Washington, DC: Brookings Institution Press.

Hoxby, C. M. (2001, Winter). Rising tide. *Education Next*.

Levin, H. M. (1998). Educational vouchers: Effectiveness, choice and costs. *Journal of Policy Analysis and Management, 17*, 373–392.

Levin, H. M. (2002, Fall). A comprehensive framework for evaluating educational vouchers. *Educational Evaluation and Policy Analysis, 24*(3), 159–174.

Levin, H. M., & Belfield, C. R. (2004, June). *Vouchers and public policy: When ideology trumps evidence*. New York: National Center for the Study of Privatization in Education, Teachers College, Columbia University.

Pons, M. (2012, October 25). How one national school voucher program fared. *The Answer Sheet*. www.washingtonpost.com/blogs/answer-sheet/wp/2012/10/25/how-the-worlds-longest-running-school-voucher-program-fared/

Rouse, C. E., & Barrow, L. (2008). *School vouchers and student achievement: Recent evidence, remaining questions*. New York: National Center for the Study of Privatization in Education, Teachers College, Columbia University.

Shaughnessy, M. F. (2008, April 8). An interview with Henry Levin: About privatization. *Education News*.

Strauss, V. (2003, September 28). Private schools leery of voucher trade-offs. *Washington Post.*

Wolf, P. (2008, April 14). School voucher programs: What the research says about parental school choice. *Brigham Young University Law Review.*

Wolf, P., Gutmann, B., Puma, M., Kisida, B., Rizzo, N., & Eissa, N. (2010, June). *Evaluation of the D.C. Opportunity Scholarship Program: Final report.* Washington, DC: National Center for Educational Evaluation and Regional Assistance, Institute of Educational Sciences.

ELEVEN

Virtual Charter Schools: Privatization on Steroids

What we're talking about here is the financialization of public education. These folks are fundamentally trying to do to public education what the banks did with home mortgages.

— Alex Molnar, National Education Policy Center,
University of Colorado, Boulder

The kids enroll. You get the money. The kids disappear.

— Gary Miron, Western Michigan University

INTRODUCTION AND ORGANIZATION

The virtual charter school, the most recent darling of the largely conservative drive for privatization, is its most rapidly growing school choice option, at least presently (Marsh, Carr-Chellman, & Sockman, 2009). But first, let's figure out what virtual charters are and the social forces driving their expansion. Next, we'll look at their development to give us a picture of their extent. We'll find out that for-profit educational management organizations (EMOs) are taking a strong lead in lobbying states to permit them to operate.

We will look at the arguments being used for virtual charters' development, and then ask how they operate and develop some of the major concerns expressed about their operation.

We'll cut to the chase immediately—by comparing how well virtual charters compete with regular schools in terms of math and reading scores (which seem to be the only, and a very limited, approach being used to evaluate how our kids are faring in school). We will investigate

141

the causes of the differences. We'll also compare graduation rates of EMOs and inquire into their rates of attrition and drop-outs.

We will also look at how children (and for that matter, people) learn, using the Gregorc personality style delineator as our touchstone—and find out that *more than two-thirds of us do not learn with the style that is required in using a virtual educational approach.*

We will find out how representative their students are in comparison with those in the five states where K12 Inc. operates, and also in the country. We'll also deal with the troubling issue of how and whether kids are socialized into becoming kindergarteners, grade school kids, middle school kids, and high schoolers if they are schooled primarily through virtual education.

We will examine some of the financial aspects of the EMOs in comparison with public schools and discover some of the advantages they have by avoiding the costs of school buildings, transportation, and other fundamentals such as accommodating special education students and English Language Learners, as public schools must. This should give us a peek into their profit margins.

Question: What do you predict they will be?

We'll look into the possibilities of irregularities—that is, gaming the system and actual fraud—in the EMO's functioning, since they are profit-making organizations. We'll cite Campbell's Law, which accurately predicts the corruption and distortion involved in the gaming going on.

We'll also utilize Henry Levin's (2002) four criteria or benchmarks, which we've used in the preceding three chapters to evaluate various findings about these schools, as we've done regarding privatization, charters, and vouchers. Levin's framework provides us with the ability to draw a sharp, insightful summary into each. Last, we'll develop a number of summary statements, and draw some conclusions and implications and even make some recommendations for policymakers.

WHAT ARE VIRTUAL CHARTERS?

For this chapter, we'll look at full-time virtual charter schools, and not at a wider array of online courses, such as delivering single courses, or a mixed combination of hybrid or blended learning.

Full-time virtual charters are also known as cyber schools or online schools. Such schools deliver their curriculum via the Internet. Most virtual schools are charters, are full-time, and are statewide in their scope, with kids working in their homes. Teachers can work in an office building or from their home—or anyplace where they can communicate with students with a computer. But while we picture in our minds the technological leaps such online virtual schools must be developing, in fact, "much of the work is completed the old fashioned way, with a pencil and paper while seated at a desk" (Saul, 2011).

Miron and Urschel (2012) estimate that about 250,000 students are enrolled in the model full-time virtual school, which is our focus, up from about 20,000 less than a decade ago. Thirty states and the District of Columbia have passed legislation permitting the creation of full-time virtual charter schools and even more states have approved permitting on-line delivery of courses. Florida, for example, mandated that every student must take an online course to graduate high school, which clearly provides quite a bonus to the online virtual EMOs.

Clearly, expansion of this form of privatization stems from the same conservative social movement (Blumer, 1946) that is vigorously supporting other forms of privatization, such as charters (chapter 9) and vouchers (chapter 10). While Levin and Belfield (2004) term this social movement libertarian, we've also considered it conservative, as discussed in chapter 10.

This movement is pushing very hard to privatize education and other governmental functions. For example, in Florida, fully 60 percent of expenses for state governmental functions have been privatized, including prisons, university bookstores, and others. Those pressing either to permit or to expand virtual charter schools tend to be the same conservative governors and legislatures supporting and expanding charters, vouchers, and privatization.

The largest educational management organization (EMO) of full-time virtual schools is K12 Inc., which had forty-eight virtual full-time schools in 2010–2011 (Miron & Urschel, 2012, p. 2). Saul notes that K12 Inc. had ninety-four thousand kids in 2011. One school that K12 Inc. has under its jurisdiction is the Agora Cyber School, which we will find interesting.

The second largest EMO is Connections Academies, which had over twenty thousand students in thirteen schools by the same year. Seven other for-profit companies have jumped into operation. By the end of 2011, Saul notes that for-profit EMOs run seventy-nine online schools in the United States.

On September 15, 2011, Pearson bought Connections Academy, which had an annual income of $190 million, for $400 million. Perhaps Pearson expects to profit from this for-profit virtual charter company. We'll see what profits these virtual charters generate.

Question: What do you think Pearson (formerly a publishing company) was thinking about?

It is interesting to note that former Bush secretary of education William Bennett was one of the founders of K12 Inc. At the time he thought that such schools would be a haven for shy children, parents worried about drugs in schools, and kids with "terrible acne" (Saul, 2011). Originally, they believed this would be a support for home schooling and wanted to charge about $1,000 per student per year. They then decided to move the idea into virtual charters. Apparently, this rather limited scenario seems to have expanded.

ARGUMENTS SUPPORTING VIRTUAL CHARTERS (MAYBE)

Using technology can lead to teachers and students communicating better, thereby improving student learning. However, this does not seem to be improving student performance. As a matter of fact, virtual charters are doing considerably poorer than regular public schools.

A second argument is that choice is promoted by virtual charters, and that such choice leads to competition, which will drive schools to compete and so to improve. We've seen in chapter 10 that research on competition is mixed. Some studies indicate no impact on the public schools, while one study indicates an impact.

A third—and unspoken—argument is that it provides *an opportunity for investment—and profit*.

Conclusion: Levin's freedom of choice criterion certainly is promoted by virtual charters.

HOW FARE THE VIRTUAL CHARTER SCHOOLS?

Not well. In fact—poorly. In fact—really *very* poorly.

The facts?

In 2010–2011, only 27.7 percent of K12 Inc. students met Adequate Yearly Progress (AYP) of the No Child Left Behind yearly testing requirement. Public schools' scores? An estimated 52 percent, almost twice that of K12 Inc. This has been constant over the past two years, according to Miron and Urschel.

The authors report that in some cases K12 Inc. schools were not able to meet the requirement of 95 percent of kids in a grade having to take the state examinations. Only seven of forty-eight full-time virtual K12 Inc. schools, 19.4 percent, achieved satisfactory progress ratings. Thus, 80.6 percent failed to do so. Reading ratings across grades 3–11 were between two and eleven percentage points below their state public school averages.

Math scores lagged fourteen to thirty-six percentage points behind public school kids, and that gap increased considerably in higher grades. *Kids did worse the longer they stayed in the virtual charters.* For example, in 2010–2011 in third grade, 60 percent of kids in K12 Inc. schools met or exceeded state standards in comparison with 76 percent in state schools. In sixth grade, 57 percent vs. 73 percent in state schools. In eighth grade, 46 percent compared with 67 percent in public schools. All were well below scores in state schools where K12 Inc. was operating.

Then it dropped precipitously to about 31 percent in grade 11 compared with public school scores of 68 percent (Miron & Urschel, p. 33).

Stanford's Center for Research in Educational Outcomes (CREDO) in 2011 evaluated student achievement in charters in Pennsylvania, which presently has the largest number of virtual charters. (Actually, one-third of charter students in the state are enrolled in eight rather large virtual charters.) CREDO conducted a rigorous study matching the virtual charter kids with similar noncharter students and made sure that the virtual kids were in their setting for at least two consecutive test events. CREDO "found that the charter students were making significantly smaller gains in learning over time than matched students in traditional public schools. While students in brick-and-mortar charter schools were slightly behind their matched peers in district schools, the gains in learning over time by students enrolled in virtual charter schools were even smaller still" (Miron & Urschel, 2012, p. 5).

Further study confirms the disparity. Math gains by the virtual charters were substantially worse than the reading findings, with the virtuals significantly behind matched peers in public schools. CREDO found all eight virtual charters in Pennsylvania scoring significantly lower than matched peers in both reading and math. CREDO found no single subject test in any of the eight virtuals favoring the kids. CREDO noted that "in every sub-group, with significant effects, cyber charter performance is lower" (Saul, 2011, p. 9).

While K12 Inc. kids were doing worse, the K12 Inc. president was claiming that they were doing as well or better than regular public schools. He cited Agora as "significantly higher than a typical school on state administered tests for growth" (Saul, p. 9). The facts, however, contradict these rosy assurances. Saul indicates that weeks before this statement, 42 percent of Agora kids tested on or above grade level in math in comparison with 75 percent of kids statewide. And 52 percent of Agora kids were at or above grade level in reading compared with 72 percent statewide.

What Is the "Churn"?

Saul states that the churn rate is the constant cycle of enrollment and withdrawal. At first, I did not quite grasp what was going on. The Agora school in Pennsylvania reported that at the end of the 2009–2010 school year, it had 4,890 students.

But 2,688 students withdrew during that year. That's a 54.9 percent dropout rate *for one year*.

However, the way Agora dealt with that was to recruit vigorously, so that at the end of the year, the total number was 170 students more than they started with.

Let's analyze this.

Clearly, Agora, a K12 Inc. school, was recruiting at a phenomenal rate. But what does this do to teaching and learning? More than half the students that teachers were dealing with kept coming in and dropping out during the year. That's why I quoted Miron at the start of this chapter: "The kids enroll. You get the money. The kids disappear."

In Colorado's virtual schools, *half* the online students *left within a year*, and when they returned they were often further behind academically than when they started. Colorado online schools generated three times the number of dropouts as kids who graduated. *One of every eight online students dropped out permanently*, which was *four times the state average.*

Wisconsin found that a small number of students were enrolled continuously over a three-year period. Their virtual charter students did better than state public school kids in reading, but worse in math. Minnesota also found lower course completion rates and higher dropout rates.

Graduation rates? On-time graduation rate for K12 Inc.—49.1 percent. Public schools—74 percent.

Question: How would *you* rate these achievements?

Conclusion: Levin's productive efficiency (getting the most out of school) is quite poor.

Really serious question: In the face of such miserable results, why the nation-wide heavy push to expand virtual charter schools?

Levin and Belfield's (2004) response is key—*ideology*. The title says it all: *Vouchers and Public Policy: When Ideology Trumps Evidence*. Obviously, it is conservative ideology to press for choice and privatization—and to ignore the obviously poor results. We'll cite Campbell's Law (1976) again, which appears to be operating: "The more any quantitative social indicator is used for social decision-making, the more subject it will be to corruption pressures and the more apt it will be to distort and corrupt the social processes it is intended to monitor."

OK, Why Such Terrible Results?

First, Miron and Urschel point to high levels of student mobility. That means a lot of kids enroll and then drop out. The authors ask if the schools are enrolling kids who are mobile or do they contribute to or cause the mobility. Second, they ask if K12 Inc. gets less money and so cannot fulfill its educating function. That does not seem to be the case, since K12 was arguing that it will increase its profitability by $20 million in fiscal 2013. The authors then state, "An alternative explanation is that the company chooses not to address the weak performance of its schools to protect its profits" (p. vii).

Miron and Urschel also refer to another explanation: inadequate or insufficient instruction. K12 has three times more students per instructor in comparison with public schools and pays reduced salaries for teachers and other staff. More on this shortly.

The authors likewise point to a problem with learning styles, as well as resources in the home. So, let's home in on learning styles to see if they can explain some odd results of virtual charters.

Learning Styles

We will use Anthony Gregorc's style delineator (1999). Gregorc postulates four (4) major styles, each with its primary learning approach. In chapter 4 we briefly used learning styles to evaluate models of teaching. Here, we use learning styles as a tool to figure out how they impact the effectiveness of virtual charters.

- Concrete Sequentials (CSs) tend to see things as black or white, see no shades of gray, love detail, just want the facts, do not see the "big picture," and are not intuitive. Occupations? Bookkeepers, engineers, pilots, CPAs—all involving detailed work. They like to run things, keep time, get things in on time. Tend to be perfectionists. Are self-motivated. Learning style? Like to work *alone* on detailed tasks. Will finish them on time, even before deadlines. About 25 percent of the American population.
- At the opposite extreme, the Abstract Randoms (ARs), who live in the world of feelings and emotions, are considered at times flaky by the CSs. Are intuitive, spontaneous, unlike the more prosaic CSs. Very concerned about people's feelings, so they focus on the emotional health of any group. Want to work in groups, need to communicate with others. Little sense of time, so assignments often come in late. Motivated to make people happy, not to complete work. About half of Americans.
- The Abstract Sequential (AS) is the "big picture," critical thinker. Loves to analyze. Impatient with people who do not perceive ideas and issues in depth. Often works in the sciences. Very independent; wants to work alone. About 3–5 percent of Americans.
- Concrete Randoms (CRs) are entrepreneurs, troubleshooters, problem solvers, prone to take huge risks physically and personally and professionally. Have many projects working simultaneously. Often daredevils, inventors, highly intuitive. Big on autonomy. Love to be challenged. Like to work alone, and will get things in late, if at all. About 15–20 percent of Americans.

Question: How do you think the learning styles of these four personalities fit into the pressure of working alone at home on a computer?

The CS students can and will do it. Their preferred learning style is to work alone. They do OK if they want to do the assignments, which they normally do. They are good soldiers and will follow orders. Thorough, self-motivated, which is exactly what this sort of learning requires. Remember, they are about 25 percent of our population.

The AR, Abstract Random: *Strongly* preferred learning style is to work in groups. They are social beings, and *need to learn in direct face-to-face contact with each other*. So, about half of American kids have a learning style diametrically opposite that required by a virtual school, even if the program sets up chat rooms. These do not meet their needs for face-to-fact contact.

AS, the Abstract Sequential: These students want to work alone, but have to find worth in any assignment or project. Have to be convinced that the teacher knows his or her stuff, or will not have respect for the teacher. Will actually test the teacher's knowledge. Have to be convinced of this, or will not want to do the assignment or project. Remember, only 3–5 percent.

CR, the Concrete Randoms: Very mercurial, leaping from project to project, called bandwagoning. No sense of getting assignments in on time, or even finishing them. Very adventurous in treating assignments, very independent. Want to work alone, but can participate. Very creative. Not too good as candidates to stick it out with assignment after assignment. About 15–20 percent of kids.

Question: What are *your conclusions* regarding taking learning styles into account in the virtual charter model of kids working alone at home on teacher assignments?

The CS will fit in. That's 25 percent of our population. The *AR does not fit in*, and is a mismatch. That's half of our population. The AS? Maybe, *if* he or she respects the teachers, who must prove they are masters of their fields. The CR? A problem, as they will not get assignments in on time, maybe not at all—but will strike out on their own (very independent).

Partial Conclusions

About *65 percent of our kids' learning styles* simply *do not fit this educational model*. Virtual charters require self-motivated kids and committed parents who will work with their kids. This helps explain in part the poor results of virtual charters, doesn't it?

Conclusion: Levin's productive efficiency—that is, getting the most out of school—is not cutting it.

WHAT'S MISSING? THE CRUCIAL SOCIALIZATION PROCESS

Question: Why do we bring in the crucial nature of the socialization process?

Second question: What is the process by which infants, children, learn to become human beings?

Obviously, through contact with people. How do kindergarteners become kindergarteners? By associating with other kids their age. How do teenagers become teenagers? By associating with other teens. Kids cannot become normal and socially appropriate for their age group by being isolated from their peers.

Herbert Blumer, the University of Chicago sociologist who focused on the processes humans use to create meanings, noted that the meanings we develop about things, people, and ideas arise from interaction with others. Thus, we are who we become through interacting. Interacting with others, then, is essential in becoming socialized human beings (1969, p. 2).

Note what Blumer is saying. We develop meanings in interaction with others. If we do not interact with people, we cannot develop the meanings we need to in order to develop as human beings. Interpersonal interaction is crucial—absolutely essential—for us to learn and to become socialized. That is how we learn to develop meanings for things, such as cars and popsicle sticks; for people, such as girls and cowboys; and for ideas, such as thoughtfulness and democracy. Formation of meaning is the underpinning for kids to develop appropriate behavior in any society.

Question: How, then, does this apply to virtual learning?

That's easy. Interacting with a computer is fine and dandy, but it is no substitute for the interaction we develop as we communicate with others. We've seen that the abstract random person *needs* to interact on a face-to-face basis with others. A person is stultified if such interaction is lacking—and it certainly is lacking in virtual learning. That's likely a major reason why the approach is so deficient in learning results, particularly for this personality.

This is also true for the other personality styles, as well, and undoubtedly contributes to the poor results for this instructional approach. Kids learn to take on various roles as they interact with people occupying those roles. They learn to become students by seeing other kids working at the student role. It's pretty difficult to do if you cannot watch other kids take on student roles.

The deputy superintendent of Memphis city schools is quoted on this topic: "The early development of children requires lots of interaction with other children for purposes of socialization, developing collaboration and teamwork, and self-definition" (Saul, 2011, p. 3).

If we look at various systems of psychological theory and practice, many note how essential social relationships are to the development of the individual. Maslow (1954), for example, establishes a hierarchy of human needs, with each step in the hierarchy having to be satisfied before one can meet the next level of needs. His third level is social needs, which he believes must be achieved before the fourth level, esteem. Thus, Maslow perceives meeting one's social needs of being able to relate effectively with others as essential for one's development.

Conclusion: Productive efficiency is seriously compromised by heavy use of the virtual learning model used in such schools. Kids certainly are not getting the most out of school.

Question: What about Levin's social cohesion benchmark?

The huge dropout rates certainly provide no support for virtual charters. This churning is harmful to forming relationships with other kids. As a matter of fact, learning in isolation does the exact opposite of providing the support indispensable to develop social cohesion. We develop social cohesion in our groups, not in isolation tapping on our keyboard.

Conclusion: Social cohesion is also compromised by the virtual charter model.

TIME TO DISCOVER WHAT THE STUDENT BODY LOOKS LIKE

Racial/Ethnic Distributions

The best data set is that of K12 Inc., reported by Miron and Urschel, so we'll use their figures. Three-quarters of students are white compared with the mean in states with K12 Inc. schools of 54.7 percent and the U.S. average of 53.9 percent. Their white population is almost half again as large.

Where does this difference come from? Not the black population, which is about even for the states and K12 Inc., of 11.3 percent and 10.7 percent, respectively (although the U.S. black population is 16.3 percent).

The difference comes from many fewer Hispanic students, which total 9.8 percent for K12 Inc. and 27.6 percent in the states, virtually three times that of K12 Inc. The U.S. Hispanic population is 23.7 percent.

Asian students also are underrepresented in K12 Inc., with 3.4 percent against 5.5 percent in states with K12 schools. The U.S. Asian population is 4.8 percent.

Free and Reduced Lunch, Special Education, and English Language Learner Status

K12 Inc. has 39.9 percent vs. 47.2 percent for the states with K12 Inc. schools. Similarly, 9.4 percent vs. 11.5 percent in special education, so that almost a tenth of K12 Inc. students are special education kids. However, English Language Learners are virtually nonexistent with 0.3 percent vs. 13.8 percent for the K12 Inc. states.

Grade Level Enrollments

Interestingly, a larger proportionate number of K12 Inc. kids are in the middle school grades, but there is a considerable dropoff from ninth through the twelfth grades. Miron and Urschel believe that the kids tend to leave the schools—that is, they do not persist in the higher grades.

Could it be that the extracurricular activities are richer and more varied in the public high schools and that this is also a factor? Or it is possible that parents run out of gas trying to teach high school subjects? Or do they feel that the model simply doesn't work as well in the high school grades?

Conclusion: It looks like Levin's criterion of equity, fairness in access to educational opportunity, is not being met.

REVENUES—COSTS—*PROFITS*

Saul (2011) reports that a Connections representative offered three plans for its services to the Virginia legislature this year:

- Option A: $7,500 per student, a student-teacher ratio of 35–40:1, an average teacher salary of $45,000.
- Option B: $6,500 for each student, a student-teacher ratio of 50:1, less experienced teachers getting $40,000.
- Option C: $4,800, with a student-teacher ratio of 60:1, with a narrower curriculum.

Question: How does this fascinating offer stack up with the schools' claims that they provide high-quality education?

Second question: How moral is it to make such an offer?

A superintendent who offered to cheapen his district's educational quality to his board would be drummed out of the profession.

K12 Inc. schools received an average of $7,393 per student for the 2008–2009 school year in comparison with $10,267 per pupil nationally. But there are interesting differences between K12 Inc. schools and public schools. Student support services cost a third of that of public schools. Operations cost one-fourth. Instruction is a bit more, since they do supply computers and need more software.

But administrative expenses for K12 Inc. are three times more, although only 16 percent is spent on administrative salaries and benefits. Thus, 17.5 percent is spent on other administrative costs, which K12 Inc. did not specify.

Teacher salaries per student are less than half of U.S. salaries, $1,054 in 2008–2009 vs. $2,219. The five states in which K12 Inc. schools are located spend $2,778 per pupil. Pupil support services were $23, in comparison with the U.S. average of $331. These services included attendance, social work, student accounting, counseling, speech, psychological, and nursing services.

Student services were $5 compared with $291 U.S. and include curriculum development, instructional staff training, media, library, and instruction-related technology services. Employee benefits were $491 vs. U.S. $2,205, less than a fourth.

Teacher/student ratios were *much larger* for K12 schools—actually being *three times* that of the public schools. Saul reported an Agora teacher who contradicted their board's claim of a pupil/teacher ratio of 40:1, saying that it was closer to 70–100:1. Some high school teachers noted that they were "managing" 270 students.

Interesting question: What is the difference between teaching and "managing"?

Saul notes that in two schools, Ohio Virtual Academy and Colorado Virtual Academy, former teachers complained that their loads were seventy-five kids, and noted that an elementary teacher with that load could only spend thirty minutes a week with each student in a forty-hour work week. Saul notes,

> With teacher salaries and benefits the biggest cost to K12, increasing student-to-teacher ratios is an easy way for the company to increase profits. Ms. Henderson, the former Agora teacher and mother of four students, said the ultimate losers are the children.
>
> "What has happened now in honors literature courses, the teachers are not able to keep up with 300 students, so they'll just cut curriculum. . . . This past week my son was exempted from the 'Great Gatsby' because of the workload of the teacher." (p. 8)

Summary of Profits

Cost advantages for K12 Inc. per student (Miron & Urschel) are "over $4,000 per pupil . . . would likely surpass $5,000 in some states" (p. 29).

Since K12 Inc. reported over 94,000 students, using the $4,000 profit per student, that comes to a profit of $37,600,000 per year. Saul notes that the president of K12 Inc. was paid $5 million in 2011.

The *New York Times* investigated this whole issue of virtual charters, and, according to Saul, focused on K12 Inc. Their conclusion was "a portrait of a company that tries to squeeze profits from public school dollars by raising enrollment, increasing teacher workload and lowering standards" (Saul, 2011, p. 2).

Morality and Profiting from Public Taxes in Education

My graduate classes are extremely uncomfortable with the morality of people profiting from educating kids.

Question: Are you? Does this affect social cohesion? If so, how?

SOME ISSUES: LEGAL, PARENT ROLES

This whole issue presently is amorphous legally. It should be interesting to see what happens and how it develops in this newish area of education.

The role of the parent is fascinating. As with homeschooling, we are asking parents to become teachers, except that most parents are not educated as teachers and do not have the subject matter knowledge to pull off teaching in any level. My graduate classes are quite concerned about their own expertise to teach all subjects in elementary school, which is the reason why departmentalization is so often a result even in the middle elementary grades. Teachers do not feel that they are knowledgeable in all fields, and so feel that they will short-circuit their kids in areas in which they feel deficient (which is usually math in elementary school).

Saul notes that a parent is called "the official 'learning coach'" by the organization (p. 6).

Several decades ago, with a shortage of teachers making it difficult to get fully qualified teachers in all classrooms, I was director of secondary education in Dover, Delaware. So I tried to hire very sharp liberal arts graduates in several areas. It was an unmitigated disaster. Every single person had lethal problems in their attempts to teach.

My analysis is simple: They didn't

- understand kids
- understand how kids learn
- understand how to develop a lesson plan
- understand how to design curriculum
- understand how to teach

Other than that, they were fine. Of course, they all failed, much to everyone's distress. But I gave that rather foolish idea up, as did most of my peers. However, I note that some variants of that line of action are being used today, particularly in inner-city schools. If you want a challenge, watch some videos of recent graduates of elite universities tell their inner-city kids that they, too, can go to Vanderbilt (or some other university that they graduated from).

Question: So why are parents, who are not educated as teachers, competent to assist in teaching their kids in all fields, including high school?

Want an example?

One kid named Romeo missed a question on the definition of matter: "'Romeo, Romeo,' his mother says. 'If you had been studying appropriately you would have found out that there are lots of properties of matter. And you got to take all those elements to build matter. Because elements are gas, solids, liquids'" (Saul, 2011, p. 7).

We obviously could cite numerous additional incidents of parent ignorance, some amusing, others pitiful, but we choose to avoid further sensationalism.

POLITICS, LOBBYING, ADVERTISING/MARKETING

According to the Saul article in the *New York Times*, K12 Inc. spent $26.5 million in advertising in 2010, which undoubtedly led to the large number of kids being enrolled even as their peers dropped out of this model of education. Saul notes that current and former teachers talk about the intense recruitment efforts to fill the ranks of the program, but these folks do not talk of any efforts to establish criteria to determine if the student can make it in the program.

Conclusion: K12 Inc.'s productive efficiency was evidently quite high if we consider lobbying politicians and advertising.

Lobbying is a full-court press for the industry. Saul noted that K12 spent $681,000 in Pennsylvania in lobbying since 2007. The state's budget secretary had been senior vice president of education and policy for K12. The National Institute on Money in State Politics thought that K12 had contributed almost $500,000 to state political candidates across the nation (p. 8).

These groups have also been creative in their lobbying efforts, bringing hordes of kids to state legislative hearings on funding for online virtuals. The president of K12 called lobbying "a core competency" of the company. That makes sense if we realize that the companies would fail if they could not replace the huge numbers of kids whose parents pull them out of the program.

GAMING AND FRAUD (REMEMBER CAMPBELL'S LAW)

Some generic issues arise regarding gaming. For example, how is the teacher to know if the child answers the quizzes rather than an older sibling or the parent? At the other end of the spectrum, how do we know if the teachers, with their unwieldy student loads, are responding rather than an older child, a spouse, or someone else? Such gaps do exist, as Glass and Welner, writing for the National Education Policy Center, noted in October 2011: "Virtual schools offer much greater opportunity for students to obtain credit for work they did not do themselves."

Evidence indicates a good deal of gaming is going on. The proof? Out of close to five thousand students in the 2009–2010 school year, Agora dismissed six hundred students for nonattendance. That's around 12 percent of their student body.

More proof? Students simply need to log in to be counted in attendance at Agora. Teachers reported that their new grading policy gave students who did not turn in their work a grade of "50" instead of a zero. Some teachers said they felt pressure to pass students with marginal performance and attendance.

Question: How does this square with the K12 Inc. statement that they have high-quality standards?

Saul (p. 2) reports:

> Some teachers at K12 Inc. schools said they felt pressured to pass students who did little work. Teachers have also questioned why some students who did no class work were allowed to remain on school rosters, potentially to allow the company to continue receiving public money for them. State auditors found that the K12-run Colorado Virtual Academy counted about 120 students for state reimbursement whose enrollment could not be verified or did not meet Colorado residency requirements. Some had never logged in.

In fact, the state audit that the Colorado Virtual Academy faced, which found that the school was charging for students who were not attending the school, forced them to repay the state $800,000. These were the kids who had never logged in, but the school was still charging the state for them.

Campbell's Law lives!

SUMMARY, CONCLUSIONS, AND IMPLICATIONS

This chapter focuses on full-time virtual charter schools, quite a few of which have arisen in the last two decades and which presently enroll over a quarter of a million kids. Over thirty states and the District of Columbia have passed legislation approving virtual charters. As with other forms of privatization, these models are supported by the freedom of choice, market-based conservative ideology presently operating in this and other nations.

We're using Henry Levin's four criteria or benchmarks (freedom of choice, productive efficiency, equity, and social cohesion) to evaluate our research findings. Major arguments supporting the virtual charter model include the assertion that technology can improve communication among teachers and students and that educational choice is improved by these models. The third argument for virtual charters is that they present opportunities for investment and profit, which certainly is being achieved.

Conclusion: Obviously, freedom of choice is strongly supported by the virtual charter movement.

As for the effectiveness of virtual charters—they aren't.

Only 27.7 percent of K12 Inc.'s virtual charters pass Annual Yearly Performance criteria—in contrast with about half of all public schools. Reading scores were between two and eleven percentage points below public schools, but math scores were considerably worse. As kids stayed in the schools, they increasingly fell further and further behind their public school peers, to the point that by the eleventh grade their math scores had collapsed to about 31 percent meeting or exceeding state standards, with the public school students scoring at 68 percent.

Stanford's Center for Research in Educational Outcomes (CREDO) found the same poor results and noted that in every subgroup, cyber charters scored lower, not a glowing accolade for the movement. Another disturbing finding is called the "churn rate" by the business, which is an enormous rate of dropout and enrollment in the schools. In the K12 Inc. Agora School, for example, the churn or dropout rate is over 54 percent per year. This makes teaching considerably more difficult, since the school also is recruiting aggressively in order to keep students and their resulting funding coming in.

About half the kids graduated on time versus 74 percent for the public schools, again, indicating major problems with retention.

We looked at reasons for these poor results and found that the high levels of student mobility (read: dropouts) were one factor. Another may be that the learning styles of the kids do not seem to fit the style required to work on assignment after assignment on the computer. That requires a self-structured, motivated, detailed learning style. Since at least half of Americans are abstract random learners, and another 15–20 percent are concrete random learners who often are not the disciplined, stick-to-it individuals who do best in the virtual model, they simply do not do well with the medium. Thus, we found that about 65 percent of students do not seem to fit the style required by the virtual school.

We conclude that Levin's criterion of productive efficiency is relatively poorly achieved.

We also conclude that this style of learning is not helpful to the socialization processes required for children to learn to become kindergarteners, elementary school kids, middle school kids, and adolescents. Kids learn to become those kids by interacting with other kids. Kids learn to become students by interaction with kids who also are taking on the role of student. Sitting behind a computer, working alone, doesn't seem to facilitate such a role.

What have we concluded so far about Levin's social cohesion criterion? How can we develop social cohesion working alone? We develop social cohesion by working in groups and by communicating in social situations, not by working alone on a computer. For this criterion, we find a clear strikeout.

The student body certainly does not represent that in U.S. public schools, since its racial/ethnic composition is skewed, with 50 percent more whites than the rest of the country. The percentage of African Americans is close to being even, but the Hispanic population comprises less than half that of the United States. Asian kids are also underrepresented, as are students needing free and reduced lunches. Similarly, a smaller percentage of special education children are enrolled, and English Language Learners are virtually nonexistent in comparison with 13 percent in the states served by K12 Inc.

Grade-level enrollments are also skewed with a larger percentage of middle school graders enrolled, dropping off rapidly in the higher high school grades.

In terms of profit, K12 and other companies appear to be a good investment. As Saul put it, "A portrait emerges of a company that tries to squeeze profits from public school dollars by raising enrollment, increasing teacher workload and lowering standards" (p. 2). We've found teachers teaching three times as many kids as the public schools and receiving less than half the salary. But administrative costs, strangely, are three times higher than their public school counterparts.

The question of the morality of profiting from the public's hard-earned tax dollars has been raised and should be taken into account by policymakers.

Parents are heavily involved as "learning coaches," although most parents are pretty amateurish when it comes to being effective teachers.

The industry (which is what it is) has been plagued by considerable gaming and fraud. Kids can get credit for work they didn't do and have been kept on rolls when they hadn't even logged in. Evidence of outright fraud has been cited. Campbell's Law certainly applies here.

The virtual charter movement, like other forms of privatization, is a product of a conservative and libertarian social movement occurring in this country and other mostly Western nations. Consequently, political influence has entered into the equation, with conservative legislatures and governors pushing to expand such programs, despite negative research findings. The lobbying, advertising, and marketing have been intensive and expensive.

Decisions by various states to increase the number of virtual charter schools have not been made based on the evidence, which is negative, but rather through extensive lobbying and the social movement of a conservative or libertarian ideology that has been developing in this country and others for two decades.

Therefore, we rate their productive efficiency quite high and effective in terms of the conservative and libertarian ideology, but quite deficient in terms of paying attention to the negative evidence regarding virtual charters' educational effectiveness.

To sum up, Glass and Welner (2011) conclude that "there exists no evidence from research that full-time virtual schooling at the K-12 level is an adequate replacement for traditional face-to-face teaching and learning" (p. 5).

For two centuries, the public schools have been operated as local school districts with an elected local school board responsible for their operation. The virtual and charter school movements have turned this approach on its head by substituting the family as the decision-making unit rather than the local school board and district. That is, the family can choose to move their children to whatever form of education they decide upon. This is resulting in considerable changes in education, both in terms of a major reduction in quality, as the above evidence proves, and in financial repercussions.

The accountability movement has resulted in the testing frenzy that has impacted American education. We recommend that we institute accountability models on the charter, voucher, and virtual charter models currently expanding. These should take into account, in order to improve their functioning, the large churn rate and poor testing results found in virtual charters.

REFERENCES AND RESOURCES

Blumer, H. (1946). Social movements. In A. M. Lee (Ed.). *Principles of sociology*. New York: Barnes & Noble.

Campbell, D. T. (1976). *Assessing the impact of planned social change*. Hanover, NH: The Public Affairs Center, Dartmouth College.

Glass, G. V., & Welner, K. G. (2011). *Online K-12 schooling in the U.S.: Uncertain private ventures in need of public regulation*. Boulder, CO: National Education Policy Center. http://nepc.colorado.edu/publication/online-k-12-schooling.

Gregorc, A. (1999). *Gregorc Style Delineator*. Columbia, CT: Gregorc Associates, Inc.

Levin, H. M. (2002). A comprehensive framework for evaluating educational vouchers. *Educational Evaluation and Policy Analysis, 24*(3), 159–174.

Levin, H. M., & Belfield, C. R. (2004, June). *Vouchers and public policy: When ideology trumps evidence*. New York: National Center for the Study of Privatization in Education, Teachers College, Columbia University.

Marsh, R., Carr-Chellman, A., & Sockman, B. (2009). Selecting silicon: Why parents choose cybercharter schools. *TechTrends: Linking Research & Practice to Improve Learning, 53*(4), 32–36.

Maslow, A. H. (1954). *Motivation and personality*. New York: Harper & Row.

Miron, G., & Urschel, J. L. (2012, July). *Understanding and improving full-time virtual schools: A study of student characteristics, school finance, and school performance in schools operated by K12 Inc*. Boulder, CO: National Education Policy Center, School of Education, University of Colorado, Boulder.

Saul, S. (2011, December 12). Profits and questions at online charter schools. *New York Times*.

TWELVE

Miracles (or Really, Mirages) for the Gullible

Be skeptical of miracle schools. . . . There are no silver bullets in education.

—Diane Ravitch

"Miracle schools": Fables and myths to support a self-serving, political agenda.

—Arthur Shapiro

Before trying to make meaningful interpretations of test results, one should always pay close attention to who is tested, and who is not.

—Walter M. Haney

INTRODUCTION AND ORGANIZATION

We begin with a brief glance at the meaning of what a miracle should look like—that is, a suspension of the laws of nature or society, which should give us plenty of cause for a skeptical look at any such claims. We will subsequently consider several criteria suggested by Gary Rubenstein and Noel Hammatt in Valerie Strauss's column, written by Diane Ravitch, to identify miracle schools. Next, although we dealt with the "Texas Miracle" in chapter 1, it deserves a quick once-over to get us started, in part because it ignited No Child Left Behind, which is still controlling education.

Let's take a look at another supposed series of miracles, as advocated by former Florida governor Jeb Bush, and try to tease out some of the assumptions involved. Despite his leaving office a couple of terms ago, his foundation still exerts considerable influence in the state and the nation. Next comes Urban Prep of Chicago as a wunderkind of the educa-

159

tional reformers, followed by the Harlem Village Academies Charter schools. We might as well include Milwaukee twenty years later to analyze the results. Also, one can hardly avoid the New Orleans experience in media hype about miracles. And then perhaps a summary, a few conclusions, and implications will prove useful.

ON MIRACLES

A number of years ago, I tried to come to grips with the notion of miracles, which really states that laws of nature or of society can be turned on their heads. The notion of laws of nature being suspended seems to emerge largely from religious literature, while those of society being upended come from other sources. Since in this book, we are dealing with areas of science, we can focus on laws of society being miraculously suspended, with students performing unusual feats of achievement despite tremendous odds. Since all science involves treating such claims with a degree of skepticism, we shall pursue that line of inquiry to determine which so-called miracles are actually realistic achievements—or merely largely unwarranted claims, usually for political or personal purposes.

Several Suggestions to See If a Miracle Really Is One

In Strauss's October 18, 2011, column of the *Answer Sheet*, Ravitch cites Gary Rubenstein and Noel Hammatt, who set up several criteria useful to recognize a miracle school:

1. A low attrition rate
2. High test scores
3. High graduation rate (for high schools)
4. High college acceptance rate (for high schools)
5. Fair representation of English-language learner (ELL) and special education students
6. A high percentage of students who qualify for free or reduced meal prices
7. Funding equivalent to the nearby "failing" school
8. No evidence that the school discriminates against low-performing students (p. 1)

To these I might add the following:

1. No evidence of gaming
2. Keep Campbell's Law in mind: "The more any qualitative social indicator is used for social decision-making, the more subject it will be to corruption's pressures and the more apt it will be to

distort and corrupt the social processes it is intended to monitor" (Campbell, 1976).

Let's see how this plays out.

THE TEXAS (REALLY, THE HOUSTON) MIRACLE

As we reported in chapter 1, the Texas Miracle was based on the so-called extraordinary success of the Houston superintendent in totally eliminating dropouts in three inner-city high schools—until an assistant principal in one of the schools, Sharpston High, blew the whistle on the superintendent's claim. Assistant principal Robert Kimball, a Vietnam veteran and retired Army lieutenant colonel, looked into the "no dropout" claim and found that of one thousand kids who entered as freshmen, only three hundred were left by the senior year, but the school actually reported no dropouts, as did two other inner-city high schools (Winerip, 2003).

Are you skeptical?

Question: How did they do that?

It's pretty easy. Threaten the principals with loss of their jobs. Screw around with kids' reasons to drop out and report them with different codes. Voilà! No dropouts. That is, until some skeptic investigates. (But if someone has the gall to be a whistleblower, go after him or her.)

Want an illustration of overweening administrative arrogance? The deputy superintendent said that the attendance would increase from 94.6 percent to 95 percent the next year. And, amazingly, he could predict that the district dropout rate would decrease from 1.5 percent to 1.3 percent the following year. That's better than anything Nostradamus could come up with.

Want another miracle? Student test results in Houston will do. The superintendent claimed kids' scores leaped up on the Texas Assessment of Academic Skills (TAAS) from 61 percent in 1991 to 86 percent in 2002. The problem is that Houston is an urban district with lots of impoverished Latinos and other minorities. Unfortunately for his credibility, ACT and SAT scores dropped slightly during that period.

Question: How did he increase scores? Simple: he just held kids back in ninth grade so they could not take the TAAS (which is given in tenth grade). Or he skipped them into eleventh grade. The evidence? In 2001, 1,160 students were in ninth grade, but only 281 students were in tenth.

Then you can run for president as the "education governor" and become the "education president," as George W. Bush did—and the conspiring superintendent can be appointed secretary of education as a reward.

Question: What was the underlying thinking? Ravitch (2011a) said it best. The Texas Miracle consisted of the simple strategy of testing and accountability. The claim was that all you had to do was to set up exams and test kids. Schools that didn't make the appropriate scores would be shamed into working harder and doing better, despite the poverty background of their kids.

Thus, the Texas Miracle was an outright lie, a complete fraud.

Unfortunately for us, this scam led us to lose our common sense, our skepticism, and accept those fictional results (or were they fantasies?) uncritically, to jump on the No Child Left Behind bandwagon fad, not to mention the annual testing requirements that were imposed nationally. And our formerly locally and state-run education system became considerably more nationalized as a result.

So, now we have annual testing as a ritual starting for kids in grade 3 and other grades yearly. This has led to a huge increase in retentions and consequent dropouts as a result, as the case study of Florida succinctly illustrates. (Chapter 6 deals with the effects of retaining kids.)

Seems like the "Texas Miracle" didn't meet the eight criteria set up by Rubenstein and Hammatt as cited by Ravitch. The attrition rate was miserable, as were test scores and graduation rates. And was there gaming! Campbell's Law obviously applies in that the indicators were used for corrupt purposes.

FLORIDA'S FRAUD (OR VISITING THE LAND OF OZ)

The fourth-grade NAEP scores are where Jeb Bush gained his educational policy credentials (which still exert considerable traction). Reuters stated:

> Former Florida Governor Jeb Bush soared to rock star status in the education world on the strength of a chart. A simple graph, it tracked fourth-grade reading scores. In 1998, when Bush was elected governor, Florida kids scored far below the national average. By the end of his second term, in 2007, they were far ahead, with especially impressive gains for low-income and minority students. (Heilig, 2012)

Let's look at the reality, particularly *the exact policy mechanisms* Governor Bush manipulated to pull this off. The governor discloses some of them in this statement in the *Washington Post* on August 13, 2006:

> We have set high expectations for all students, and in key grades we have eliminated social promotion, the harmful practice of pushing unprepared students ahead. . . . Our emphasis on accountability is a big reason our schools are improving, our students are performing at higher levels and we're closing the achievement gap between poor and minority students and their peers. (Bush & Bloomberg, 2006)

Haney (2006) punctures the illusions (or are they delusions?) sponsored by the man behind the curtain: "It turns out that the apparent dramatic gains in grade 4 NAEP math results are simply an indirect reflection of the fact that in 2003–04, Florida started flunking many more students, disproportionally minority students, to repeat grade 3" (p. 3).

How many more? Over 29,000 third graders! That's about 10–12 percent. But who flunked? Disproportionally more black and Hispanic kids. That percent is instructive in terms of Bush's claim that they were reducing the achievement gap between poor and minority kids and those in the middle class. The difference in failure rates?

- whites—about 4–6 percent
- Hispanics and blacks—15–20 percent

Haney then concludes,

> Hence it is clear what caused the dramatic jump in grade 4 NAEP results for 2005. Florida had started flunking more children before they reached grade 4. . . . Thus, it is clear that the NAEP grade 4 results for 2005 reflected not any dramatic improvements in elementary education in the state. Rather they were an indirect reflection of Florida policy that resulted in two to three times larger percentages of minority than White children being flunked to repeat grade 3. (pp. 6–7)

Question: What is the *policy mechanism* Bush used to increase scores?

It certainly wasn't his insistence that we have to start holding schools accountable for results. It wasn't his insistence that all we had to do was to hold kids to high standards. His mechanism? *Failing large numbers* of poor-achieving kids, and holding them back one year. When you flunk kids, they'll be a year older, they'll have matured more, and thus they will do better on tests.

We know that some kids, particularly immature boys, develop more slowly, but by fourth grade they seem to catch up. So, kids who should be in fourth grade will do better on tests they have to repeat in third grade. But, as we reported carefully in chapter 6 on failing kids, about 65 percent of kids will drop out after failing once.

Question: What about Bush's boast that his policies had reduced the achievement gap between poor and minority kids and their peers? If you hold kids back a year, they'll do better on the tests because they mature. And notice that about three times more minorities were held back. When the huge extent of failed numbers of kids emerged, his comment was "It breaks my heart, but it's for their own good."

Haney concludes, "The apparent dramatic improvement in 2005 grade 4 NAEP scores in Florida are illusory" (p. 13).

To underscore my point about kids being flunked in grade 3 so that they'll be a year older and will do better on the tests, Haney notes,

> The Florida case—what might be called the Florida fraud—helps to illustrate a fundamental point about interpretation of test results in general and NAEP results in particular. Before trying to make mean-

ingful interpretations of test results, one should always play close attention to who is tested and who is not. (p. 7)

A HARD LOOK AT SOME CLAIMS OF THE MIRACLE WORKERS

Since former Florida governor Jeb Bush is taking his claims as the educational governor national, it may be useful to analyze his and other miracle workers' claims about their stunning success. A key statement is this one: "The No Child Left Behind Act of 2001 sent an enormously important message to politicians and educators across America. Stop making excuses for low student achievement and start holding your schools accountable for results" (Bush & Bloomberg, 2006). Further points referred to earlier include the following:

- Set high expectations for all students
- Eliminate social promotion
- Grade all schools on student performance
- Thus informing everyone how well or poorly the school is performing
- This emphasis on accountability is the reason schools and kids are improving
- We're closing the achievement gap

Let's look at his assumptions: All you have to do is test and hold people accountable and the kids will score higher on tests. The underlying assumptions are that all kids are developmentally at the same place—utter nonsense—and that social conditions, such as poverty levels, have no impact on kids. Unfortunately, the PISA results (as we saw in chapter 1) show that poverty is directly responsible for kids' achievement. It also assumes that teachers and kids aren't working hard enough, so they need to be held accountable and punished.

Our Conclusions

At this point in time, and unlike any other profession, educational policy and practice have been shanghaied by noneducators such as politicians, economists, and statisticians, who have imposed ideological free-market solutions that are driving educational reform. As they impose their solutions, we can perceive their common mind-set:

They do not know how kids learn and that they learn differently.
They do not know or care that kids develop differently.
They know little regarding how to teach kids.
They seem equally ignorant about how teachers work, usually working collaboratively.

They haven't the slightest idea that schools work best as cooperative enterprises.

They believe that we motivate kids and teachers by punishing and humiliating them (such as by grading schools A–F).

CHICAGO'S URBAN PREP

Recently, Secretary of Education Arne Duncan hailed this school as the usual "miracle." So let's give it a once-over. The assertion is that all the kids, 100 percent, who graduated were accepted into a college, which looks pretty good. But looking at the facts provides a different insight.

The school started with 150 kids, but, unfortunately, only 107 hung around long enough to graduate. As Ravitch notes, the graduates regrettably achieved test scores much lower than the average for the Chicago public school students. Gary Rubenstein notes, "Only 15 percent met Illinois' Prairie State assessment standards, which includes math, reading and the ACT. While 100 percent were accepted into college, zero percent were rated by the state as 'college ready'" (Ravitch, 2011d).

Even more unfortunately, only 17 percent passed state tests, in comparison with 64 percent in the low-performing Chicago Public School District (Ravitch, 2011c).

Conclusions include that they have generated a high attrition rate, but low graduation rate and test scores. Does it seem that gaming the system is occurring?

This is a miracle?

HARLEM VILLAGE ACADEMIES CHARTER SCHOOLS

"All that holds Village Academies together is Deborah Kenny's unrelenting ambition and greed" (Rubenstein, 2012, p. 1, quoting former teacher).

Village Academies' Web page touts its results:

- No. 1 school in Harlem (NY) for eighth grade reading and math
- 100 percent proficient in math for three straight years
- Near perfect New York Regents passing rate

In 2010–2011, Rubenstein notes that HVA had 55 percent free and 13 percent reduced lunches compared with the district's 74 percent free and 5 percent reduced. Its Limited English Proficient (LEP) students were 3 percent compared with the district's 11 percent.

Suspensions in HVA were 38 percent for at least one day vs. 7 percent for the whole district, which is quite high, obviously.

But student attrition is significant, with sixty-six fifth graders in 2007–2008 shrinking to only sixteen by 2010–2011. This is a 75 percent attrition rate; yet during that time the school's population increased.

Rubenstein inquired into the high rate of passing and found that none of the students took the Geometry or Algebra II/Trigonometry Regents exams. Consequently, the 100 percent passing rate stems from students taking the ninth-grade Algebra Regents tests. Rubenstein inquired into this and the school responded that "they actually had 90 students taking Geometry (noting nothing about Algebra II) and that 82 percent passed. But since they only had 80 students who could feasibly qualify to take this test, this seems unlikely" (p. 3). He was trying to get more data as he wrote his article.

A key indicator of organizational problems is staff turnover:

- 53 percent in 2007–2008
- 38 percent in 2008–2009
- 61 percent in 2009–2010

This compares with 19 percent teacher turnover for the district (which is pretty high itself). My own experience as a top administrator in several school systems and in consulting with numerous others is to look very carefully at turnover rates as a symptom of dysfunction and the existence of problems. Rubenstein certainly considered these figures alarming and inquired into the dynamics involved by interviewing a teacher who left as an expert witness.

My own experience relates to her testimony. I was a teacher in a highly regarded high school in a Chicago suburb. The chair of the English department was Dr. Charles Ruggles, who was considered a national expert in English education. I asked him which he thought was the best English department in the country and, without hesitation, he said that it was New Trier Township High School's department in Winnetka, Illinois, a highly upscale suburb of Chicago. So, somewhat innocently, I asked why he didn't shoot for that goal.

His reply was very interesting and insightful. He said that he could not drive people to achieve such a goal. To reach that point, he and the teachers would have to work themselves to the bone, sacrificing their personal lives, working night and day, and living just for that goal.

In fact, the teacher Rubenstein interviewed said that this was essentially what the director of the school was doing—pressuring young, idealistic teachers to work "seven weeks over the summer, teaching on multiple Saturdays, and averaging 12-hour work days during the week. . . . basically work your teachers to death, and you'll see the results. . . . When teachers are leaving left and right because they're asked to perform superhuman feats for little compensation, the idea of 'community' vanishes" (p. 4). She also noted that the school "was one of the worst offenders of creating and sustaining the myth that teachers can solve everything" (p. 3). This teacher likewise observed that the principal paid herself almost nine times as much as her teachers and was the highest-paid charter school executive in New York City.

Rubenstein ends, "In summary: HVA, no miracle for you" (p. 4).

MILWAUKEE TWENTY YEARS LATER—LESSONS LEARNED

Ravitch (2011b) summarizes what we've learned about the first voucher program:

> Look at what happened in Milwaukee, where researchers used to argue about whether vouchers were working. The argument is over. After 20 years of vouchers, even voucher advocates admit that students in voucher schools are doing no better than students in regular public schools and students in charters. And all three sectors are doing poorly.
>
> The theory of vouchers and charters is that competition will cause achievement to go up in public schools, and a rising tide will lift all boats. But according to the latest National Assessment of Educational Progress, black students in Milwaukee public schools score below black students in Mississippi, Alabama and Louisiana. And voucher students do no better! So voucher advocates now say that the goal of vouchers is not to improve test scores but to increase parental involvement or to provide choice for its own sake. That is called moving the goal posts. (p. 2)

Alas, still no miracle.

NEW ORLEANS'S STATE RECOVERY SCHOOL DISTRICT

The miracle supposedly developed by the district was touted in the *New York Times* in October 2011, which stated that before Hurricane Katrina, more than 60 percent of kids attended a failing school and presently only 18 percent do.

Question: Can you figure out the unasked questions to analyze this potentially remarkable result?

Diane Ravitch in Strauss (2011) analyzes this stunning statement and asks the following questions:

- Are the students in New Orleans the same ones who were in the schools before the hurricane?
- How many of the city's poorest children returned?
- What is the definition of a "failing school"?
- Was the definition the same pre- and post-hurricane?
- What methods are the presumably better schools using to produce such miracles? (p. 2)

Before Katrina devastated New Orleans, the New Orleans Recovery District was established by law and was allowed to take over any school rated below the state average. These essentially were nonfailing schools, as Deshotels noted (2013). After the hurricane, there was a mad scramble by the various charter operators to attract the best students. Also some of the better connected charter operators such as KIPP were able to get huge grants from both government and private foundations and therefore were able to pick the most motivated students and supportive parents by offering an enriched program. As a result, out of 70 charters now operating in the N.O. RSD, 5 are rated as "B" schools, 5 are rated as "C" schools and the rest are D's and F's.

Considerable hype was given to this development, but we'd better look at the facts. Unfortunately, the New Orleans RSD is rated above only one district, St. Helena, which is also poverty stricken and also run by RSD. That is, it is sixty-ninth of seventy districts. Deshotels states simply, "Taken as a whole, the RSD is dead last in the state!" (p. 2). And he also notes, "It does not work." (p. 1)

The state awarded a D or an F as a grade to 87 percent of the schools in the Recovery District.

He comes to this conclusion because when Louisiana tried to expand the model, it took over twelve other schools and converted them to charters. All of them continue to be rated "F," and on average they have declined slightly rather than improving and have experienced an enrollment decline of 39 percent on average.

Deshotels notes that the New Orleans Recovery District is the second-lowest-performing large school district in the nation, ranking above only Washington, D.C.

Ravitch (2012) notes that the statewide average in Louisiana of students who reached basic levels or above was 75 percent. In the New Orleans Recovery School District? Forty-nine percent. Six charters/vouchers are above this state average, with two very close to it. The rest start to fall off the cliff.

Conclusion? Smoke and mirrors, gaming us.

SUMMARY, CONCLUSIONS, AND IMPLICATIONS

We can go on, but why bother? The KIPP schools could be examined, but their financing is thousands of dollars above local schools, thus failing the criterion established by Rubenstein and Hammatt that funding has to be relatively similar to local schools to be considered. This also applies to Geoffrey Canady's Harlem Children's Zone School. It should be mentioned here that he dumped his first class of kids who didn't develop the results he and his board wanted. It's pretty hard to do that in any public school, although (as many systems learned) if you make sure that the bottom 10 percent don't take the tests (as in Florida), you'll look pretty good.

We examined what a miracle supposedly is supposed to look like in the real social world, and used Rubenstein and Hammatt's criteria to recognize a miracle school and then used them to evaluate the schools designated as miracles. Unfortunately, they all failed, starting with the Texas/Houston miracle, which claimed that dropouts were reduced to zero in three inner-city high schools using testing and accountability as their golden elixir to success.

Then we noted the Florida fraud, which was accomplished by failing the lower 10 percent of kids, which raised scores considerably. We pointed out that noneducators, such as politicians, businessmen, statisticians, and economists, seem to be claiming that they have the solution to educational ills, except that they don't. We cited Chicago's Urban Prep as another collapsed miracle, as are the Harlem Village Academies Charter Schools.

We also noted Milwaukee twenty years later, which Ravitch noted as not doing any better than regular schools, although their students are faring miserably in comparison with similar populations in other cities. And we finished the list of miracles with the New Orleans experience, which turned out to be disastrous.

Conclusions? Implications?

Lots of gaming. Too many hucksters (my thanks to Dr. Terri Wonder for that one: personal communication, Monday, April 8, 2013). Too many foolish pop culture beliefs, such as "poverty doesn't matter" and "hard work can overcome all odds." This sounds a lot like mythical Lake Wobegon, where all the women are strong, the men are handsome, and the kids are all above average.

Question: What else do you conclude?

Second question: Why do we believe such nonsense?

Let's head for the last chapter: "Major Reforms That Really Work."

REFERENCES AND RESOURCES

Bush, J., & Bloomberg, M. (2006, August 13). How to help our students: Building on the "No Child" law. *Washington Post.*

Campbell, D. T. (1976). Assessing the impact of planned social change. The Public Affairs Center, Dartmouth College, Hanover, New Hampshire.

Deshotels, M. (2013, January 11). Miracle results of school takeovers . . . not in Louisiana! *Louisiana Educator.*

Haney, W. M. (2006). Evidence in education under NCLB (and how Florida boosted NAEP score and reduced the race gap). Center for the Study of Testing, Evaluation and Education Policy, Lynch School of Education, Boston College, MA. Paper presented at the Hechinger Institute "Broad Seminar for K-12 Reporters," Grace Dodge Hall, Teachers College, Columbia University, New York City, September 8–10, 2006.

Heilig, J. V. (2012, November 28). Lurking in the Bushes: Peeking at Florida education miracle. *Cloaking Inequity.* http://cloakinginequity.com/2012/11/28/lurking-in-the-bushes-peeking-at-florida-education-miracle/

Ravitch, D. (2011a, April 5). The Texas Miracle revisited. *Bridging Differences.* http://blogs.edweek.org/edweek/Bridging-Differences/2011/04/the_texas_miracle_revisited.html

Ravitch, D. (2011b, April 13). Miracle schools, vouchers and all that educational flim-flam. *NiemanWatchdog*. http://www.niemanwatchdog.org/index.cfm?fuseaction=ask_this.view&askthisid=503

Ravitch, D. (2011c, May 31). Waiting for a school miracle. *New York Times*.

Ravitch, D. (2011d, December 6). Do you believe in miracles? *Bridging Differences*. http://blogs.edweek.org/edweek/Bridging-Differences/2011/12/do_you_believe_in_miracles.html?utm_source=twitterfeed&utm_medium=twitter

Ravitch, D. (2012, June 11). No miracle in New Orleans. *Diane Ravitch's Blog*. http://dianeravitch.net/2012/06/11/no-miracle-in-new-orleans/

Rubenstein, G. (2012, June 14). Another "miracle school" debunked: Harlem Village Academies. *Seattle Education*. http://seattleeducation2010.wordpress.com/2012/06/14/another-miracle-school-debunked-harlem-village-academies/

Strauss, V. (2011, October 18). Ravitch: Why miracle schools aren't really miracles. *The Answer Sheet*. www.washingtonpost.com/blogs/answer-sheet/post/ravitch-why-miracle-schools-arent-really-miracles/2011/10/18/gIQAM62RuL_blog.html

Winerip, M. (2003, August 13). On education: The "zero dropout" miracle: Alas! Alack! A Texas tall tale. *New York Times*.

THIRTEEN

Major Reforms That Really Work

When your knowledge changes, the universe changes.
We are what we know.
— James Burke, *The Day the Universe Changed*

INTRODUCTION AND ORGANIZATION

The purpose and organization of this chapter are pretty simple. Simply investigate several major reforms that really work—the ones that make a positive difference in kids' and teachers' lives and improve teaching and learning. Doesn't that make sense? However, we need some limits, so we'll exclude subject matter (math, English, social studies) reforms, since you can't deal with the whole world.

The first reform is that of decentralizing schools into smaller, more workable units, since so many are far too big and impersonal for the intimacy necessary for both kids and teachers (and administrators) to feel needed by the school and district. Some call such units small learning communities (SLCs); other names are halls, small schools, or schools-within-a-school.

Related to small learning communities are professional learning communities (PLCs), another reform that works if properly implemented (that means full faculty involvement). Next, Project Star in Tennessee was a carefully designed, well-researched major study in which small class size improved academic performance and reduced the achievement gap.

A quality universal preschool such as the system France developed, and took seventeen years to implement fully, is another important and effective reform. Learning centers are another reform that has been around for quite some time; these are effective when implemented with faculty involvement and support.

Constructivist teaching and leadership approaches often generate improved schools and classes. The model designed to improve education in Finland, which includes constructivist elements, is worth investigation for its systemic classroom-based approach to deal with issues and problems immediately.

Project-based learning, which can include simulations are extremely effective, inasmuch as they get students heavily involved. Some coaching and supervisory models stimulated by the Gates Foundation and other current reform models seem to have considerable impact on facilitating teachers to improve classroom practice. Cooperative learning is related to these models.

Continuous progress or nongraded or ungraded models seem to support kids in their classroom efforts, as does the practice of looping, widely used in many American, Swedish, and Finnish schools. We'll look at an astute technological program based on constructivist principles, in which each elementary student had a computer, as an example of successful reform.

We cannot spend too much time on each model or we'll end up with a humongous book that might scare people off with its size and weight. And we have to stop at some place or, again, we'll end up with too much to digest. We might as well follow the format set earlier and come up with a summary, some conclusions, and implications worth thinking about.

Question: What reforms do *you* perceive as effective in improving teaching and learning?

SCHOOL SIZE: DECENTRALIZING LARGE SCHOOLS INTO SMALLER UNITS

In a small school, everyone is needed.
—Stanton Leggett, premier educational consultant

If you really want to increase test scores (and, presumably, learning), in low achieving schools with high levels of poverty . . . just reduce the size of the student body.
—Paul Abramson, educational consultant, editor, and columnist

Want some facts about too large schools?

A high school of two thousand generates twice as many dropouts per thousand kids as a school of six hundred. In a high school of one thousand no one can tell an intruder from a student.

Poverty is the killer in education, isn't it? Want a structured approach to reduce that power? Small schools cut poverty's power over achievement by 80–90 percent in reading, writing, and mathematics (Bickel & Howley, 2002). That's why Abramson is quoted at the beginning of this section.

For our purposes, a small school is one in which everyone knows everyone, so we're talking about no more than five hundred to six hundred kids. That's about the outer limit for a principal and faculty to know everyone. The British infant schools believe that schools should be much smaller, in the range of two hundred fifty to three hundred, so it can be much more personalized, which is what little kids need. The Finns go with two to three hundred on the elementary school level.

OK, let's get started. The father of administration, Chester Barnard (1938), pointed to three indispensable elements for any organization to be effective:

- a clear, shared purpose
- a system of cooperation to achieve the shared purpose
- a system of communication to communicate the purposes in order to achieve them

Let's see how this plays out in large versus small organizations. The charts on the following pages are a brief summary from Shapiro, *Making Large Schools Work* (2009).

Since relational trust is so crucial for schools to improve, schools with low trust levels have little chance of improving academic achievement despite the huge pressure of NCLB, Common Core Standards, and so forth.

We can expand the factors and categories to compare the advantages and disadvantages of large and small schools, but it seems pretty clear the smaller schools hold many more advantages. Bryk, Deabster, Easton, Luppescu, and Thum (1994) stated that "teachers in small schools are much more satisfied." Hare and Heap (2001) noted that small schools are "the single most effective way to retain teachers" in a study of urban, rural, and suburban superintendents.

PROFESSIONAL LEARNING COMMUNITIES (PLCS)

Ruebel (2012) cites Huffman and Hipp (2003), who contend that a professional learning community (PLC) is "the most powerful professional development and change strategy available" (p. 4). The focus of a PLC is on improving student learning. Ruebel notes that Vescio, Ross, and Adams in 2008 reviewed six studies that focused on the relationship between teachers' participation in PLCs and student achievement. They noted that "all six studies revealed that student learning improved when teachers worked in PLCs" (p. 1).

Component	Large	Small
1. Purpose	Large student body requires a large faculty, limiting sharing of information. People interact with their departments or grade levels, losing sense of shared school purpose (Oxley, 1989, p. 29).	Faculty and students can develop shared sense of purpose. Since people feel they belong, they buy into goals, developing greater sense of participating and belonging.
2. Cooperation	Cooperation is harder to develop the further one is from power sources. Departments and teams become fulcrums for loyalty.	We cooperate more readily in small units. We feel closer to each other and more important *because everyone is needed.*
3. Communication	Becomes top-down in large organizations. The communication system becomes formal and requires going through channels, so it becomes hierarchical and difficult. Purpose and cooperation tend to become lost. We interact with our own formal and informal structures.	Communication is simpler and faster. Everyone becomes informed, since information becomes informal. The organization becomes *a small face-to-face folk society*, since everyone knows everyone.
Lines of communication	Generally long and generates misunderstanding.	Can be short and direct; therefore, more effective.
4. Student achievement, graduation rate, attendance, violence	Generates decreased student achievement, lower graduation rates and attendance, and more violence.	The value of small schools in increasing achievement, graduation rates, satisfaction, and improving behavior has been "confirmed with a clarity and level of confidence rare in the annals of education research" (Raywid, 1999). Greater academic achievement (Fowler & Walberg, 1991).
	Reduces relational trust, (see #5, Culture & Climate), thus reducing achievement (Bryk & Schneider, 2002).	With increased relational trust, achievement rises. Student performance and test scores improve. "Better behaved" (Godfredson, 1985).

Advantages and Disadvantages of Large and Small Schools

A. Poverty, the Achievement Gap	"The correlation between poverty and low achievement can be as high as ten times stronger" (Eckman & Howley, 1997).	Greater equity in achievement (Lee & Smith, 1995). See Bickel & Howley's statement on page 170.
5. Climate and Culture	Greater social distance, far less trust. Reduced sense of developing a stake in the school.	Close social distance. People feel part of the operation of the school. Much greater participation: three to twenty times greater in extracurricular activities (Barker & Gump, 1964).
A. Behavior/Relationships Establishing relationships with each other for both students and teachers is essential. People need relationships to be healthy emotionally.	Social distance marked. Many kids who are marginal become alienated because they cannot establish positive relationships. In large schools, teachers do not know each other.	Personalized, sense of community easy to establish. Essentially a folk community with face-to-face contact daily with each other. "We're like a family."
B. Trust-distrust Trust essential for effective human relationships and leadership, essential for organizations to become effective.	Trust harder to establish when social distance exists.	Much easier to establish when we know everyone.
Relational trust, based on social respect, competence, integrity, and personal regard for others, is crucial (Bryk & Schneider, 2002). Without it, it is virtually impossible for schools to improve academically.	Relational trust harder to develop.	Easier to develop. Only 14 percent of schools with low relational trust able to improve academically, vs. 50 percent with high levels of relational trust (Bryk & Schneider, 2002).
6. Roles		
A. Of principal	More distant, more of an authority figure. Develops a crisis mentality of putting out fires.	More of a head teacher. Authority barrier can be removed, resulting in improved instructional leadership.

Advantages and Disadvantages of Large and Small Schools

B. Of Teachers	Teacher becomes primary control agent. Causes student-teacher relationships to erode. Often feel powerless, pawns. Departments become basic unit in secondary schools.	Students can become primary control agents because everything is so visible. Feel more effective, have bigger voice in decision-making.
C. Of Students	Student separated from faculty. Cliques often form to protect individuals against the organization because they feel powerless. Students passive, such as rarely take any initiative in developing curriculum.	Student-teacher contact maximized, producing more effective relationships with each other. Teachers get to know students and vice versa. No one is a stranger. Student roles can be expanded. Can be proactive. Student needs can be met better. Cooperation enhanced. Students develop a higher sense of satisfaction.

Advantages and Disadvantages of Large and Small Schools

Professional learning communities consist of small groups of teachers who work together to improve their teaching skills and techniques to facilitate greater learning for kids. One of the pioneers of professional learning communities, Richard DuFour (2004), lays out the "big ideas" supporting the movement:

1. a focus on ensuring that kids learn
2. developing a culture of collaboration
3. a focus on results

Essentially, the PLC is a vehicle for teachers meeting in small groups to improve their classroom practice. One of the requirements is that the teachers meet regularly to examine their teaching processes to improve them. Often it is crucial that teams be involved as teams so that they can work on common issues, concerns, and problems.

Obviously, issues of trust, acceptance of others, and respect must eventually be dealt with for any PLC to be successful. I once asked a high-status elementary teacher involved in a PLC how it was working out. She said that she had video-taped herself and found that she was talking about 75 percent of the time. She said that her goal was to reduce that to 70 percent for the next taping. She felt that her PLC teammates were supportive, accepting, and made thoughtful suggestions to each other. She thought that the acceptance and search for ideas and processes that worked were key.

The processes that the teacher described and analyzed are crucial to a PLC being effective in improving teachers' professional practices. In the model cited above, the principal at first was not involved; instead, a nonjudgmental university professor served as a facilitator.

DuFour and Eaker (1999) note that a school that has managed to establish a PLC has a culture that supports such practices as collective inquiry. They are involved in forming collaborative teams that focus on continuous improvement and tend to be results oriented. If the school's culture is not supportive, the PLC cannot work, so teachers must be involved in the process.

Additionally, teachers have to decide to give up being defensive and to open themselves up to objective comments and evaluation. That this is not easy is an understatement. But if people are defensive, the processes for personal and professional growth become reduced. Improving one's professional practice takes time, introspection, and self-honesty, among other sometimes difficult processes. But the PLC can be quite helpful in improving one's professional practice and one's professional self, especially if it develops a subculture that is nonjudgmental, accepting, and professional. A later section will deal with the expansion of some interesting coaching and supervisory practices that can be and are helping teachers improve their professional practice.

THE ADVANTAGES OF SMALL CLASS SIZE: PROJECT STAR

One of the best researched projects to determine whether small class size was beneficial was undertaken in Tennessee. Project STAR (Student/ Teacher Achievement Ratio) was a four-year reform effort that took place in Tennessee from 1985 to 1989 to determine whether students attending small classes in grades K–3 had higher academic achievement than their peers in larger classes. The state was also interested in the effect of reducing class size on minority student achievement, which is a huge problem in the United States.

It was a controlled, randomized, large-scale experiment, which Boyd-Zaharias (1999) called "one of the most important educational investigations ever carried out and illustrates the kind and magnitude of research needed in the field of education to strengthen schools" (p. 1).

All Tennessee elementary schools were invited to participate, with seventy-nine qualifying with their K–3 classes. Kids were randomly assigned on entering kindergarten to one of three classes: a small (S) class with thirteen to seventeen kids; a second class labeled (I), with twenty-two to twenty-six students; or a regular class of twenty-two to twenty-six with a full-time teaching aide, called an RA. The kids remained in the classes in the study for four years. Interestingly, the teachers received no special instruction during the first year; also, they were randomly assigned to different classes every year.

STAR then tracked the academic achievement of the kids in grades 4–6, which they called the Lasting Benefits Study. This study revealed that students who had been in small classes for more than one year retained an academic advantage over peers in large classes through eighth grade—that is, for four years after leaving the smaller classes.

For kids who spent only one year in the small class, the benefits did not seem to last beyond middle school. If kids spent three years in smaller classes, the benefits generated 4.5 months ahead of their peers in grade 4, 4.2 months in grade 6, and 5.4 months in grade 8.

Thus, the impact continued. Kids in smaller classes were more likely to take the SAT or ACT. They found also that "decreased disciplinary problems contributed to a more positive learning environment in which there were fewer distractions from academics" (p. 94).

Interestingly, the presence of aides had no significant impact on academic achievement, while class size did. As for minority versus white student scores, the impact was considerable: "While all students did better in small classes, the gains in effect size for minorities were approximately twice the gains of whites, reducing the achievement gap" (p. 91).

Implications of this study might include the suggestion that teachers might have benefited from in-service work on improving teaching techniques for small groups. Since teachers were not given in-service, one wonders whether this would have improved results.

QUALITY UNIVERSAL PRESCHOOLS

Most European nations have established quality universal preschools for their kids since they have a more expansive view of social services than does the United States. France, for example, implemented its system over a seventeen-year period, so as we in the United States edge into this schooling, we should expect ups and downs and a slow process of implementation. Many of the European systems have developed high-quality programs, with fully credentialed teachers. An iffy figure of about 48 percent of U.S. kids may be in some form of preschool.

The American provisions for preschool range from excellent models, usually in posh suburbs, to storefront or home operations ranging from good to just baby-sitting. Do you think that the supposedly richest nation on earth ought to do a better job for its little kids?

Let's get at what preschool is all about. Fu (2003) insists that preschool is not meant to prepare kids for kindergarten, just as the purpose of elementary school is not to prepare kids for middle school. So, let's focus on what a preschool learning environment is and then what should children learn. Fu states that "knowledge and understanding are constructed through social interactions" (p. 1). Fu also notes, "The aim is to construct a teaching and learning environment in which children and teachers are given opportunities to make decisions, pursue authentic questions and concerns, connect what is known to the unknown, and be successful as they explore, test ideas, and discover through play, informal teaching activities and projects" (p. 1).

We might turn to an economist to get an estimation of the value of a quality preschool. James Heckman (2013), a Nobel Prize–winning economics professor at the University of Chicago, points to the economic benefit of preschool. (What else would you expect from an economist?) "It pays off 7 to 10 percent per annum for each dollar invested . . . [while] the stock market between 1945 and 2008 was a 6 or 7 percent return" (p. 2).

Heckman also pointed out that kids learn "soft skills," such as learning to play with others, that are more difficult to learn after early childhood and tend to have a lasting impact. He noted that, obviously, many kids learn these skills at home, but disadvantaged kids may not get such lessons from their parents. As a consequence, Heckman stated that preschool experience reduces inequality and promotes social mobility, obviously both social goods. Reardon (2013) notes that the rich (in contrast to the middle- and low-income parents) have "access to higher quality child care and preschool" (p. 4).

Fu concludes that "preschools teach children the early skills for literacy and science and mathematics development in an environment that encourages learning through social relationships" (p. 2).

CONSTRUCTIVIST TEACHING APPROACHES

The overwhelming consensus as the twentieth century closed has been that knowledge is constructed.
—D. C. Phillips, *Constructivism in Education*

Constructivism has become the reigning paradigm in teacher education in America today.
—S. Housefather, *Educational Horizons*

It may sound a bit odd, but every single one of us *constructs* the way we look at and perceive things. If we think carefully about that, we can see that it is valid when we look at how twins construct their worlds. If we're a twin, do we see things exactly the same way as our twin? Of course not. Does our brother or sister (if we're lucky enough to have one or more) look at things the same way as we do? As we grow, we develop different perceptions of our family, people, money, school, music, sports, and work.

I remember that when my brother and I described our mother, my wife exclaimed, "You're describing two entirely different women." My wife, who is a twin, picks up on twins way before I do. And, unlike her younger twin, she is almost always able to predict which twin is the older.

Question: OK, what am I saying? As we grow older we develop different experiences that affect our feelings, beliefs, values, and perceptions. We develop meanings for things different from others. Constructivism simply means that because each one of us has different experiences, we slowly build different ways of looking at the same things, and we develop different perceptions, even of the very same things. The best illustration of this is that different people can describe an accident quite differently.

An early scientist who was a pioneer in the field of constructivism was Piaget, who as far back as 1954 titled a book *The Construction of Reality in the Child*, essentially asserting that different kids develop different perceptions of the same things (as my brother and I did regarding our mother). Piaget, being a shrewd person, concentrated on finding out how kids build their understandings of things, of how various things work in their world. And he discovered that they develop quite different beliefs, ideas, and values in the process based upon their previous experiences and knowledge.

We've pretty well established support for D. C. Phillips's quote at the beginning of this section, that knowledge is constructed. Phillips gives us some real insights with the following statements, in which he targeted the nature of constructivism:

> This . . . type of constructivist view is that learners actively construct their own ("internal," as some would say) sets of meanings or understandings; knowledge is not a mere *copy* of the external world, nor is knowledge acquired by passive absorption or by simple transference from one person (a teacher) to another (a learner or knower). In sum, knowledge is *made*, not *acquired*. (2000, p. 7)

That's quite a mouthful, isn't it?

Question: How does this play out in the classroom? A simple comparison of a classical/traditional approach with a model of a constructivist approach will provide some fascinating insights. It is taken from Shapiro (2008).

A Classical/Traditional Model

Claudia Geocaris, a science teacher, provided quite an insightful analysis of her former approach to teaching her area of science. She realized after a while that she was pretty ineffective, as you will see. Her structure for the class, as well as the processes she had developed, led her to recognize their shortcomings. Note who made *all* the decisions—and the impact of that on the kids' involvement (or lack of involvement) due to her strong need for control.

> In the past years *I* took a traditional approach with a complex, but vitally important scientific concept. What is DNA and how does it contribute to genetics and the diversity of life? *I* usually presented material to students through lectures and labs. *I* explained key scientific discoveries and told students about the theories that resulted from the research. After presenting the material, *I* expected students to understand the relationships among DNA, RNA, proteins, and genetics. Although many students did, others did not; moreover, my students did not exhibit high levels of student engagement. (1996/1997, 72; emphasis added)

It is interesting that Ms. Geocaris finally figured out that she wasn't particularly effective and changed her approach. Since it was *her* class, which *she* ran, why would she expect the kids to leap up with excitement?

A Constructivist Teaching Model

Sue Sharp left her middle school team, blew into the classroom, set up her laptop, and typed out the agenda for the day:

> State on your post-meeting reaction form (PMR) your long-term goals and today's objectives.

> Schedule for groups:

> > The Warriors: Greek armor, weapons, war strategies
> > The Tradesmen: Economic life: role of local, overseas trade, agriculture, diet, products
> > The Politicians: Political organizations and structure, who makes decisions, what is the involvement of the various social classes?
> > The Fashioneers: Roles of genders, dress, costumes, responsibilities, styles
> > The Artists: Drama, comedy, architecture, arts, sculpture, materials used

> > Review of today's work
> > Planning, objectives for tomorrow
> > Materials, other resources needed
> > Wrap-up, assessment on the group planning or PMR form

Briefly comparing and contrasting these two approaches provides insight into constructivist versus traditional approaches.

- Passive vs. active learner—which approach structures student roles to be active or passive?
- Individual vs. social system (group)—Ms. Sharp treats kids as in social systems.

- Motivation—Ms. Sharp uses Maslow's hierarchy of human needs (1954) to meet her students' needs. Ms. Geocaris seems unaware of her kids' needs.
- Which model focuses on higher-order cognitive levels, active decision-making, problem solving, and reflection? Actually, in traditional classes, kids can make decisions: go along with the teacher, pay little or no attention, sabotage.
- Which group is learning to plan?
- How are the classrooms organized? Rows, groups?
- Which students have a decision about what they study?
- Which integrates assessment within the context of the daily classroom?
- In which is responsibility not only encouraged but also structured by its organization?

We can ask more, but it's pretty clear which is more effective. We see simply no comparison.

CLASSROOM LEARNING CENTERS

Learning centers are one of the greatest opportunities for creativity and actually having fun that any teacher (usually elementary or middle school) can create. They've been around quite a while, too. Fredericks (2005) notes, "A *learning center* is a space set aside in the classroom that allows easy access to a variety of learning materials in an interesting and productive manner" (p. 224). Cindee Rubenstein of Broward County, Florida, thinks that work in centers should be cooperative (personal communication, April 20, 2013).

Centers provide a terrific opportunity to individualize teaching because they can be set up in a variety of ways in which students can work alone or with others on a project, or a topic, or a concept, a skill, a theme, or what have you. The center can be used to introduce material, or it can be used during the course of presenting material or after the original presentation to expand on the lesson, according to the interests or needs or talents of kids.

Learning centers can be designed in a huge number of ways, and they can be used to involve students in their design, content, processes, and products. Obviously, involving students generates a sense of ownership. I once taught U.S. history in a high school, and one of the kids brought in original letters from a great-great uncle who fought in the Civil War, written to his parents and siblings. To say that the school was astounded was an understatement. We even copied them at the request of the students and with the permission of the family.

Centers can be enrichment centers, or skill centers, or exploratory in nature. Centers can be used for a student or a group to illustrate a concept, process, or topic. I've found that kids respond positively to encouragement to participate in designing centers, and particularly in bringing in materials for them.

Abcteach.com (2009) suggests organizational approaches, such as making use of

- themes (transportation, symbiosis, cooperation)
- learning styles (auditory, tactile, visual, etc.)
- subjects (math, English, history, biology)

Obviously, depending upon the experience of the kids, ground rules have to be developed. We've found that it is quite useful to consult with the kids regarding these. When the kids are involved in creating and agreeing to such rules, they are much more likely to be followed.

Centers often are placed in nooks, some with rugs designating the space. Centers can be organized in baskets or plastic boxes for storage before and after use, thus expanding considerably the teacher's repertoire of materials and supplies. To individualize further, checklists can be provided for kids to check the activities or projects they're working on and completing. Planning forms can be used to structure work, plan ahead, and self-evaluate, like the tongue-in-cheek Post-Meeting Reaction Form (really a group planning form) developed by Herbert Thelen with a team of us at his teaching-learning lab at the University of Chicago (see the next page). Obviously, this is an accountability mechanism with a feedback aspect.

Forms can be developed with student input about each student's contribution to the project and the overall success of the project. That is, self grading and group grading forms (if a group is involved) can be developed.

PROJECT-BASED LEARNING MODELS, INCLUDING SIMULATIONS

It's clear that the learning system established in the preceding section on constructivism and constructivist teaching, Ms. Sharp's approach, is a project-based model. We can design any number of projects and simulations depending upon our imagination and creativity.

RECENT COACHING/SUPERVISORY MODELS

Heather Holder, peer evaluator at Hillsborough Community Public Schools in Tampa, Florida, reports an interesting, interlocking coaching/ supervisory system established by the Hillsborough Public Schools (2013). The program is supported by a Bill and Melinda Gates seven-year grant of $100 million. Several programs have developed, including the following:

POST MEETING REACTION (PMR) FORM
GROUP PLANNING FORM

A.   Date: _____

C.   Class _____ D. Pd. _____

B.   Name of Group _____

E.   Recorder _____

F.   Long Range Goals   1.) _____

                           2.) _____

                           3.) _____

G.   Task(s) for Today   1.) _____

                           2.) _____

                           3.) _____

H.   Amount Accomplished   I.   What helped you? _____

100%

50%

0%

J.   What blocked you? _____

K.   Task(s) for Tomorrow

_____

_____

L.   What Resources Do You Need For Tomorrow?

        Human   _____

        Material   _____

Post-Meeting Reaction Form (originally created by Herbert Thelen, but modified by Arthur Shapiro)

- A mentoring program for the first two years of teaching for all new teachers
- A peer evaluator program for all teachers to provide formative feedback focusing on instructional strategies starting with their third year of teaching
- A peer connectors program at each school to improve communication and help teachers understand and utilize the Charlotte Danielson Framework for Teaching

- The Danielson Framework's four domains (planning and preparation, classroom environment, instruction, and professional responsibilities) comprise the basis for teacher observations and evaluation
- Professional learning communities, which focus on Danielson's domains

Clearly, this integrated system is designed to facilitate teachers' professional development. It also has compensation aspects, as required by recent state law.

COOPERATIVE LEARNING

According to Fredericks (2005), cooperative learning is built on a four-step process:

1. Presentation of content
2. Teamwork, such as Jigsaw, Student Teams-Achievement Divisions (STAD), and think-pair-share to work to grasp the material/ideas/processes
3. Individual assessment, since each student must make sure that they "get" the ideas and so forth
4. Team recognition, particularly of the team's efforts to make sure that every member learns the specific material

Note that this model reduces students' dependence upon the teacher for answers, promoting student efforts at critical and independent thinking. A key for success is the process of forming groups, which has been hinted at in chapter 11, where we discussed using the Gregorc personality style delineator (1999) to form groups that are balanced according to learning style.

TECHNOLOGY THAT STIMULATES CONSTRUCTIVISM

Laptop computers have been shown to improve organization, teaching, and learning in classrooms where each student and teacher received his or her own laptop, termed one-on-one. Today, the trend is toward less expensive tablet computers for communication, research, connectivity, and creativity. Goals were to increase time on task, collaborative learning, test scores, and student self-reliance.

Dr. Lynne Brown Menard, assistant principal, Manatee County Schools, Florida, helmed a study (2010) showing that teachers' perceptions of the use of technology led to the above goals being achieved, as well as an increase in constructivist practices: "Constructivism is a learning or meaning-making theory, that offers an explanation of the nature of knowledge and how human beings learn. It maintains that individuals create or construct new understandings through the connection of what they already know and believe, together with new found learning, and draw on their own conclusions" (Brooks & Brooks, 1999, p. 4).

The new technology stimulated students and teachers to work collaboratively, which led to high degrees of motivation, with participants taking ownership of their and their group's work. Classrooms became highly creative, with students' expertise being recognized by faculty to the extent that teacher and student roles became blurred, since many students had developed greater expertise than teachers. Teachers learned to use the strengths of the student "experts" to aid instruction and to provide leadership. Thus, the culture of the classrooms changed over time, with teachers asserting that they couldn't teach any other way once they had laptops. Teachers became more and more constructivist in their classroom strategies.

Of course, after a short time, students began to reach out beyond the classroom, involving other students and teachers, schools, districts, states, and countries in their projects and research. While the original purpose of the project was to use technology in the classroom, the outcome was a new vision, a constructivist and collaborative model of learning, teaching, and leadership.

MORE MODELS DESERVING ATTENTION

See chapter 6 for a discussion of Finland's system for quality education: the continuous progress, nongrading, or multi-age grading systems, and looping. Montessori schools also seem to have strong staying power in our multifaceted school system, with good cause. So does the Trump high school model, which uses flexible modular scheduling and allocates time according to need, not a rigid time, for every subject.

SUMMARY, CONCLUSIONS, AND IMPLICATIONS

This all-too-brief once-over of reforms that work should give hope to those of us depressed at the generally destructive, too often ideologically based ideas being widely pushed, legislated, and/or mandated in the United States to reform our schools. After cheerfully reviewing each of the previous chapters, my grad students unanimously urged me to lay out reforms, or models, or processes that work. They became depressed by the frauds, fads, and fantasies/fictions that are being supported and forced down our collective throats nationally, regionally, and locally.

So, that's why this last chapter is written. What should we conclude and imply from it?

Popular beliefs without a research basis fall flat on their faces. Testing and punishing do not work, and neither does forcing. In actual fact, some of our kids are doing quite well. It's the many in poverty who are not. So forcing, punishing, coercing, meritizing, and VAMing become distractions that fail to get to the heart of improving schools—they never deal with poverty.

Decentralizing schools into smaller units works, does not cost more, and is highly effective in reducing the achievement gap. Virtually everyone is much happier and more relaxed in decentralized small schools because they work better. Professional learning communities (PLCs) help teachers improve their professional practice, as did the small classes in Project STAR, which also help kids learn better.

We seem to be on our way to universal preschools in America—it's about time. And it's also about time to expand our constructivist teaching models and dump our teaching to the test, which virtually everyone cordially despises. Classroom learning centers offer excellent opportunities for students to increase their independence, a major value in our culture.

Analyzing other models for insight into how we can improve is a useful strategy, and Finland's system provides precisely such food for thought. The Finns trust their teachers—in contrast to some in our society who disparage ours. Theirs is an integrated, carefully thought-out system that immediately focuses on any student having problems to facilitate their learning. It also is less expensive than ours.

Project-based learning offers many positive aspects for student and faculty growth and improved function, as do new supervisory and coaching models being used in some districts. We have cited one that is designed as an integrated system that focuses on coaching to improve teaching and learning. Continuous progress can assist in finessing the foolish practice of retaining kids, and it is worthwhile for meeting student and teacher needs.

We have also included a new approach to utilizing technology in the classroom, which consisted of providing each student and teacher a computer in a number of classrooms. The program was quite successful in stimulating creative responses, which led to blurring teacher and student roles because the kids were often more technologically expert than faculty. As teachers and students worked together, they developed more constructivist practices, which began to change the culture of the classrooms.

REFERENCES AND RESOURCES

Abcteach.com (2009).

Barker, R. G., & Gump, P. V. (1964). *Big school, small school*. Stanford, CA: Stanford University Press.

Barnard, C. I. (1938). *The functions of the executive*. Cambridge, MA: Harvard University Press.

Bickel, R., & Howley, C. B. (2002, March). The influence of scale. *American School Board Journal, 189*(3), 28–30.

Boyd-Zaharias, J. (1999, Summer). Project STAR: The story of the Tennessee class-size study. *American Educator*.

Brooks, J. G., & Brooks, M. G. (1999). The courage to be constructivist. *Educational Leadership, 57*(3), 18–24.

Bryk, A. S., Deabster, P. E., Easton, J. Q., Luppescu, S., & Thum, Y. M. (1994). Measuring achievement gains in the Chicago Public Schools. *Education and Urban Society, 26*(3), 3.

Bryk, A. S., & Schneider, B. (2002). *Trust in schools: A core resource for improvement*. New York: Russell Sage Foundation.

DuFour, R. (2004, May). What is a professional learning community? *Educational Leadership, 61*(6), 6–11.

DuFour, R., & Eaker, R. (1999). *Professional learning communities at work: Best practices for enhancing student achievement*. Bloomington, IN: National Education Service.

Eckman, J. M., & Howley, C. B. (Eds.). (1997). *Sustainable small schools: A handbook for rural communities*. Charleston, WV: Eric Clearinghouse on Rural and Small Schools. Appalachia Educational Laboratory.

Fowler, W. J. Jr., & Walberg, H. J. (1991). School size, characteristics, and outcomes. *Educational Evaluation and Policy Analysis, 13*(2), 189–202.

Fredericks, A. (2005). *The complete idiot's guide to success as a teacher*. Royersford, PA: Alpha.

Fu, V. R. (2003, March). Learning and teaching in pre-school. *PBS Teachers. Early Childhood*.

Geocaris, C. (1996/1997). Increasing student engagement: A mystery solved. *Educational Leadership, 54*(4), 72–75.

Godfredson, D. C. (1985). *School size and school disorder*. Baltimore, MD: Johns Hopkins University, Center for Social Organization of Schools [ERIC Document Retrieval Service No. ED261456].

Gregorc, A. F. (1999). *Gregorc Style Delineator*. Columbia, CT: Gregorc Associates, Inc.

Hare, D., & Heap, J. (2001). *Effective teacher recruitment and retention strategies in the Midwest: Who is making use of them?* Naperville, IL: North Central Regional Educational Laboratory.

Heckman, J. (2013, March 19). Return on investment can beat stock market. *WTTW: Chicago Tonight, Evaluating Universal Preschool*.

Holder, H. (2013, April). Report on feedback offered in HCPS (Hillsborough County Public Schools). Manuscript submitted for publication.

Huffman, J. B., & Hipp, K. K. (2003). *Reculturing schools as professional learning communities*. Lanham, MD: Rowman & Littlefield.

Lee, V., & Smith, J. (1995). Effects of high school restructuring and size on gains in achievement and engagement for early secondary school students. *Sociology of Education, 68*(4), 241–270.

Maslow, A. H. (1954). *Motivation and personality*. New York: Harper & Row.

Menard, L. B. (2013, May 1). Ideas that work: Using technology to stimulate collaborative learning, teaching and leadership opportunities. Manuscript submitted for publication.

Oxley, D. (1989). Smaller is better. *American Educator, 13*(1), 28–31, 42–51.

Phillips, D. C. (Ed.). (2000). *Constructivism in education: Opinions and second opinions on controversial issues*. Ninety-ninth Yearbook of the National Society for the Study of Education, Part I. Chicago: University of Chicago Press.

Piaget, J. (1954). *The construction of reality in the child*. New York: Basic Books.

Raywid, M. (1999). *Current literature on small schools*. Charleston, WV: Clearinghouse on Rural Education and Small Schools, Appalachia Educational Laboratory.

Reardon, S. (2013, April 27). No rich child left behind. *Opinionator, New York Times.* http://opinionator.blogs.nytimes.com/2013/04/27/no-rich-child-left-behind/?_r=0

Ruebel, K. K. (2012, January). Professional learning communities. AMLE Research Summary. http://www.amle.org/Research/ResearchSummaries/PLCs/tabid/2535/Default.aspx

Shapiro, A. (2008). *The effective constructivist leader.* Lanham, MD: Rowman & Littlefield.

Shapiro, A. (2009). *Making large schools work: The advantages of small schools.* Lanham, MD: Rowman & Littlefield.

Thelen, H. (1959). Post Meeting Reaction Form: Group Planning Form.

Vescio, V., Ross, D., & Adams, A. (2008). A review of research on the impact of professional learning communities on teaching practice and student learning. *Teaching and Teacher Education, 24*(1), 80–91.

About the Author

Arthur Shapiro (PhD, University of Chicago) is a theoretically based practitioner who is professor of education in the College of Education at the University of South Florida, Tampa, Florida.

He has been a high school, middle school, and elementary school teacher; senior high school principal; director of secondary education; assistant superintendent; and superintendent of schools, all in nationally prominent districts. He has developed nongraded high schools and elementary schools, as well as schools of choice. His experience covers working in and with public and private schools in inner-city, urban, suburban, and rural settings, plus two nationally famous laboratory schools, one being John Dewey's Lab School at the University of Chicago. He has also served on two boards of education, chairing the education committee of one.

His teaching is based on modeling a constructivist philosophy and approach, for which he received the TIP award for excellence in teaching.

Dr. Shapiro's writing and consulting are empirically based on his wide experience. He is a pioneer in the small schools and small learning communities (SLC) movement, having published on and developed decentralized schools. He consults internationally and nationally on leadership, organization, and management; change strategies and developing comprehensive system-wide planning models that work; personality and learning styles; conflict resolution strategies; team and trust building; and related areas.

He was lead author of an analysis and comprehensive recommendations to improve the Republic of Macedonia's radical school reform, which decentralized its system into independent school districts (all 2,500 schools). He also provided expertise in analyzing the radical school reform of the school system of the Republic of Georgia, with recommendations for improvement.

His major publications include three of the first five books on constructivist leadership, the first new theory of leadership since the late 1970s, and the first theories of curriculum and supervision.

Dr. Shapiro served on the Working Committee for Desegregation of the Hillsborough County Schools in Florida as the only outsider, as well as on the Committee for Instructional Design. He has been cochair of numerous dissertation committees, also serving on university, college, and departmental committees. He is vice president of the professor union known as the United Faculty of Florida and is an officer of the University Senate.

He admires his talented wife, Sue, and two adult children—Marc, who has a PhD in political science and policy analysis and is an international consultant, and Alana Shapiro Thompson, who teaches English literature at Tennessee State University in Nashville.

Unfortunately (and sadly), he is an unrequited, almost compulsive, punster, much to the chagrin of his decreasing number of friends.